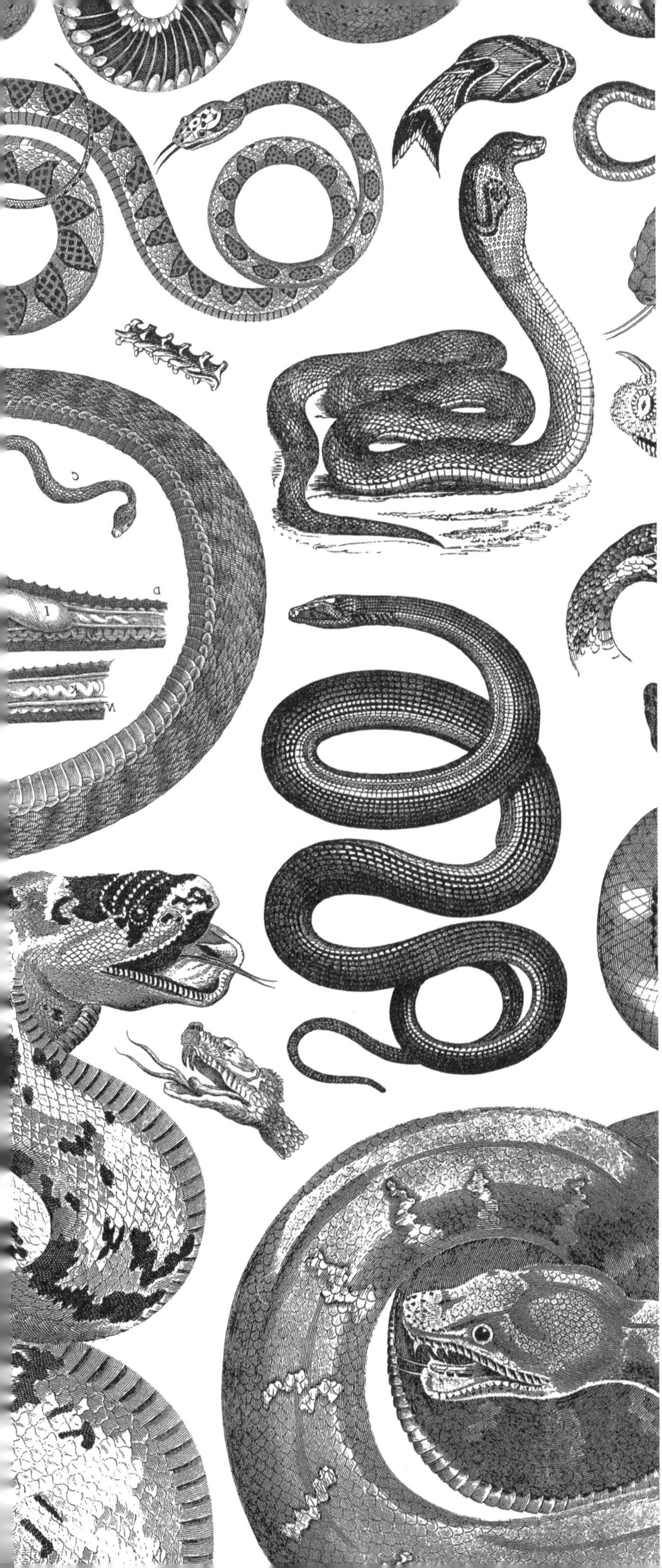

SNAKES & OTHER REPTILES

AN IMAGE ARCHIVE FOR
ARTISTS *And* DESIGNERS

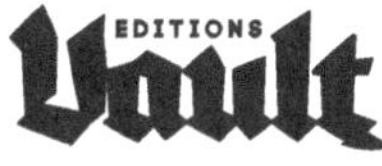

INTRODUCTION

Reptiles are cold-blooded, air-breathing vertebrates (animals with a backbone) covered in hard, waterproof scales made of keratin. Cold-blooded animals do not maintain a constant body temperature. They rely on external factors and behaviours, such as basking in sunlight to warm their bodies and keep their metabolism working. All reptiles shed their scales. For example, snakes will rub their head on a sharp rock to create a tear in their skin and begin easing themselves out of their old skin. Crocodiles and alligators shed their scales individually by rubbing against trees and rocks. There are several major groups of living reptiles: Testudines (turtles), Tuatara (reptiles native to New Zealand), Squamata - (lizards, snakes and worm lizards) and Crocodilia (crocodiles, alligators, caiman, and gavialidae.)

This pictorial archive features a comprehensive collection of 327 images of snakes and other animals in the class Reptilia. Discover striking images of deadly hyper-venomous viper and cobra snakes, prey squeezing constrictors including boas and pythons, anacondas, adders, rattlesnakes, sea snakes, snake skeletons, and more. Explore highly detailed renderings of crocodiles attacking their prey, basking caiman and congregations of alligators. *Snakes and Other Reptiles* also showcases a diverse and extensive range of lizard and turtle imagery.

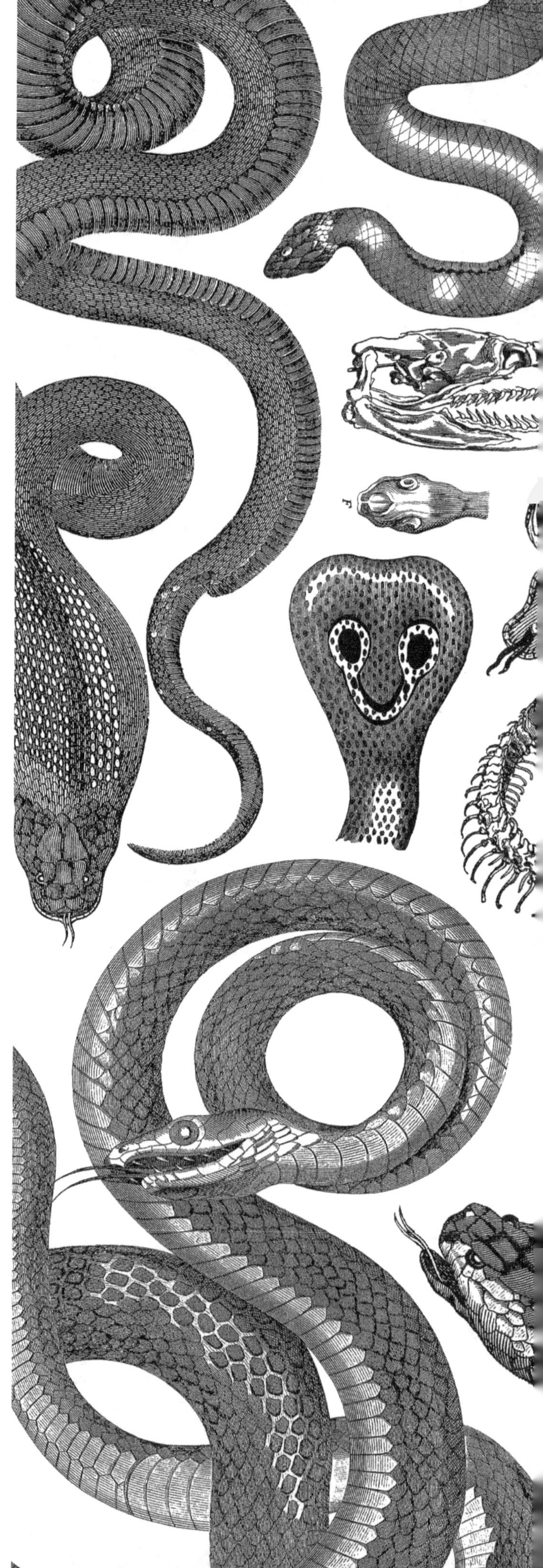

TABLE OF CONTENTS

Snakes	01-65
Crocodilia	66-72
Lizards	73-88
Turtles	89-96

DOWNLOAD YOUR FILES

Downloading your files is simple. To access your digital files, please go
to the last page of this book and follow the instructions.

For technical assistance, please email:
info@vaulteditions.com

Copyright

Bibliographical Note

This book is a new work created by Vault Editions Ltd.

ISBN: 978-1-925968-88-0

SNAKES & OTHER REPTILES

VAULT EDITIONS

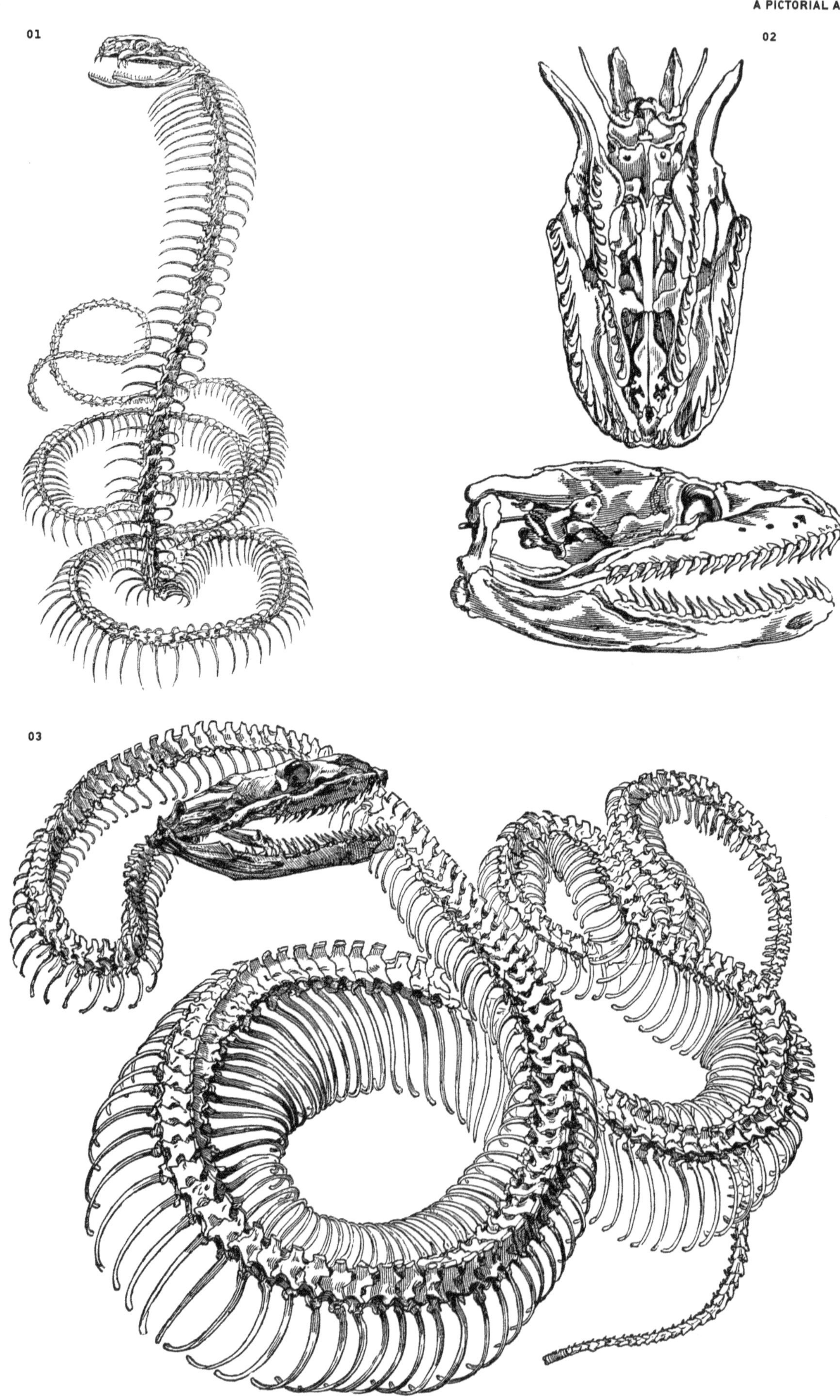
01
02
03

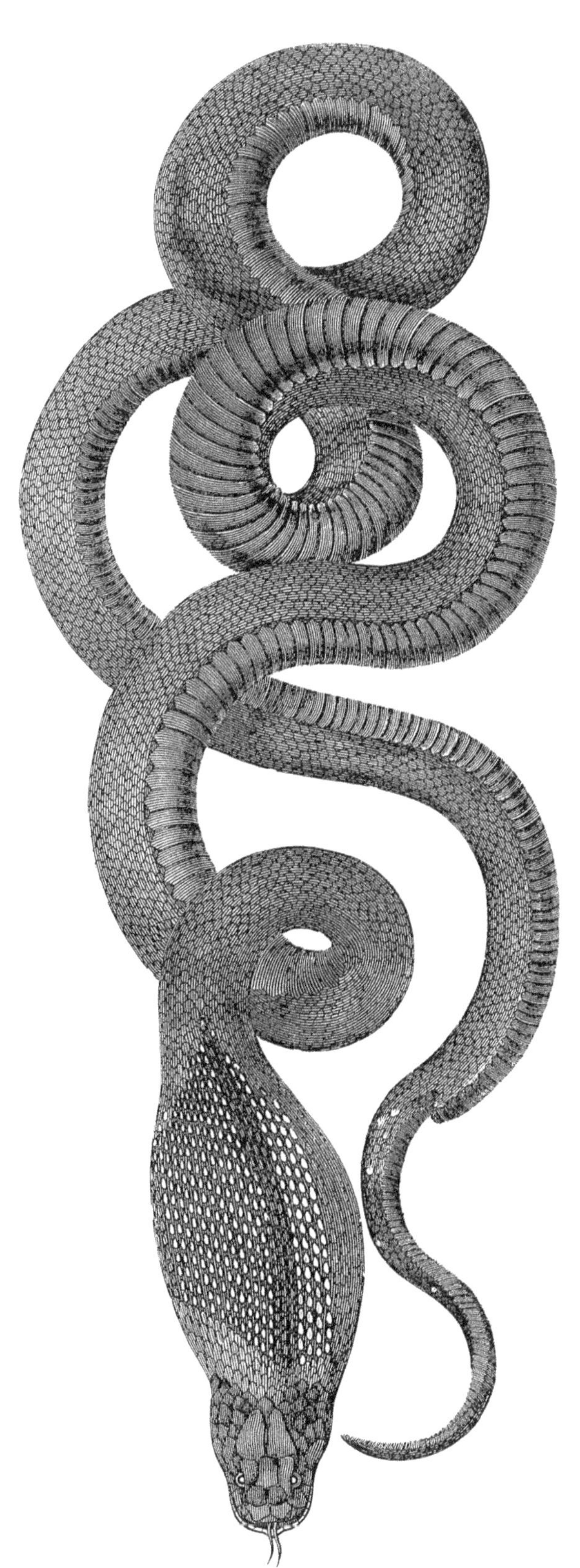

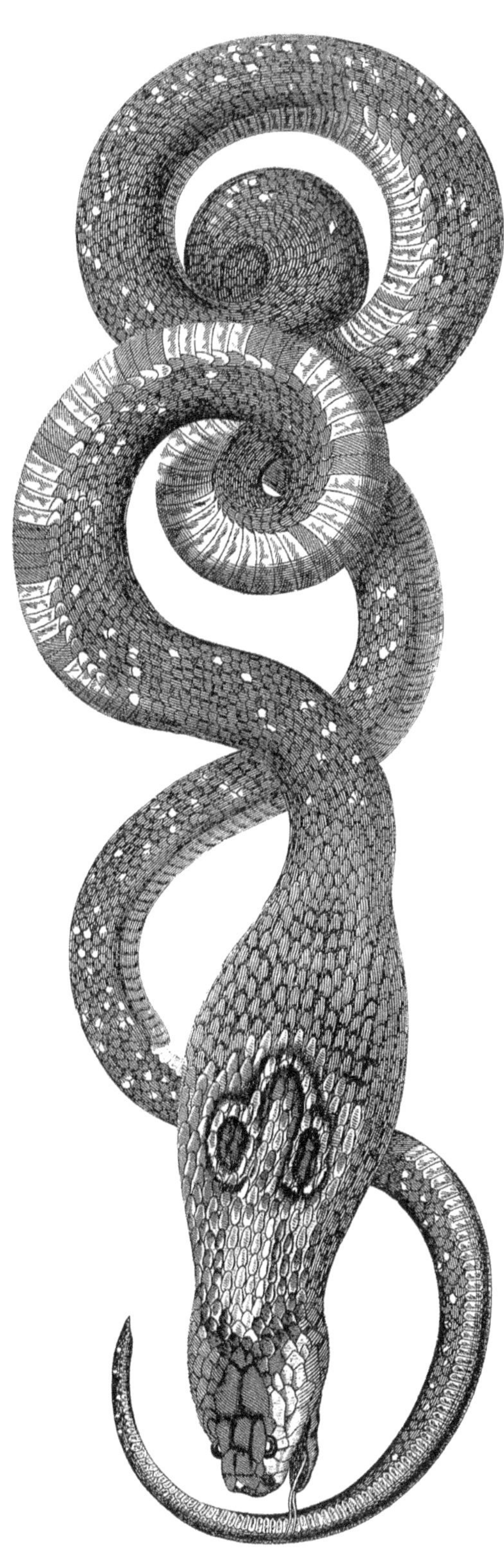

06

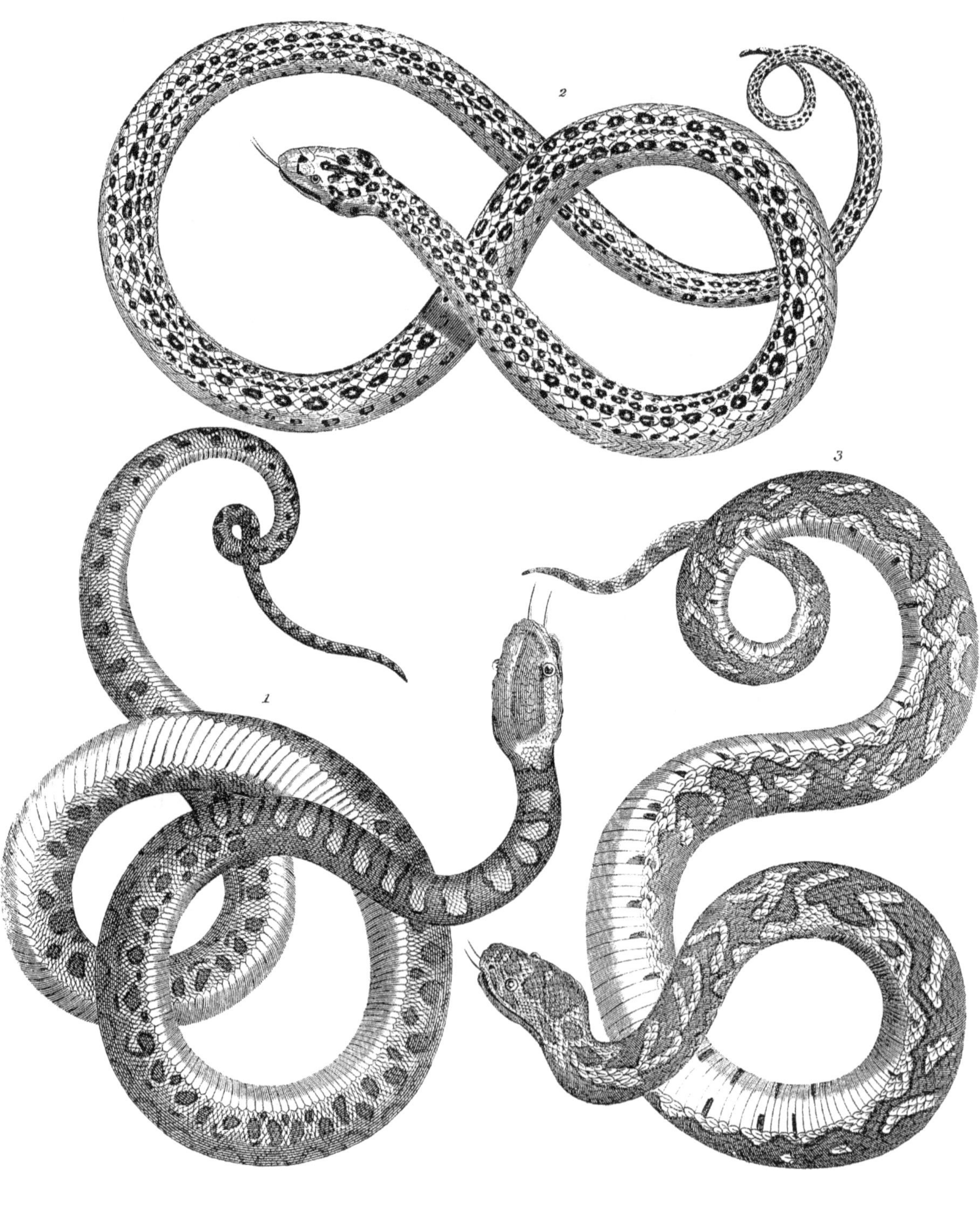

07

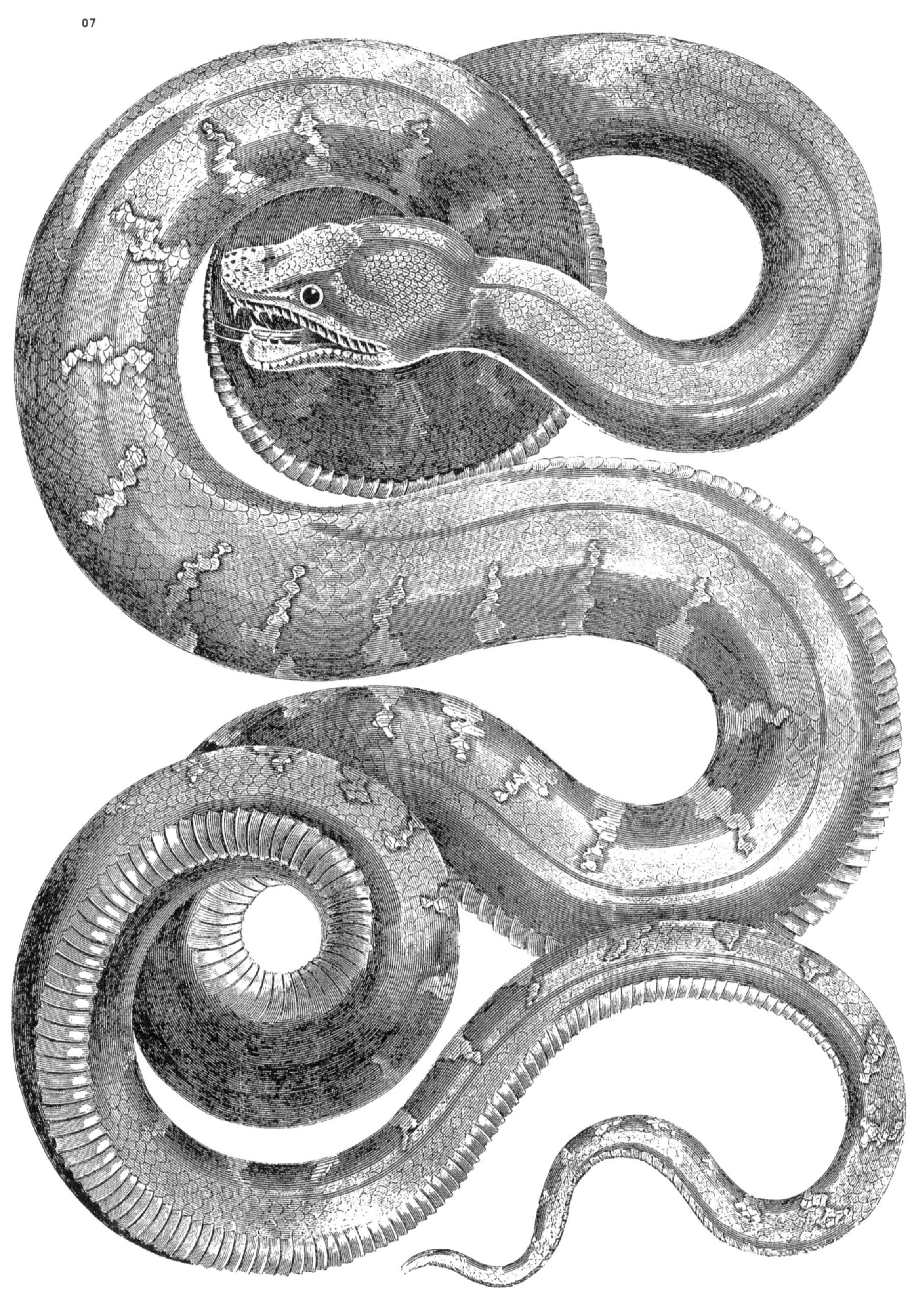

08

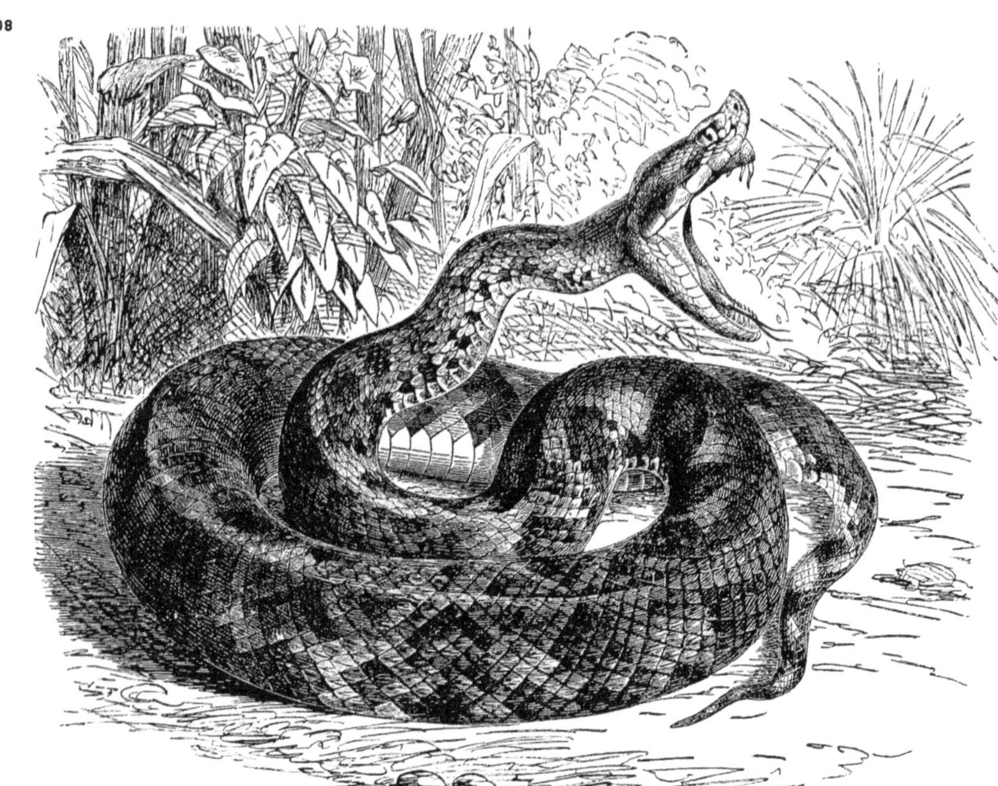

09

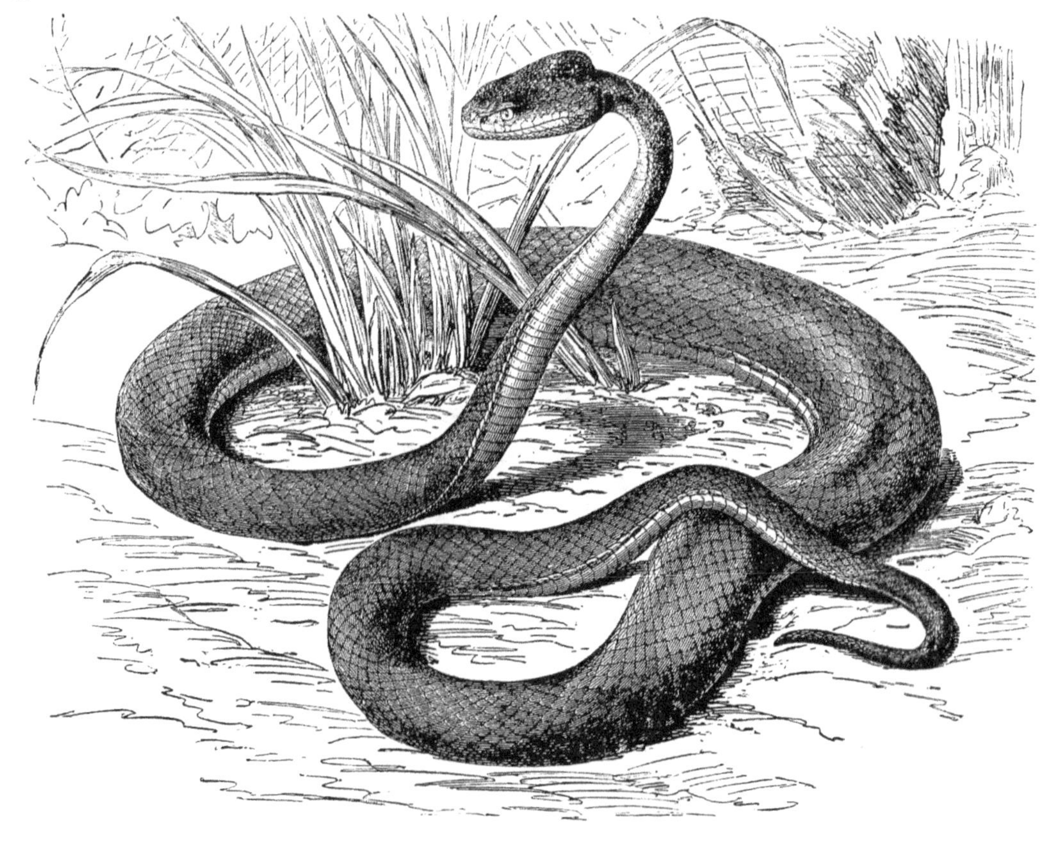

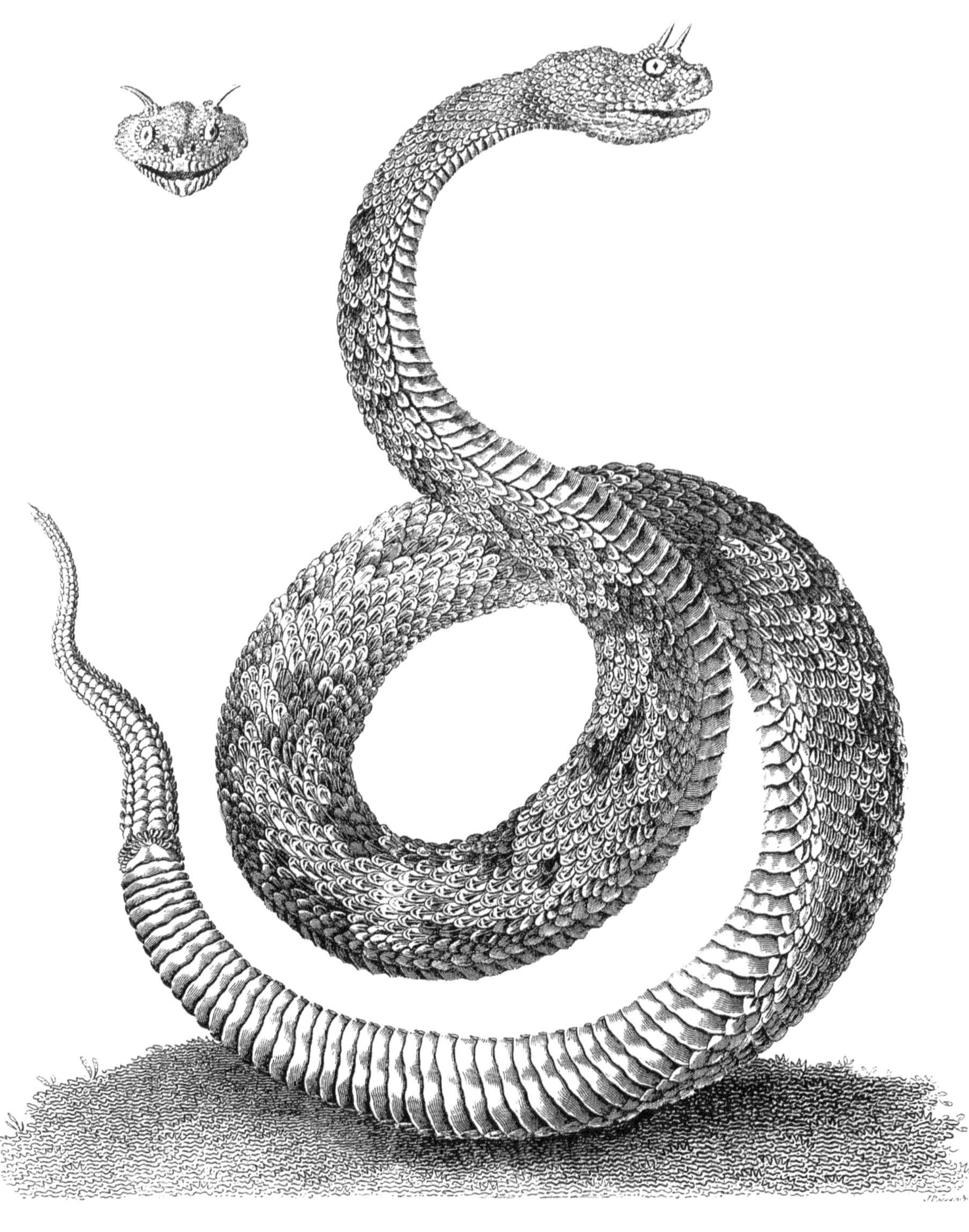

11

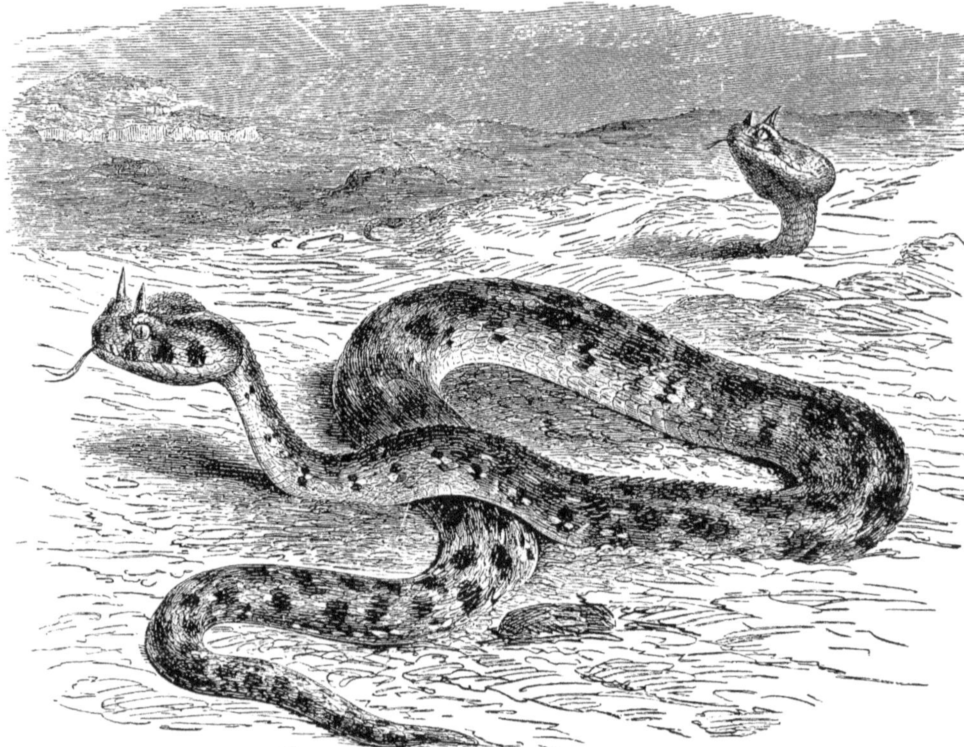

12

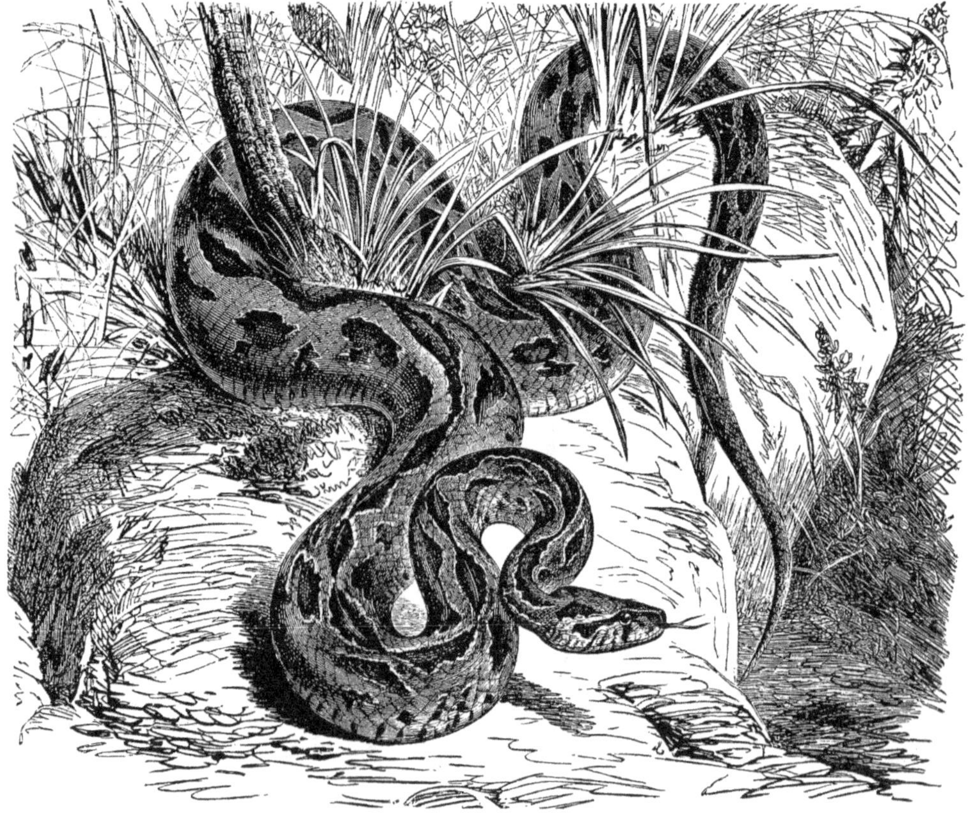

13

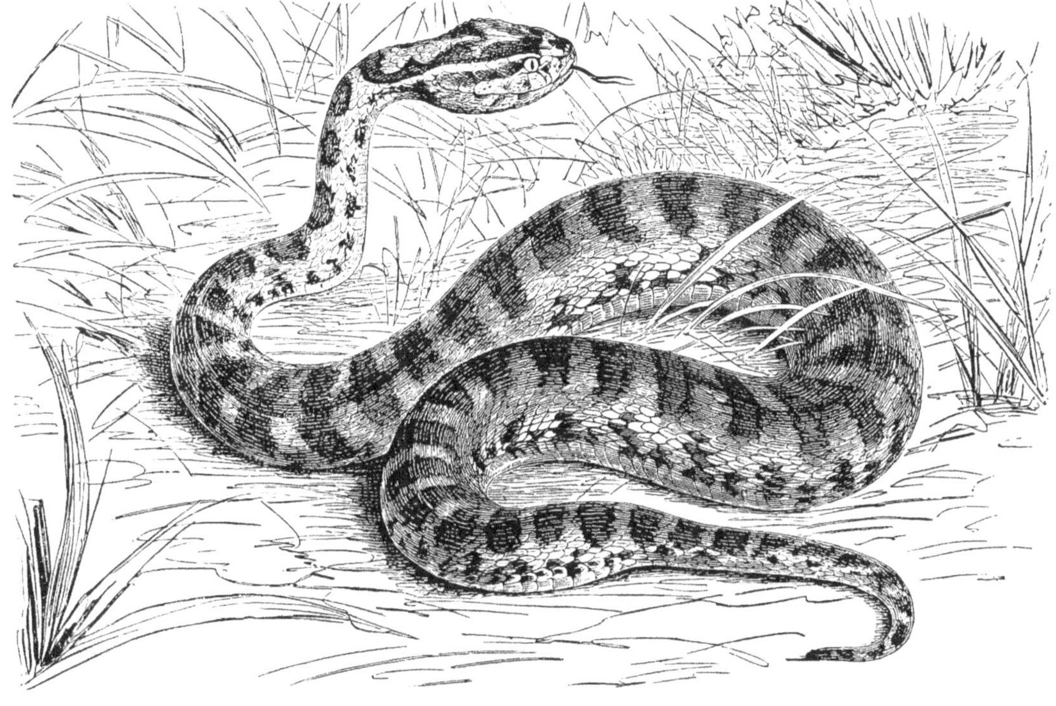

14

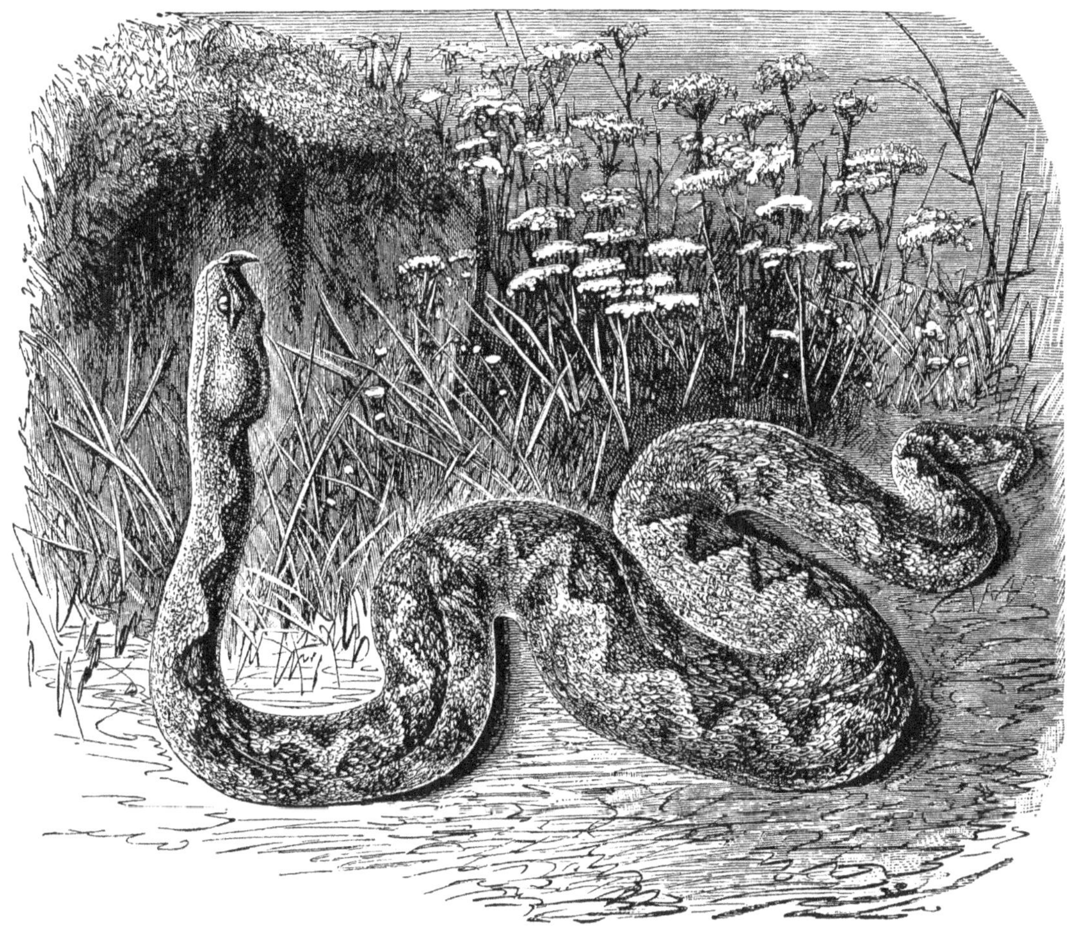

SNAKES

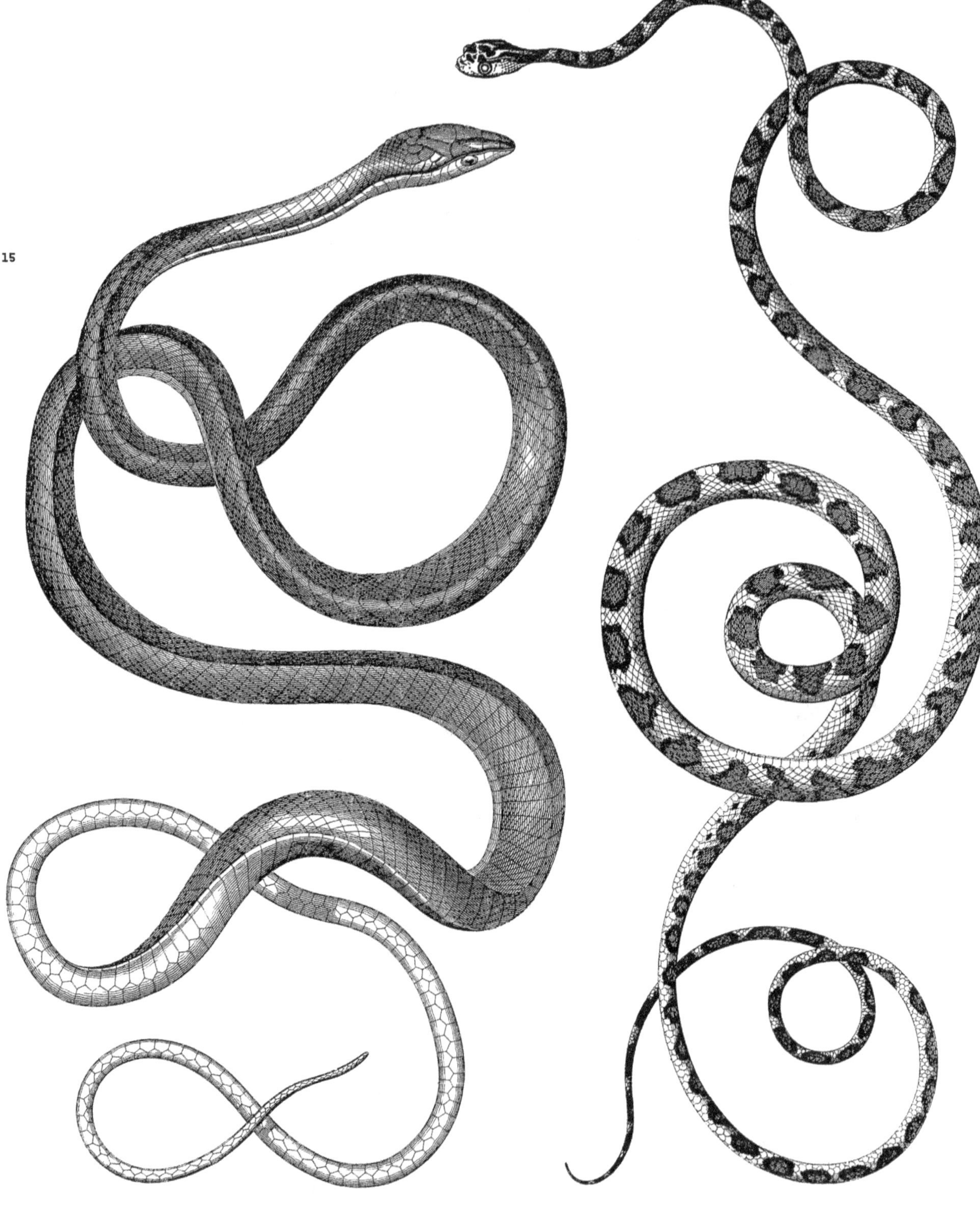
16
15

17

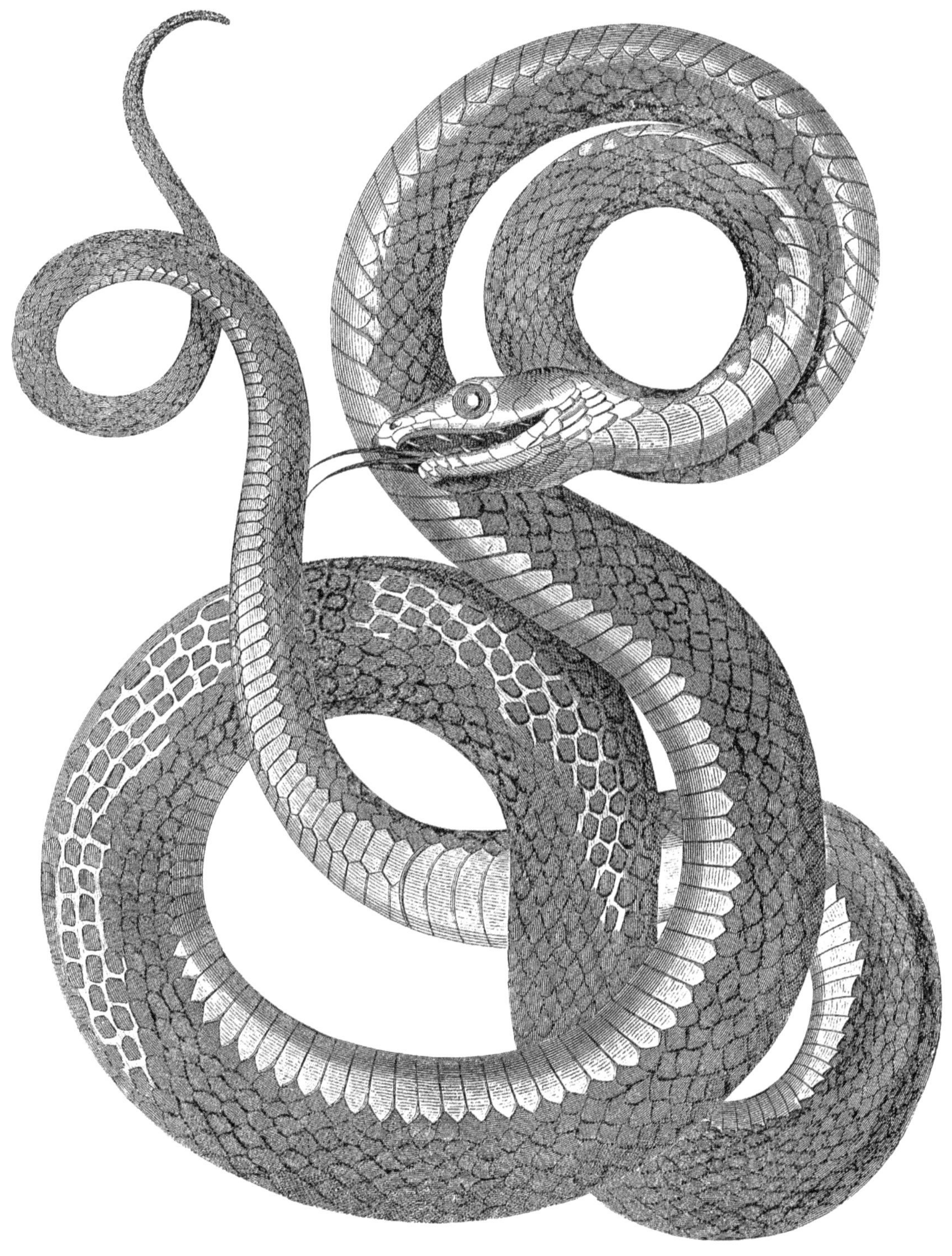

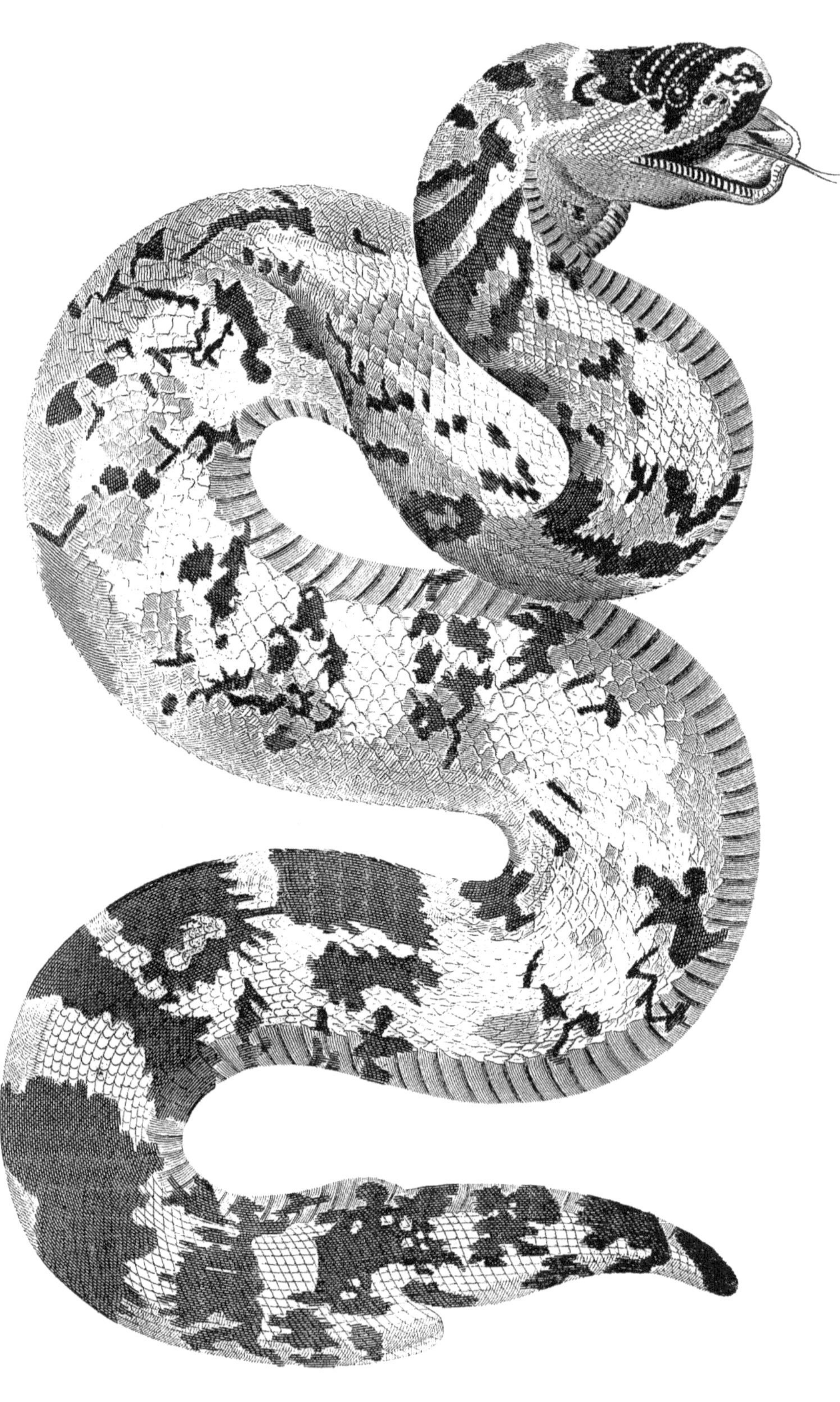

19

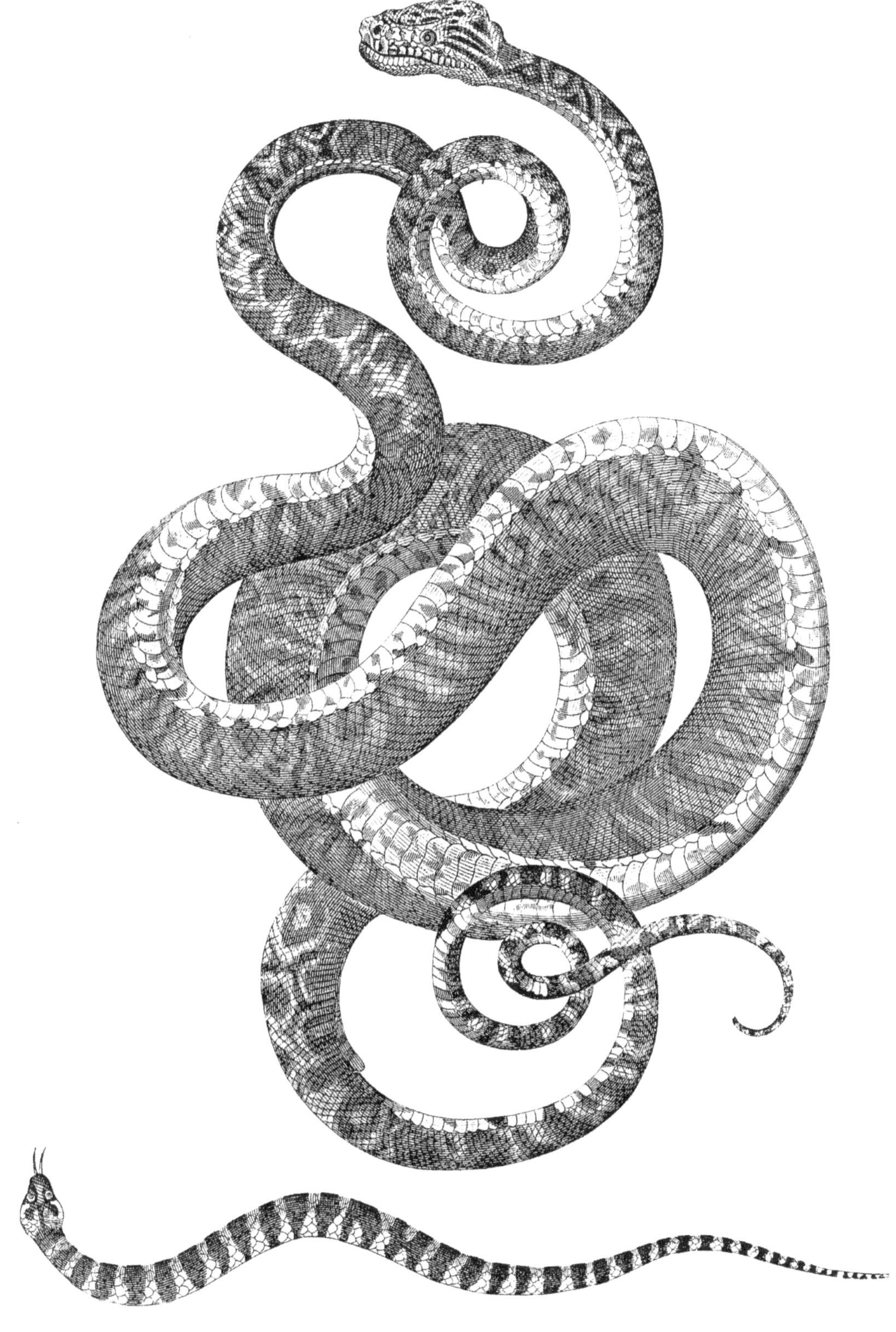

SNAKES

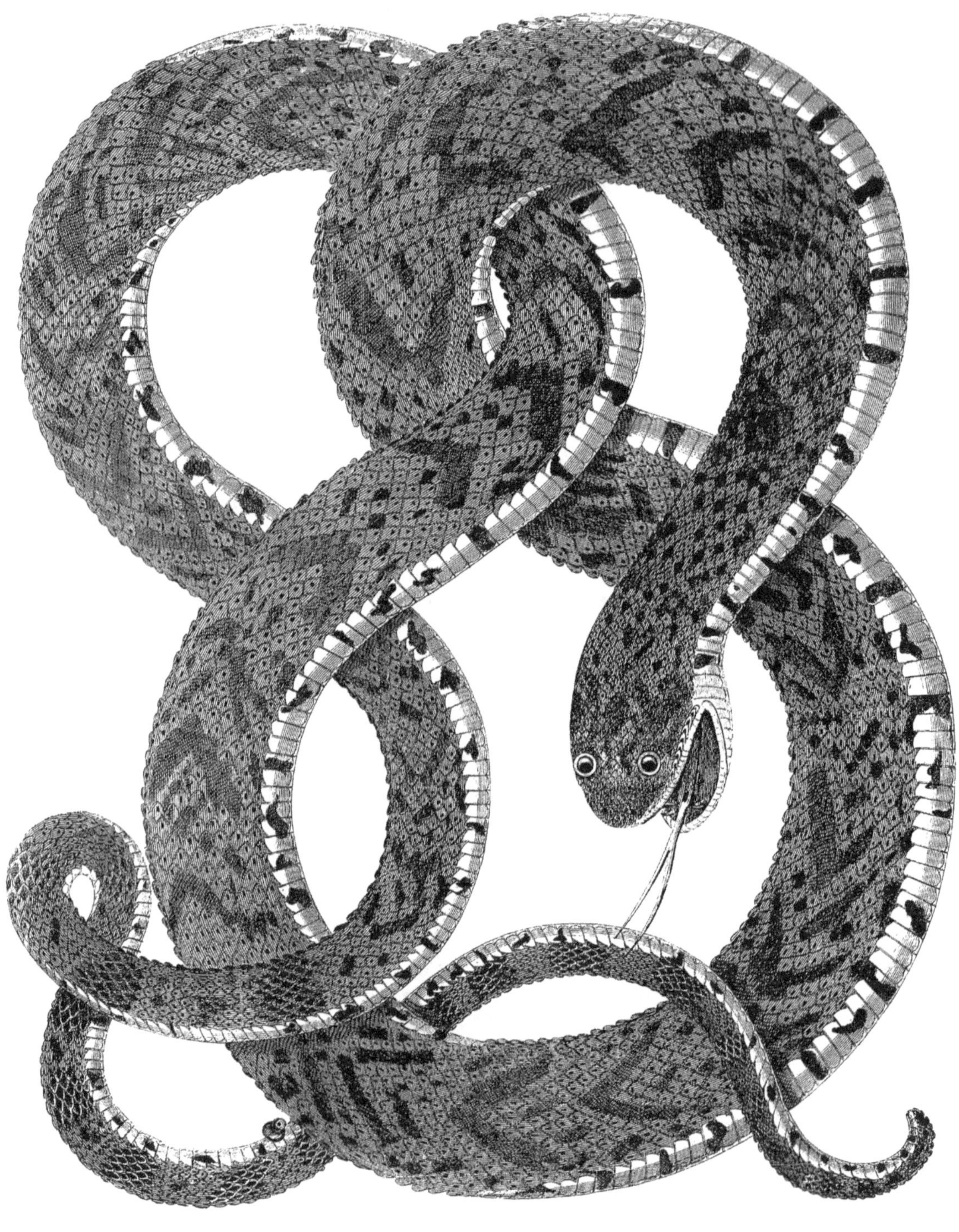

21

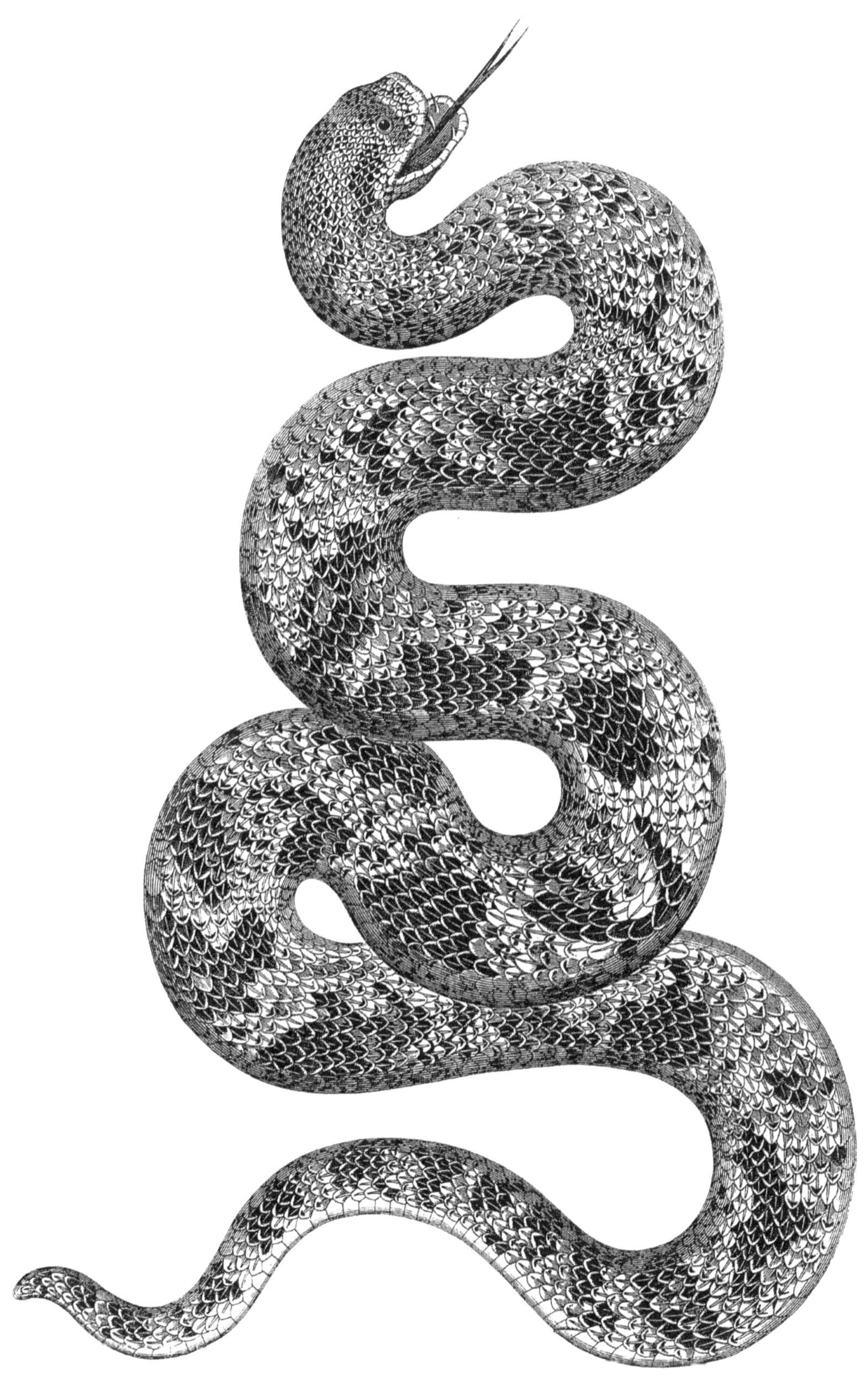

SNAKES & OTHER REPTILES

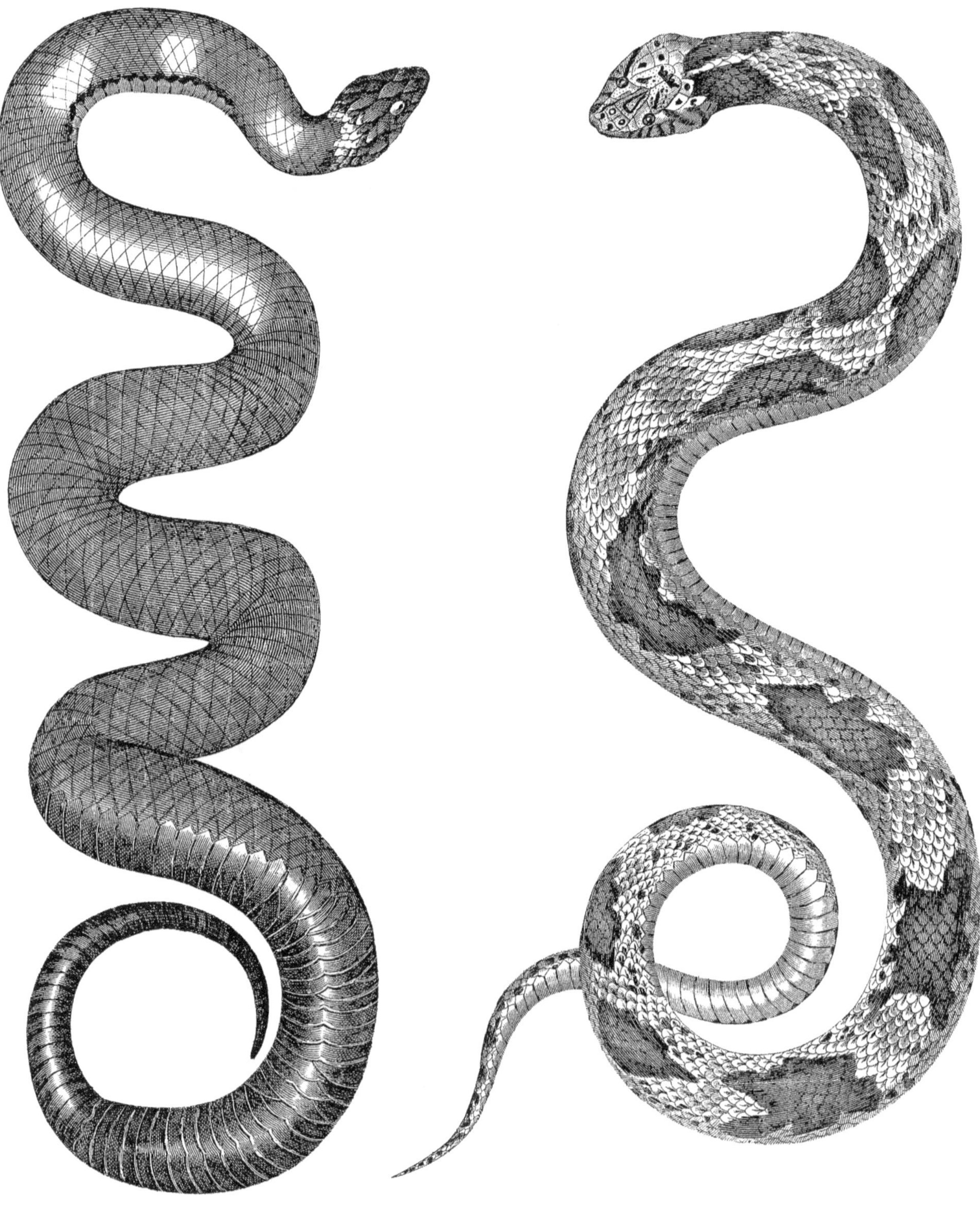

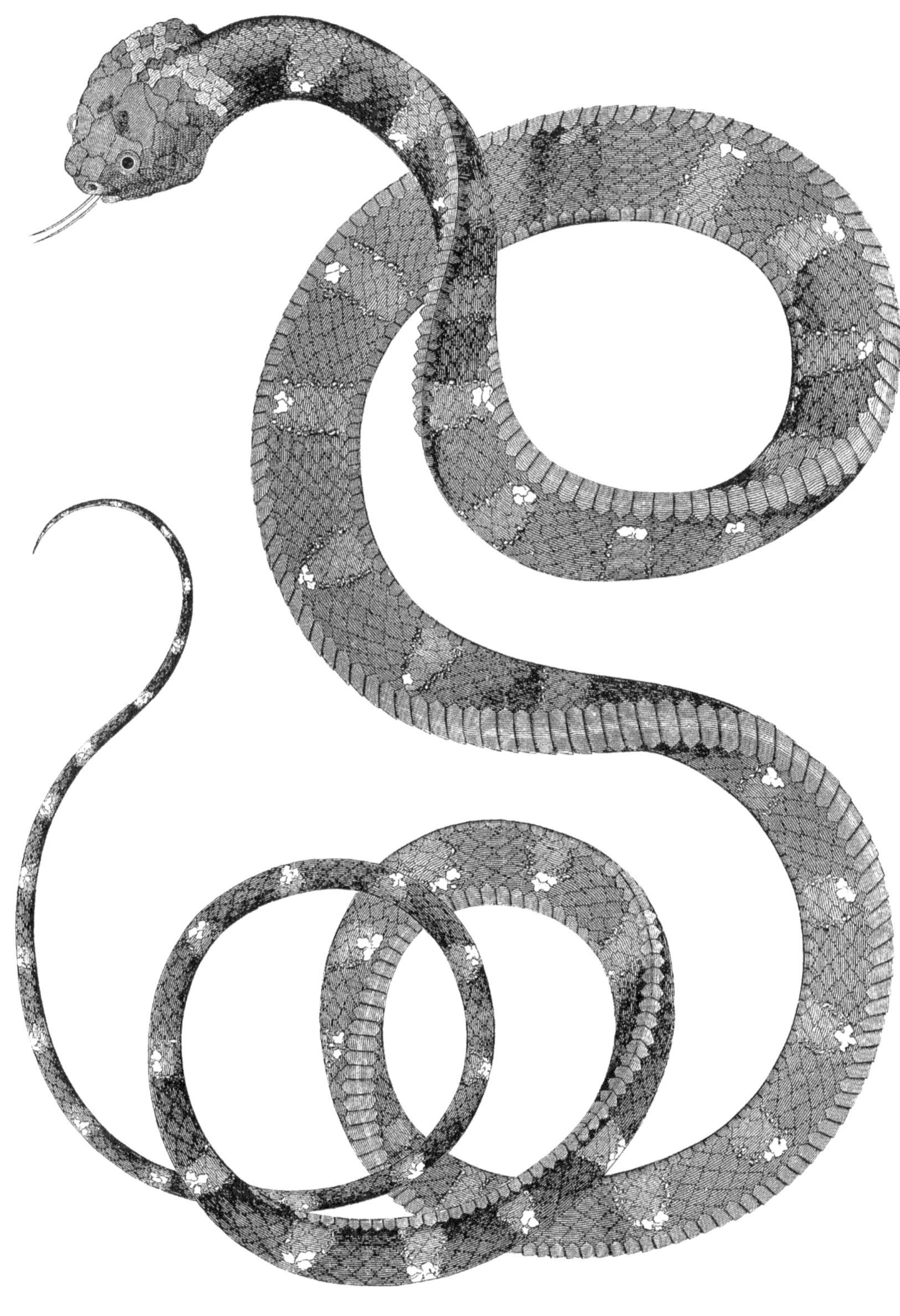

25

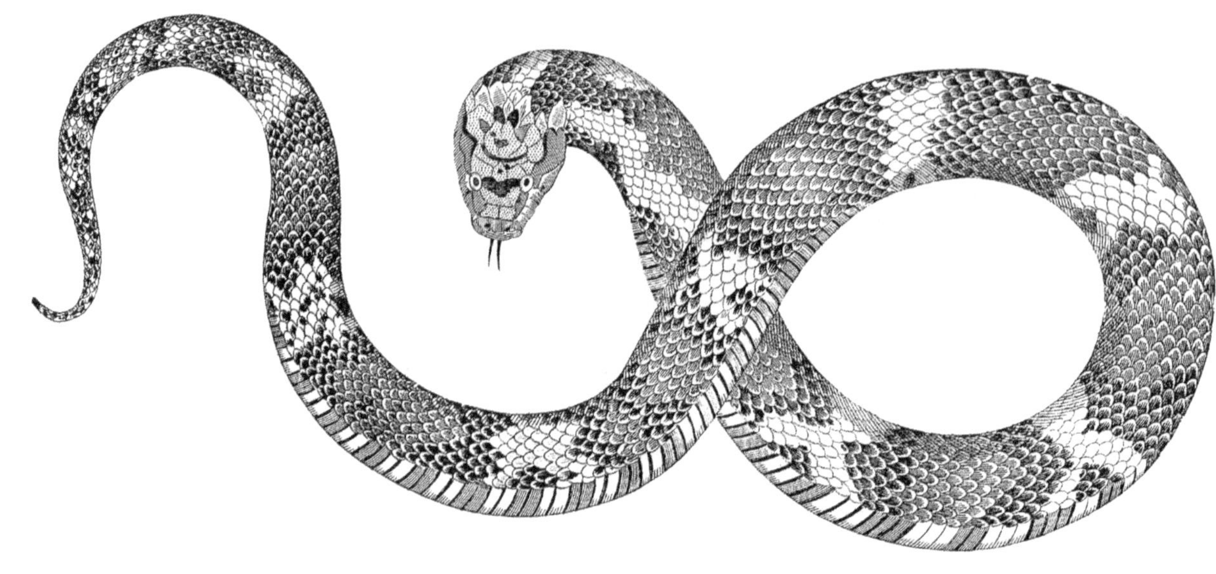

26

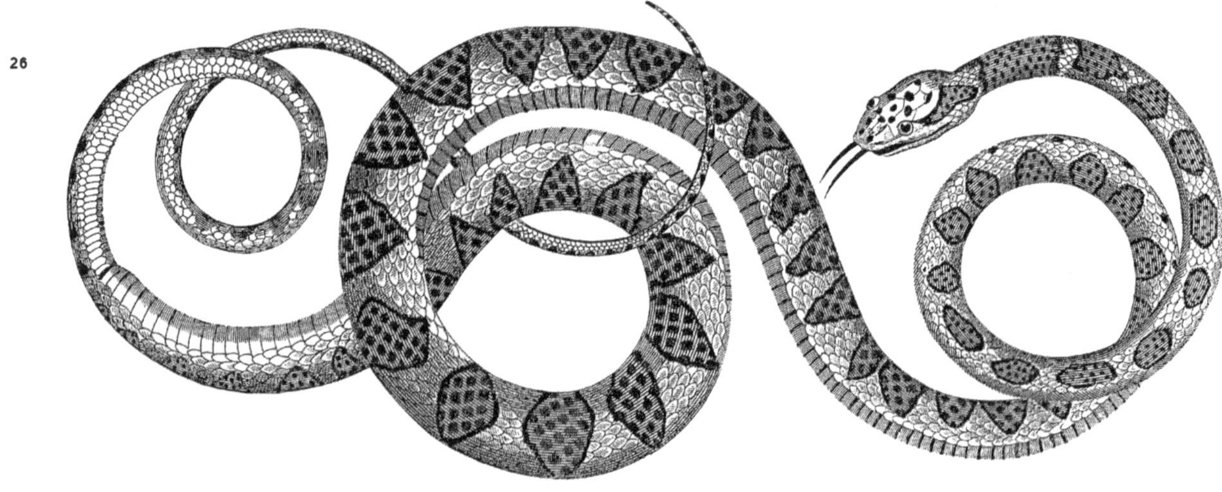

27

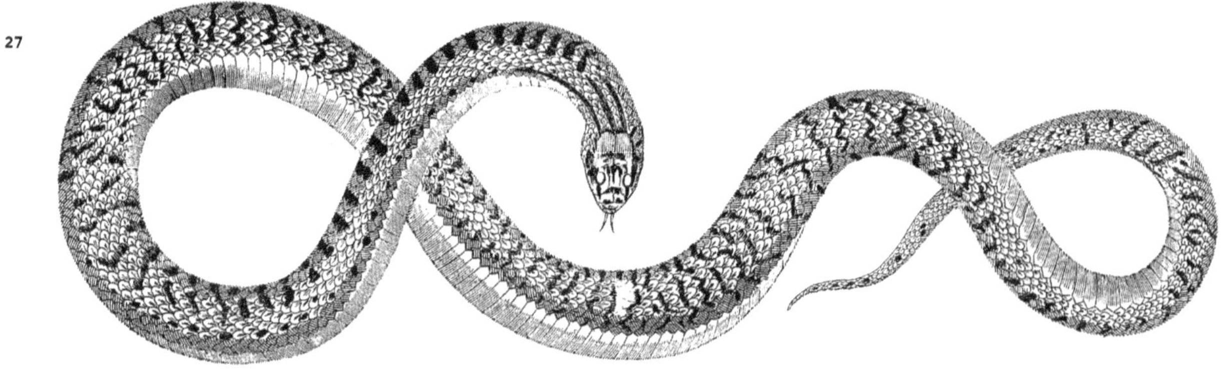

28

29

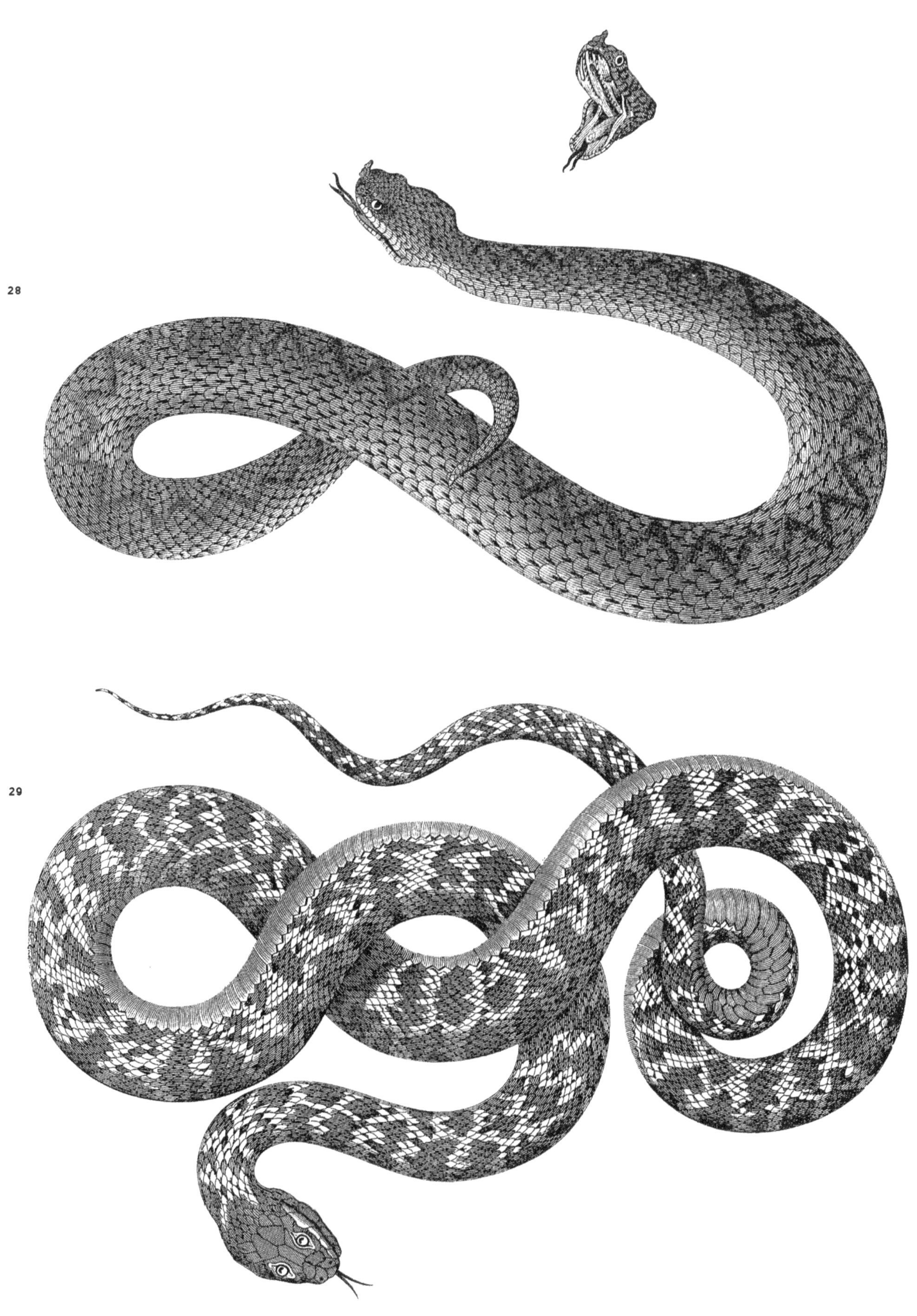

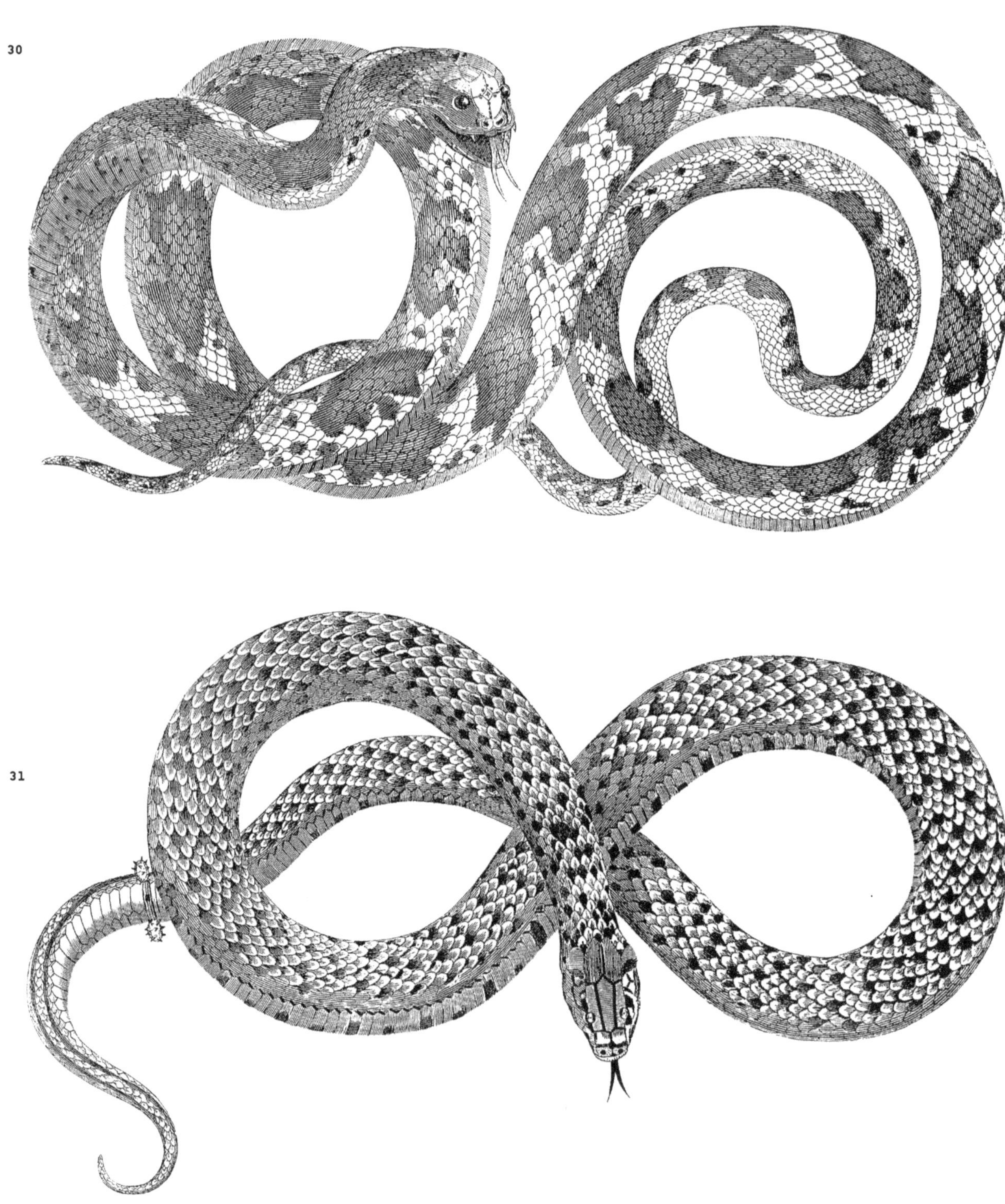

30

31

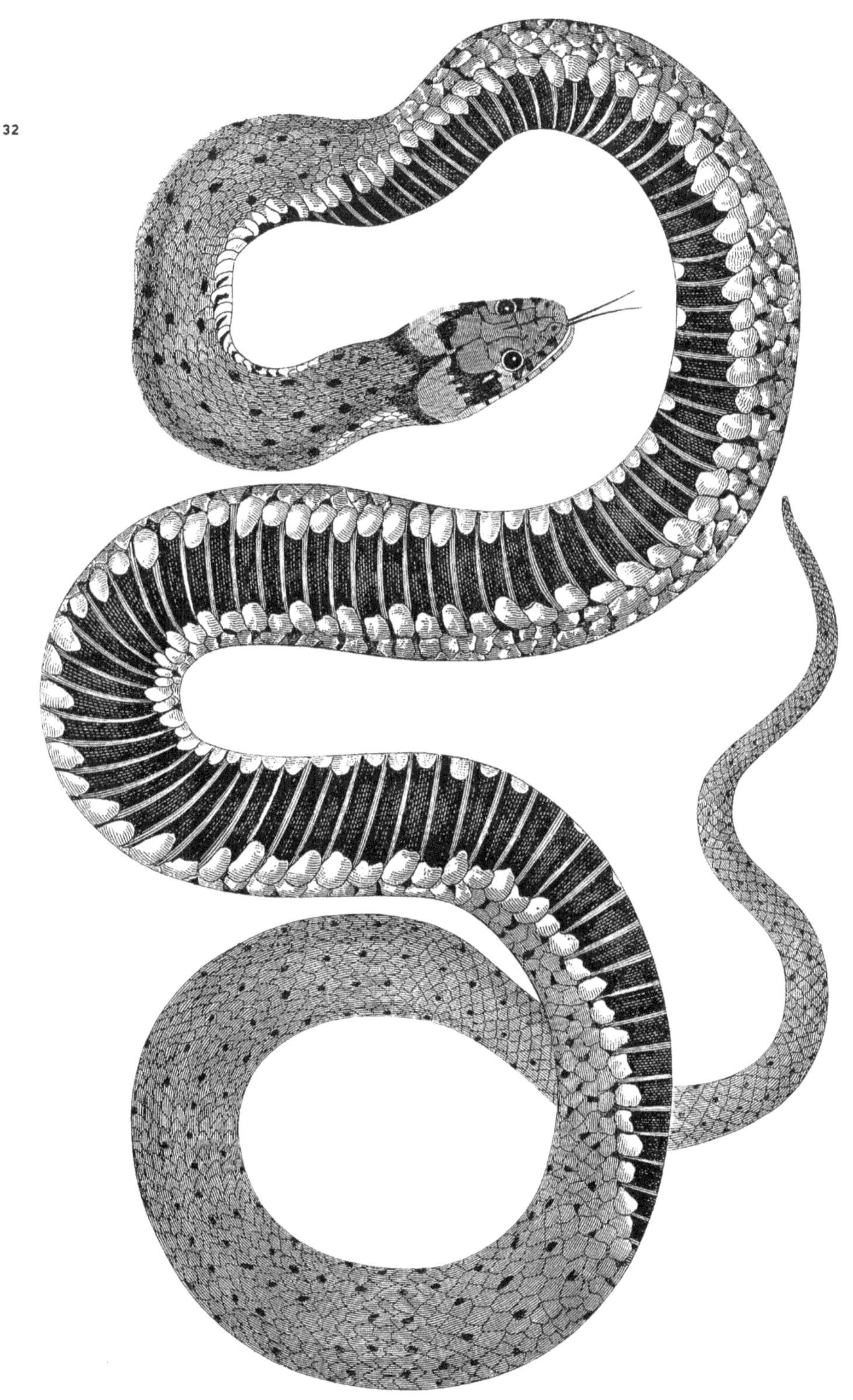

32

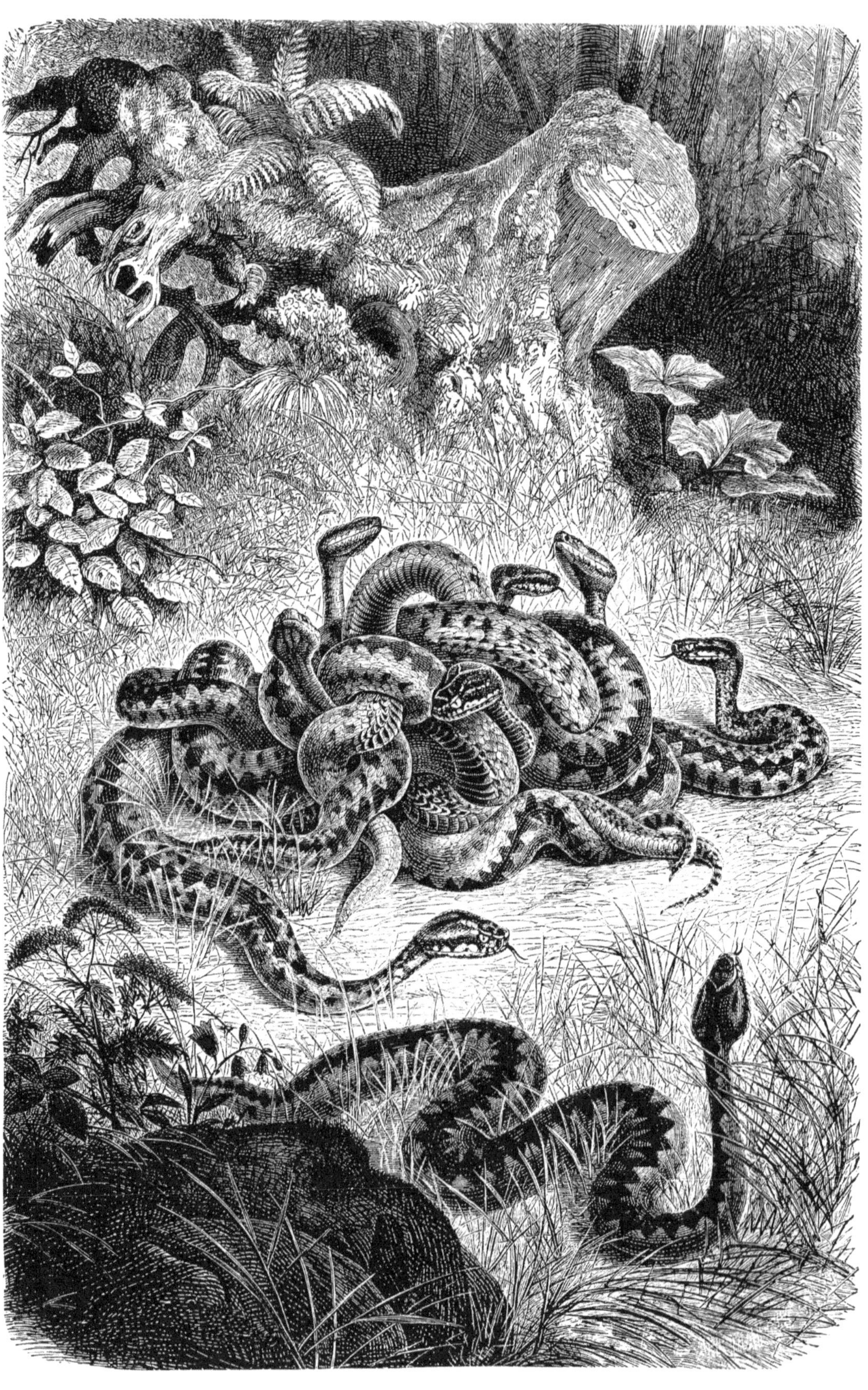

34

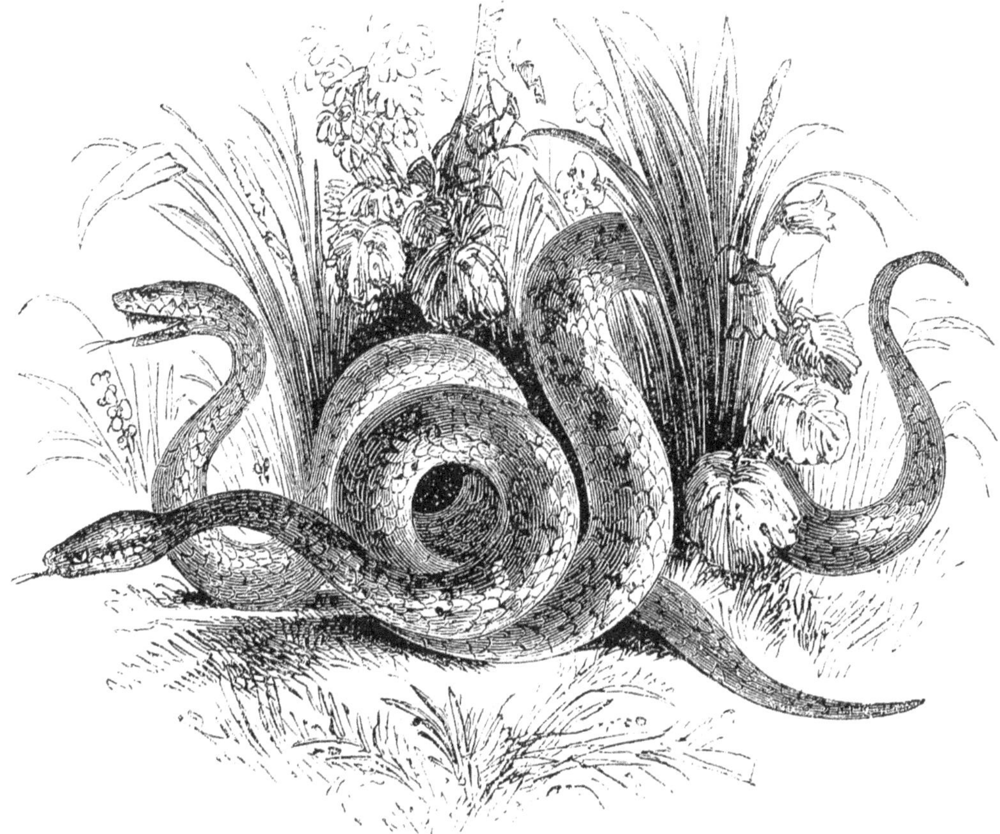

35

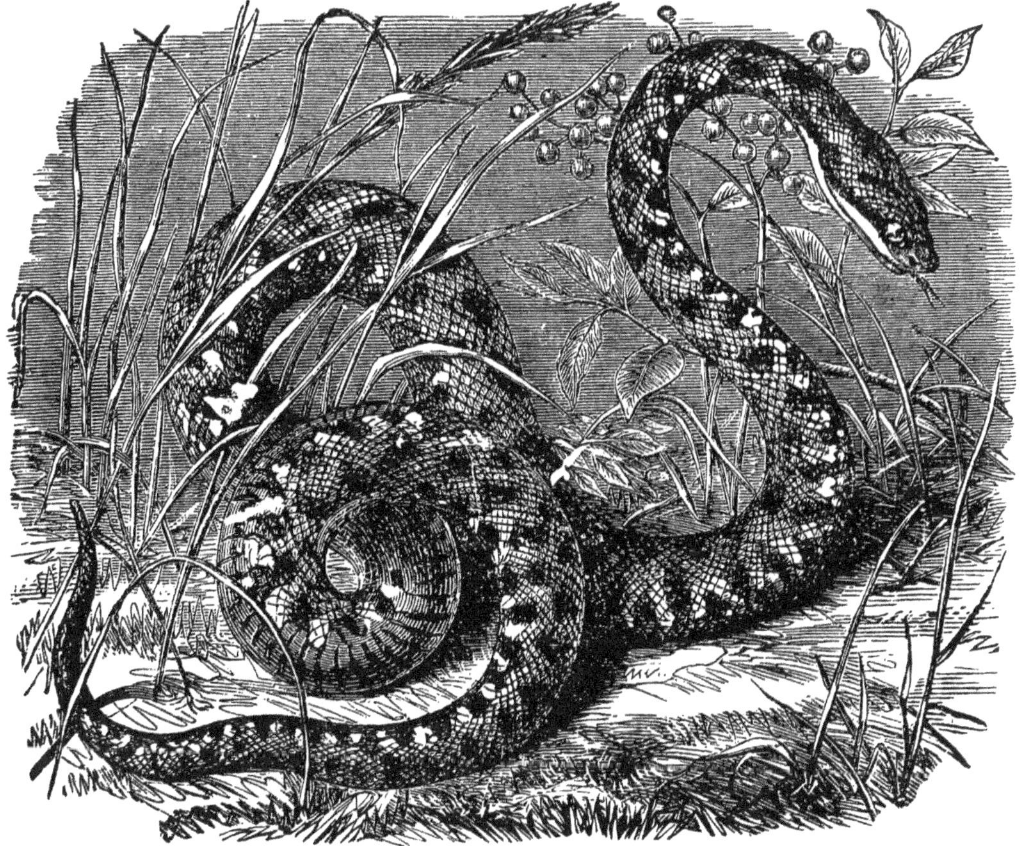

36

37

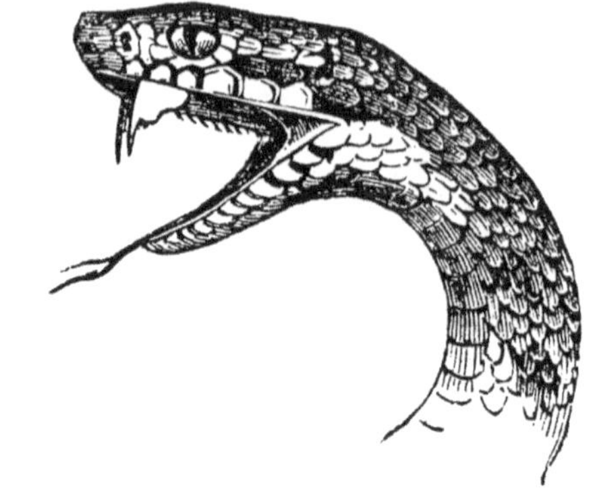

38

39

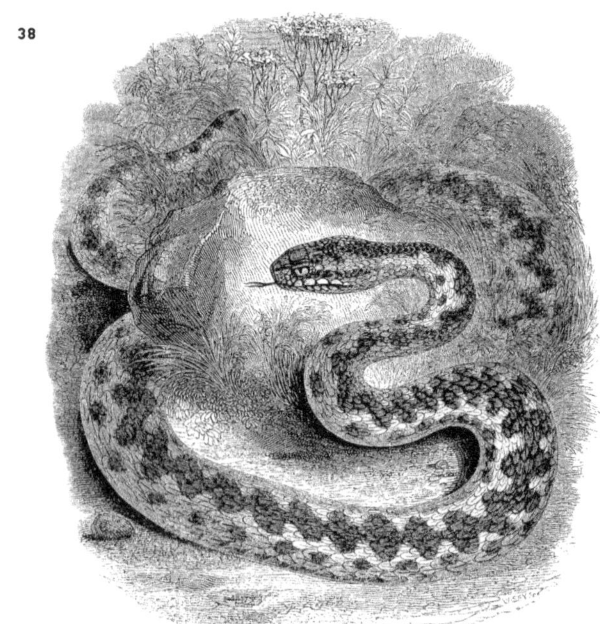

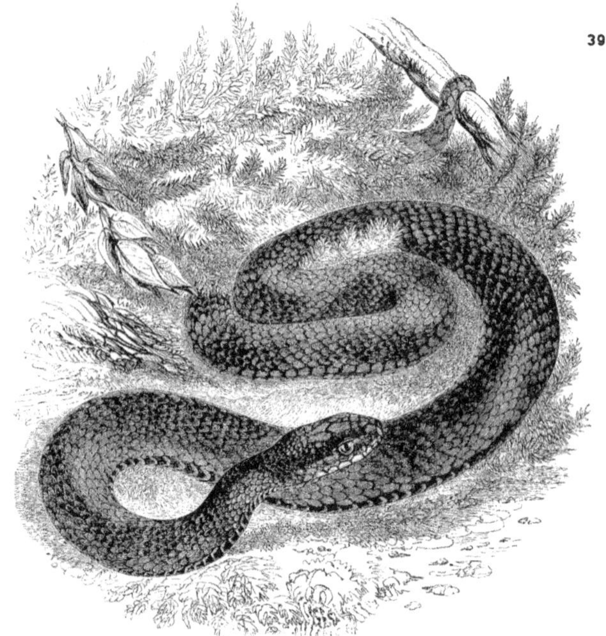

40

41

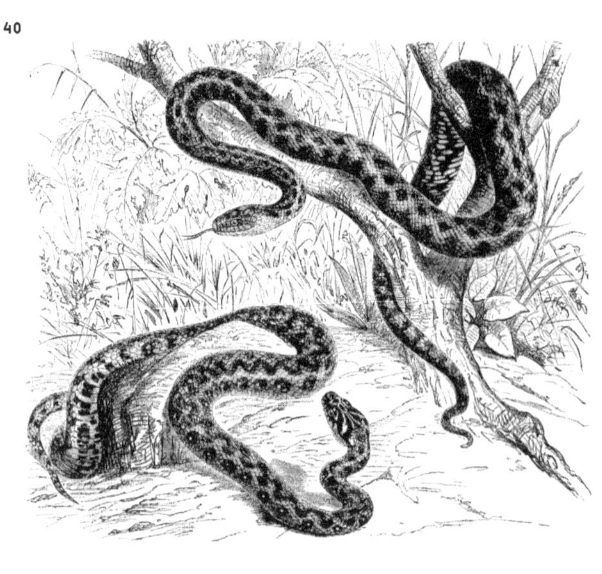

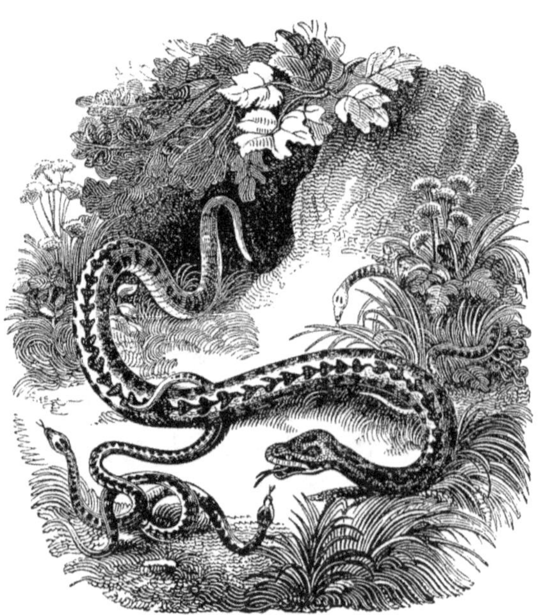

42

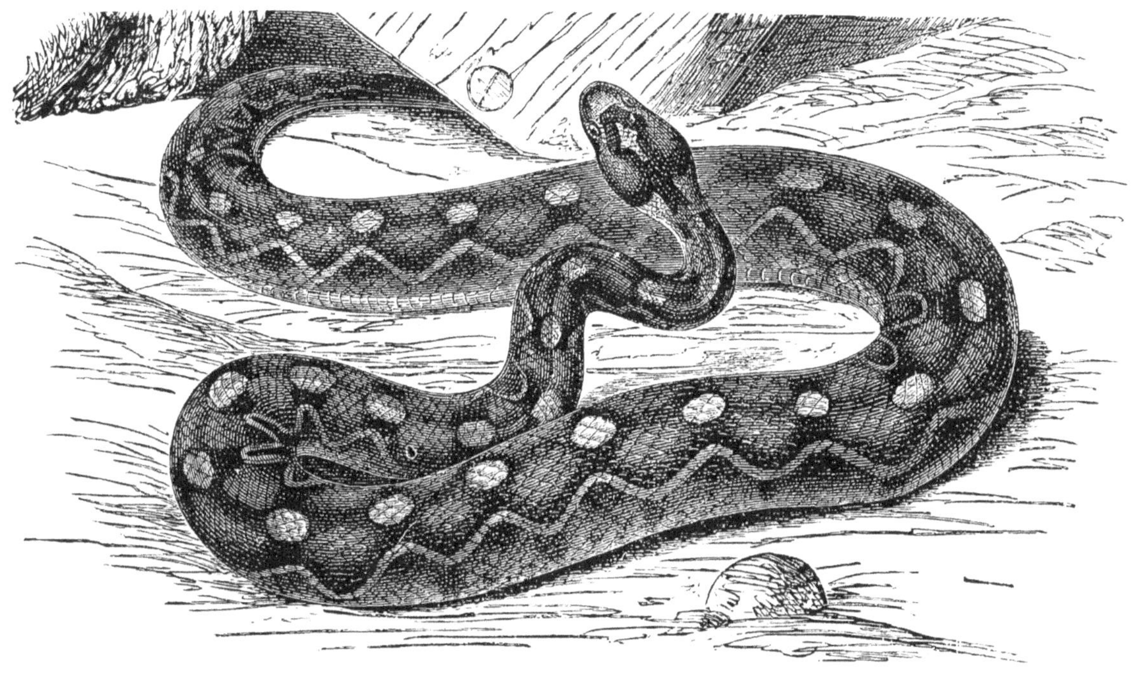

43

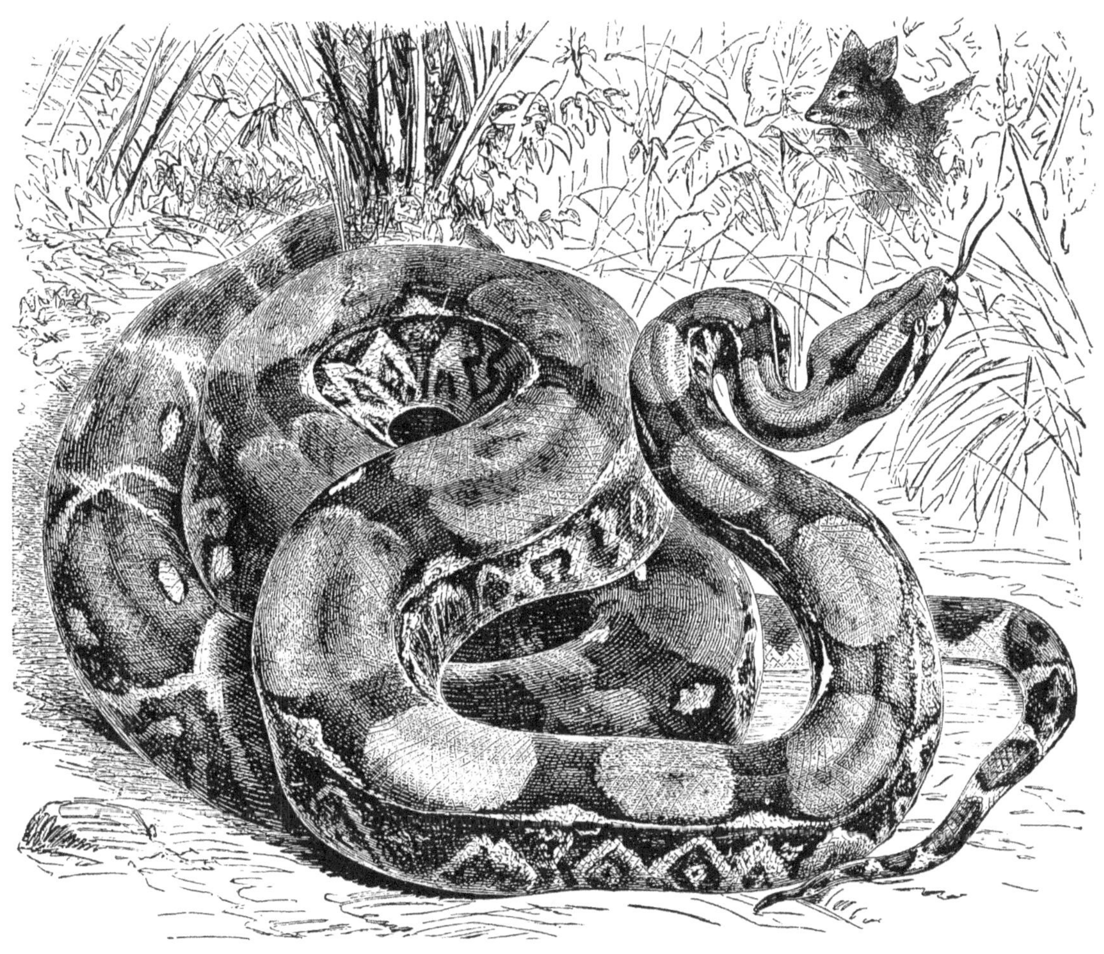

44

45

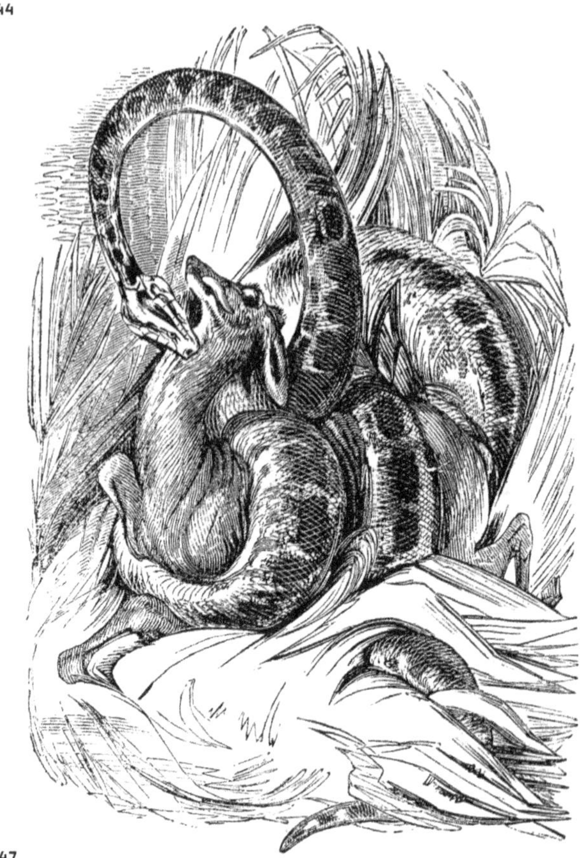

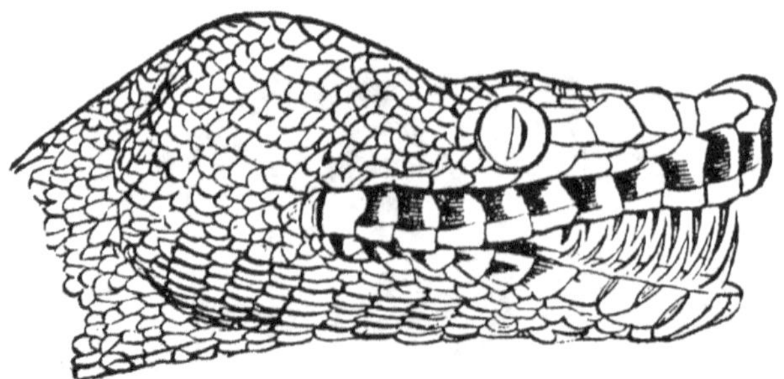

46

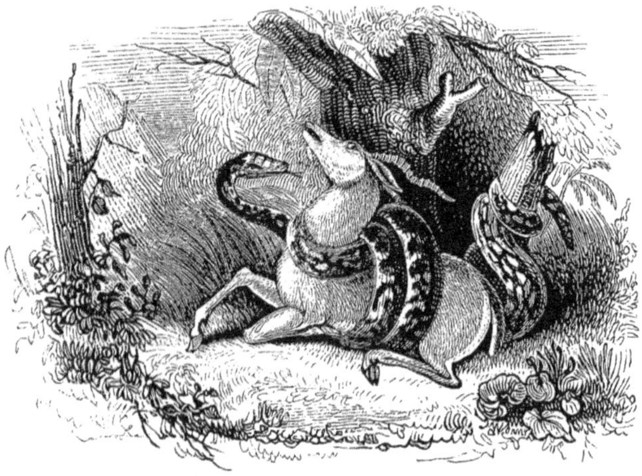

47

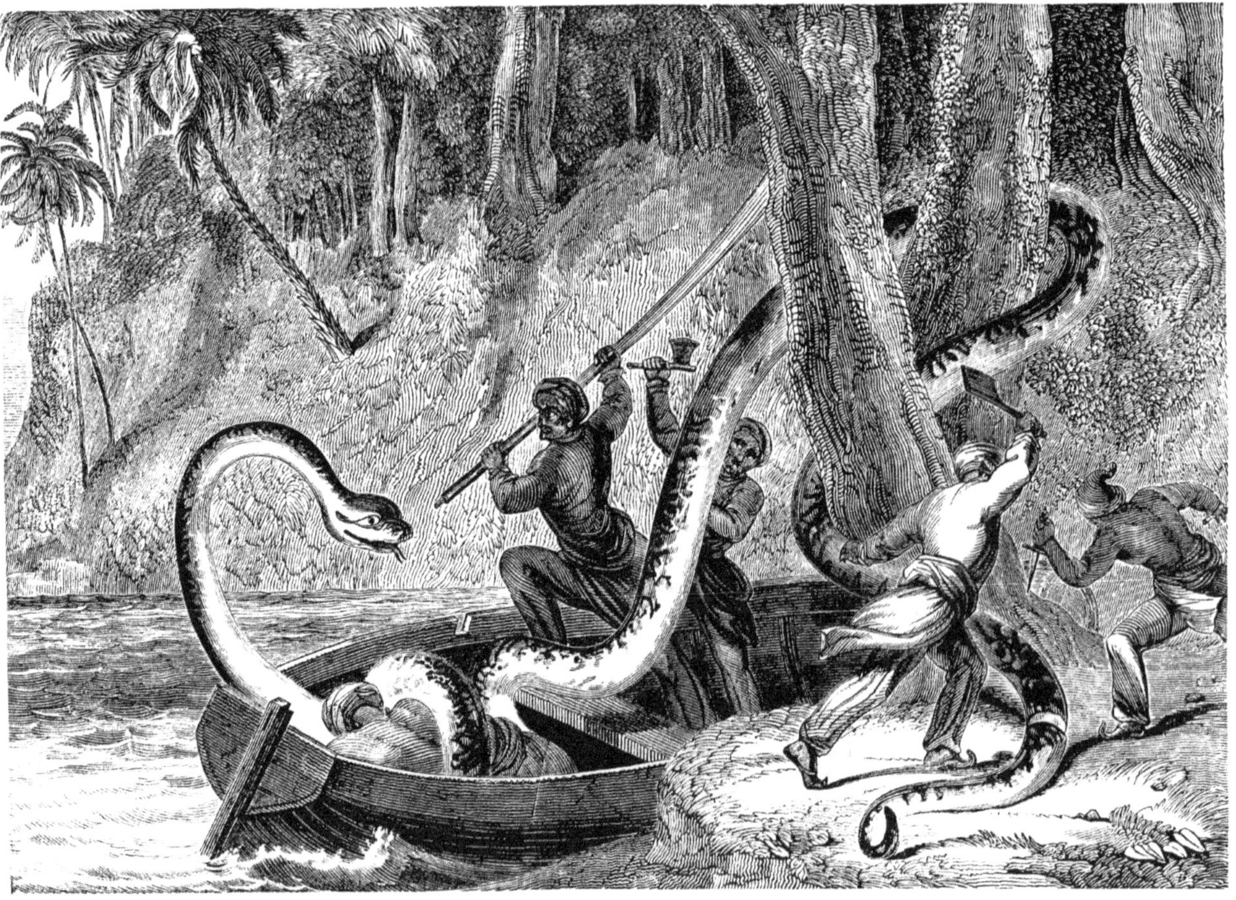

SNAKES

48

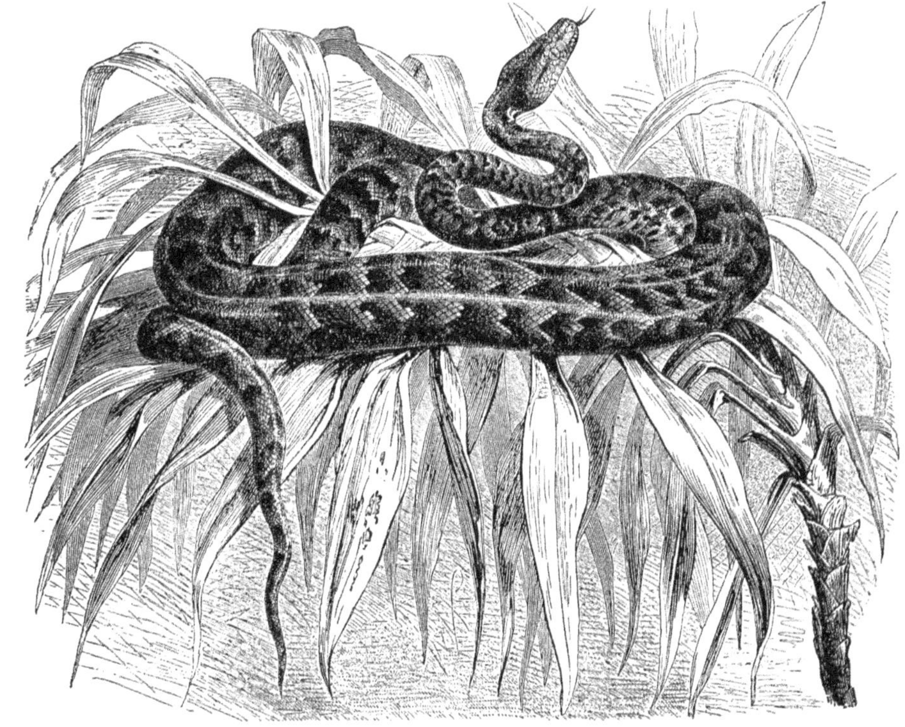

49

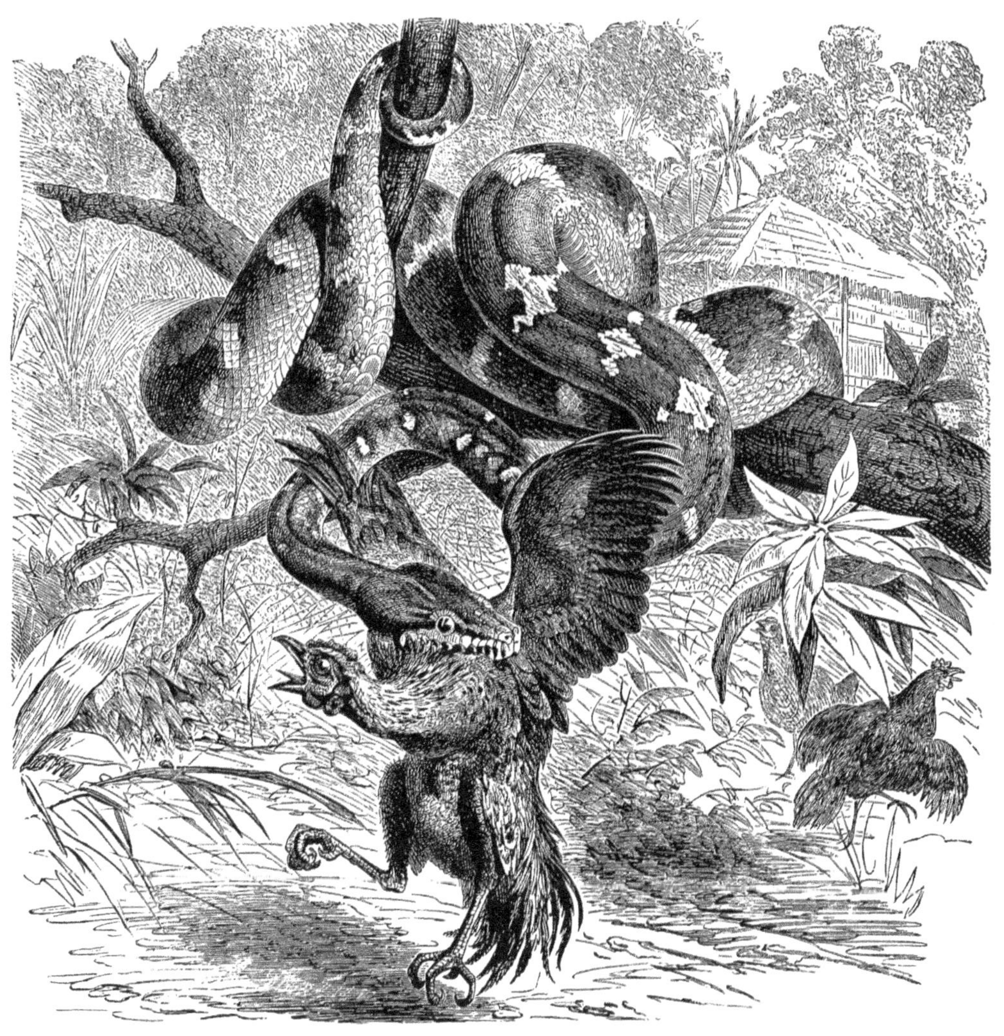

SNAKES

50

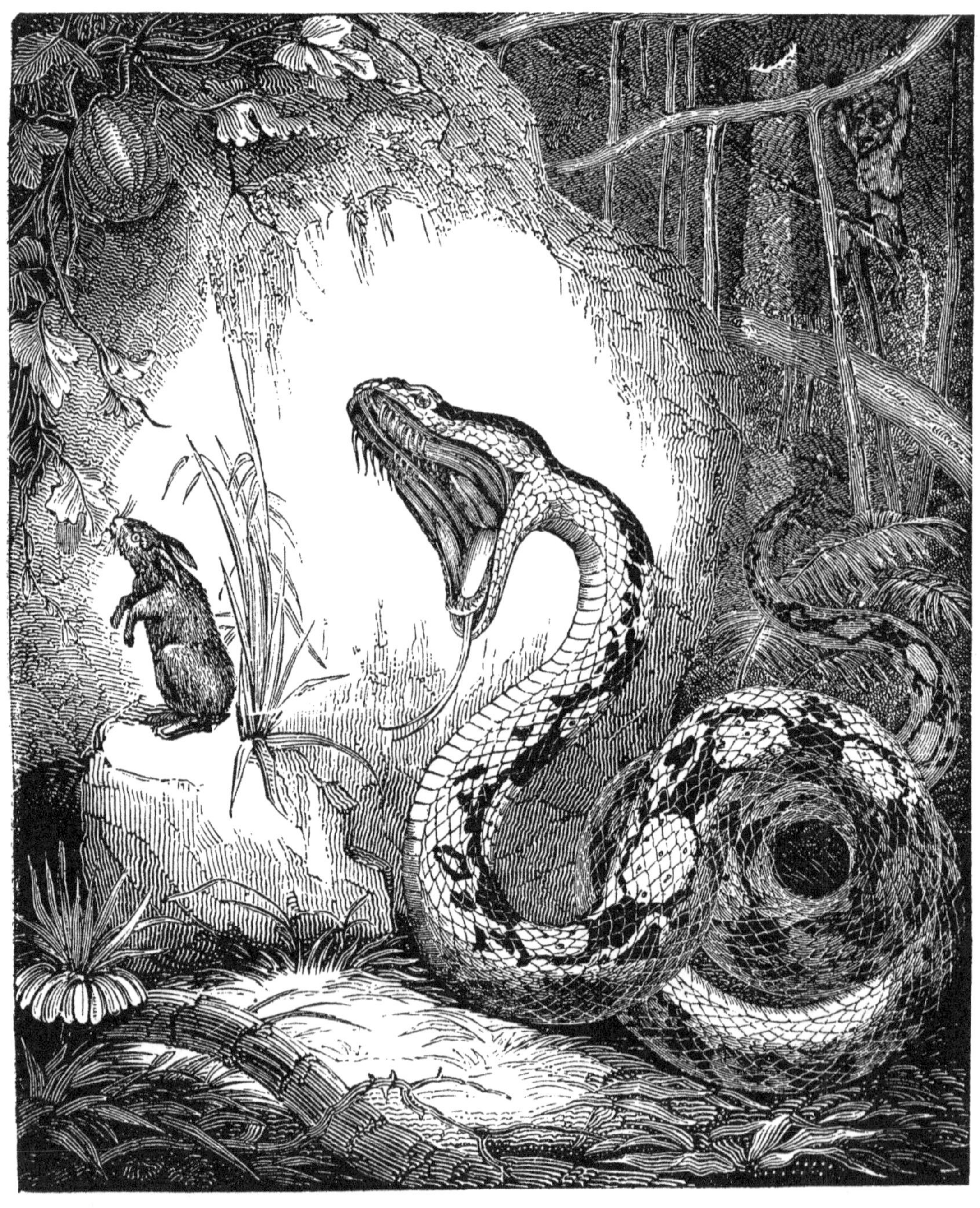

51

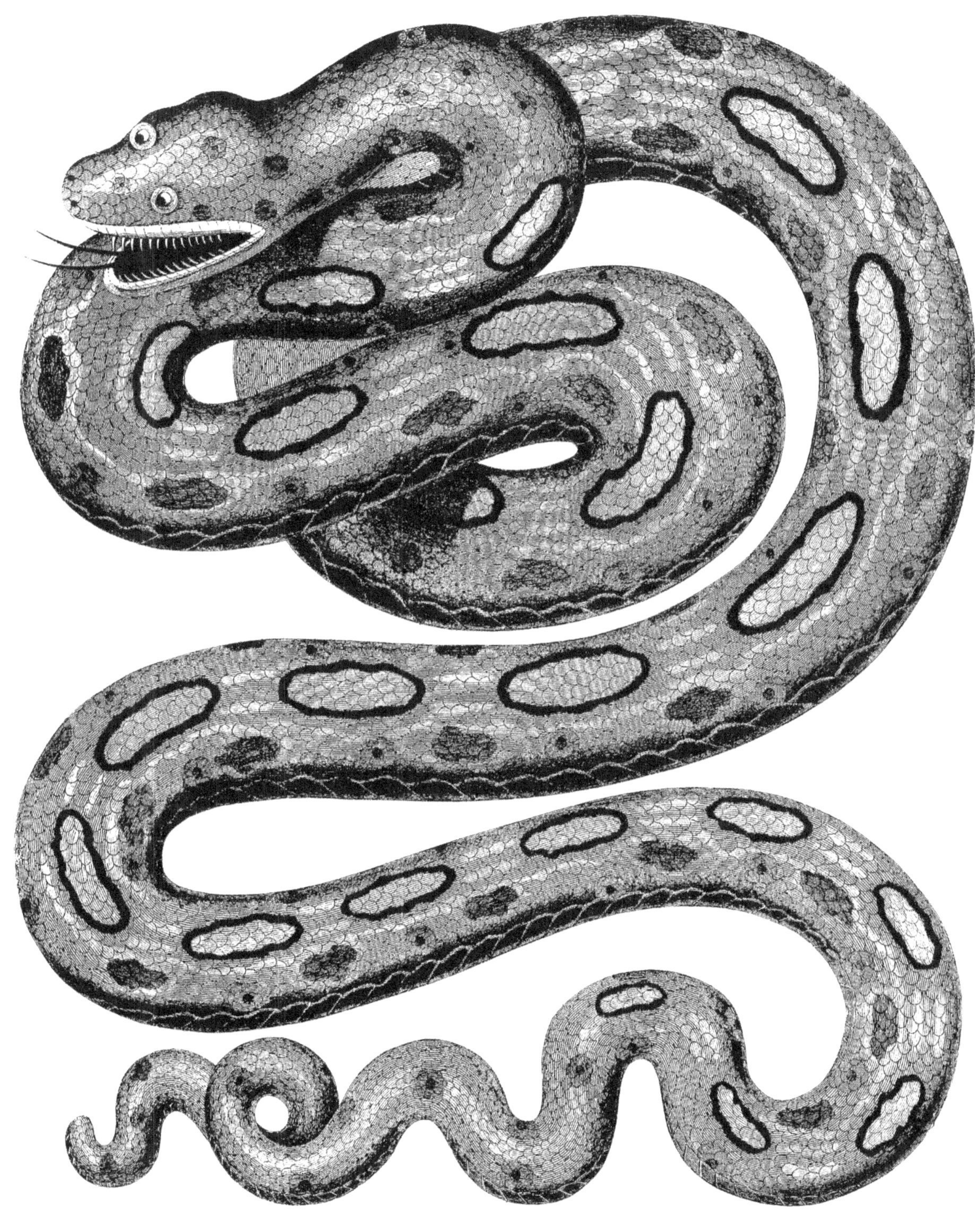

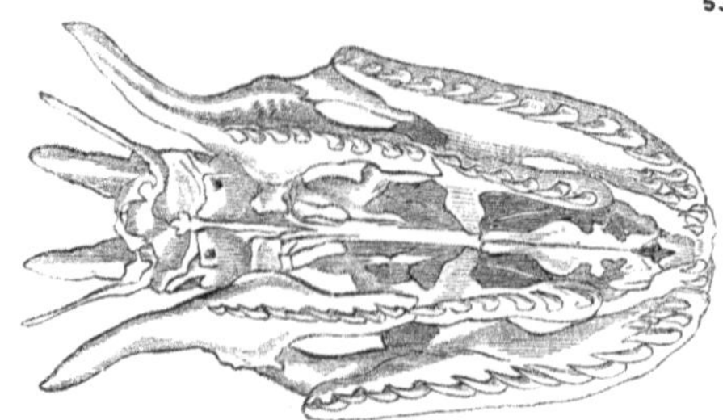

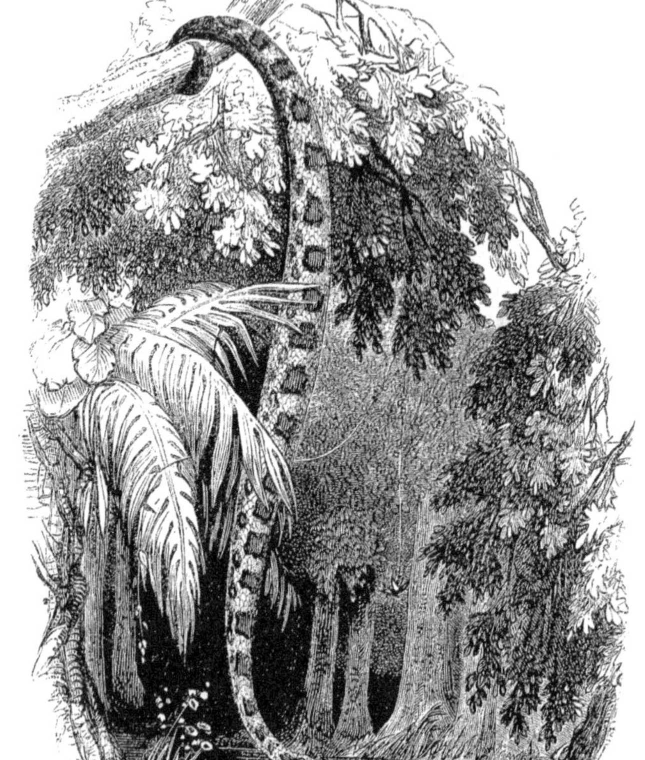

54

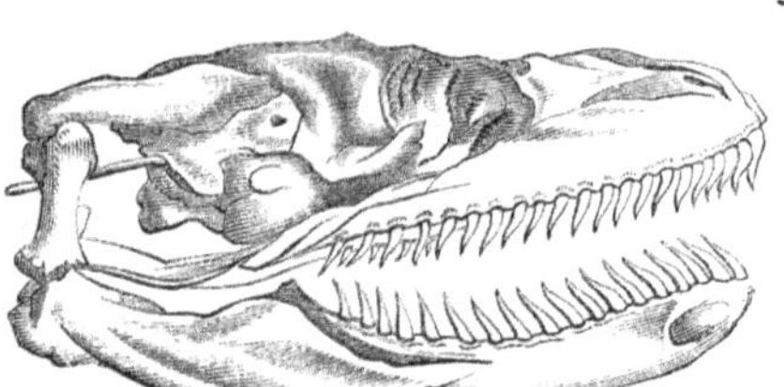

55

56

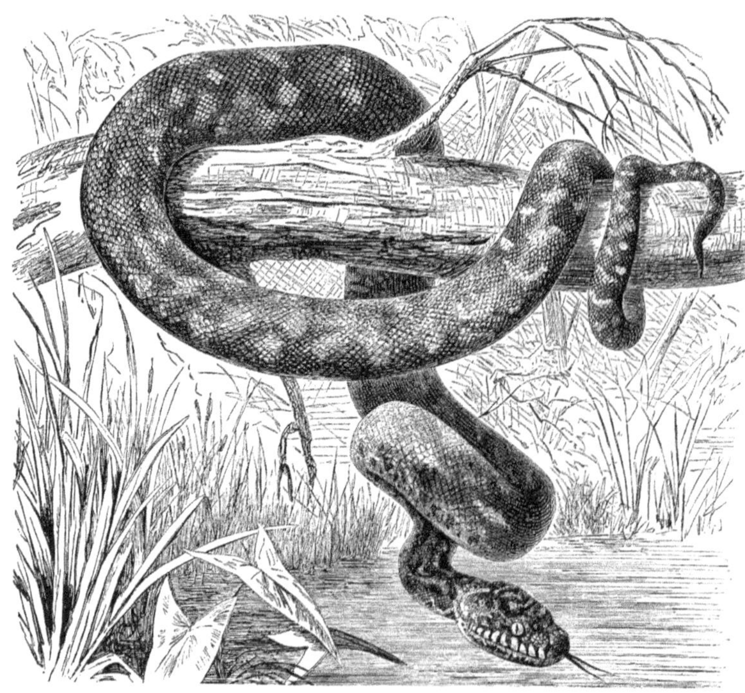

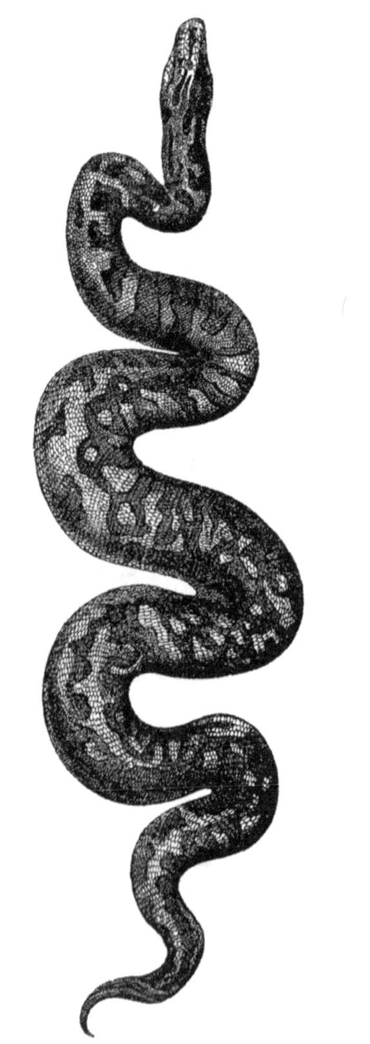

57

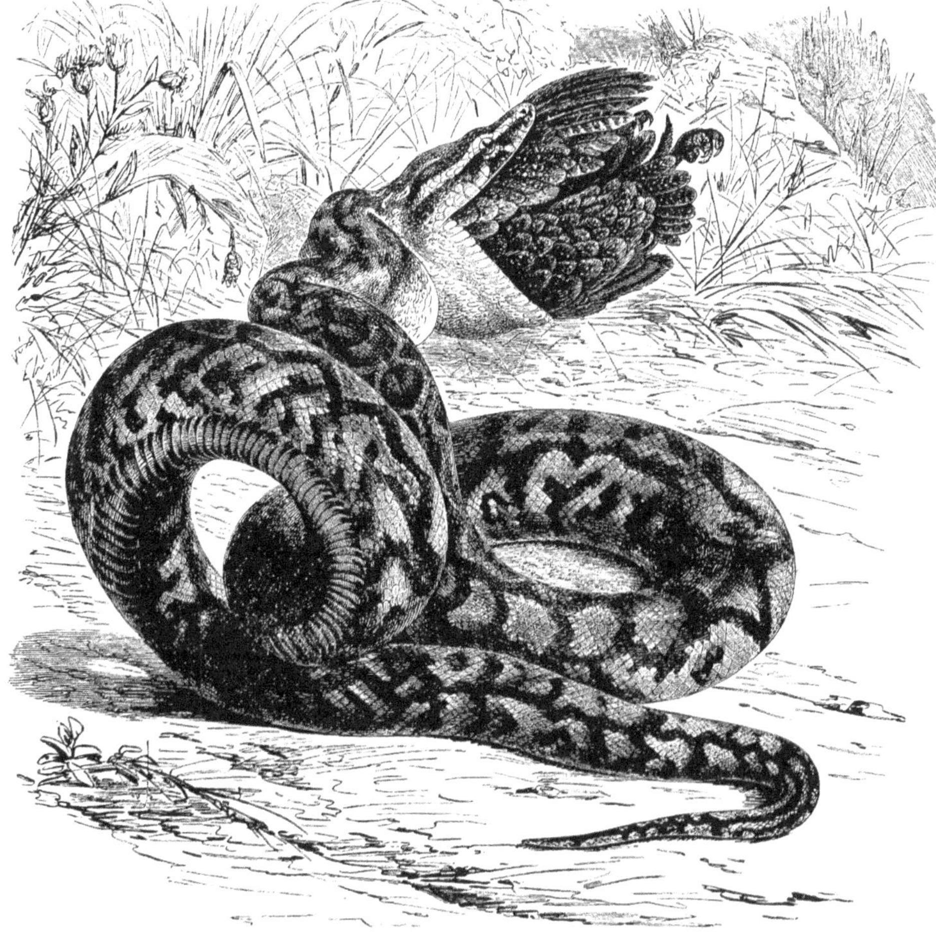

58

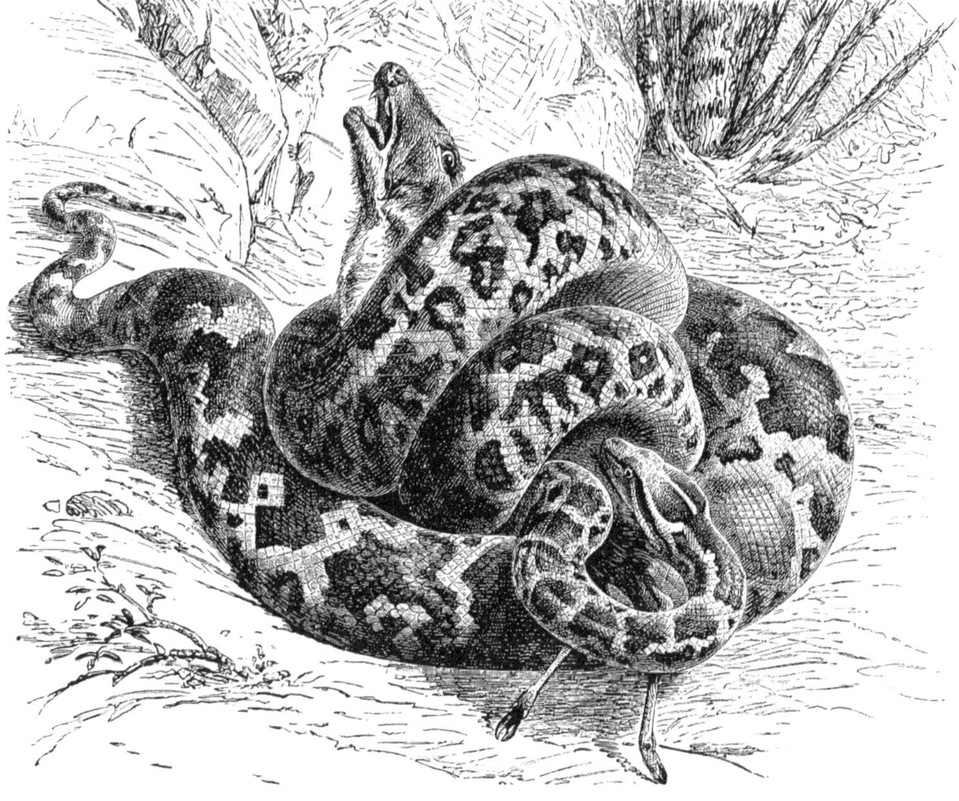

59

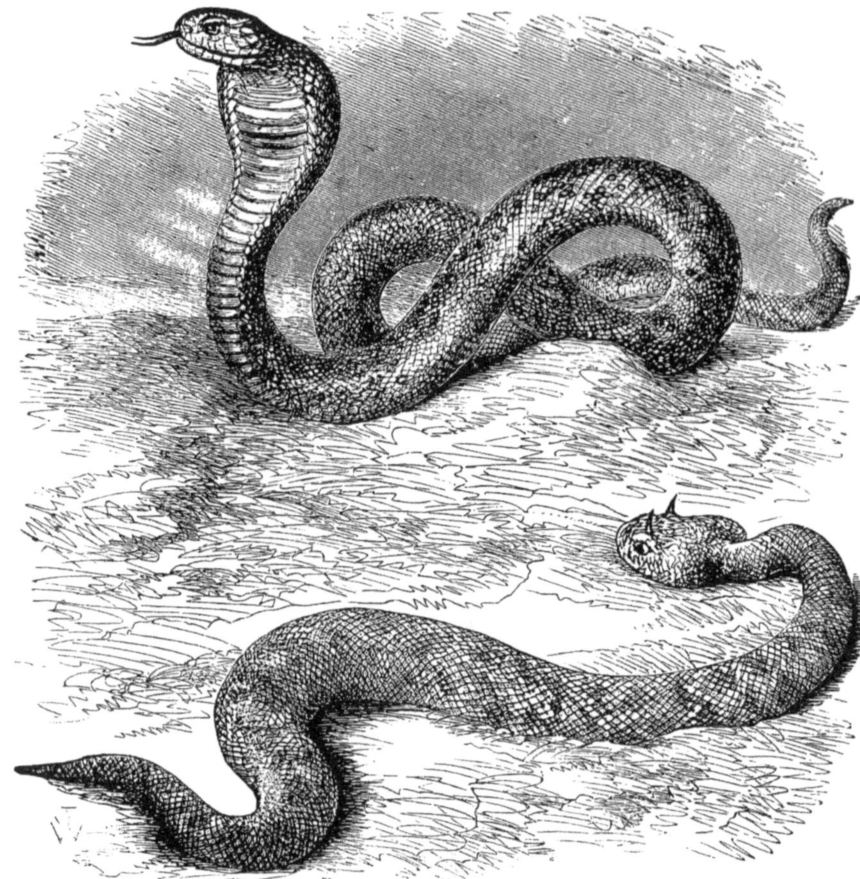

60

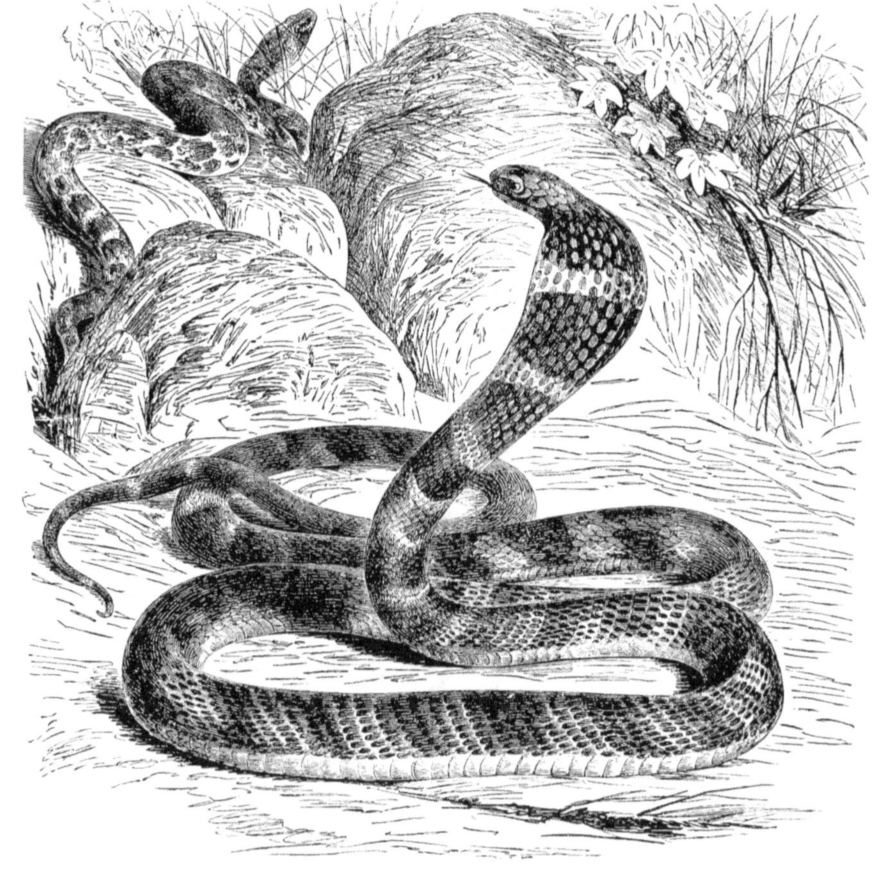

61

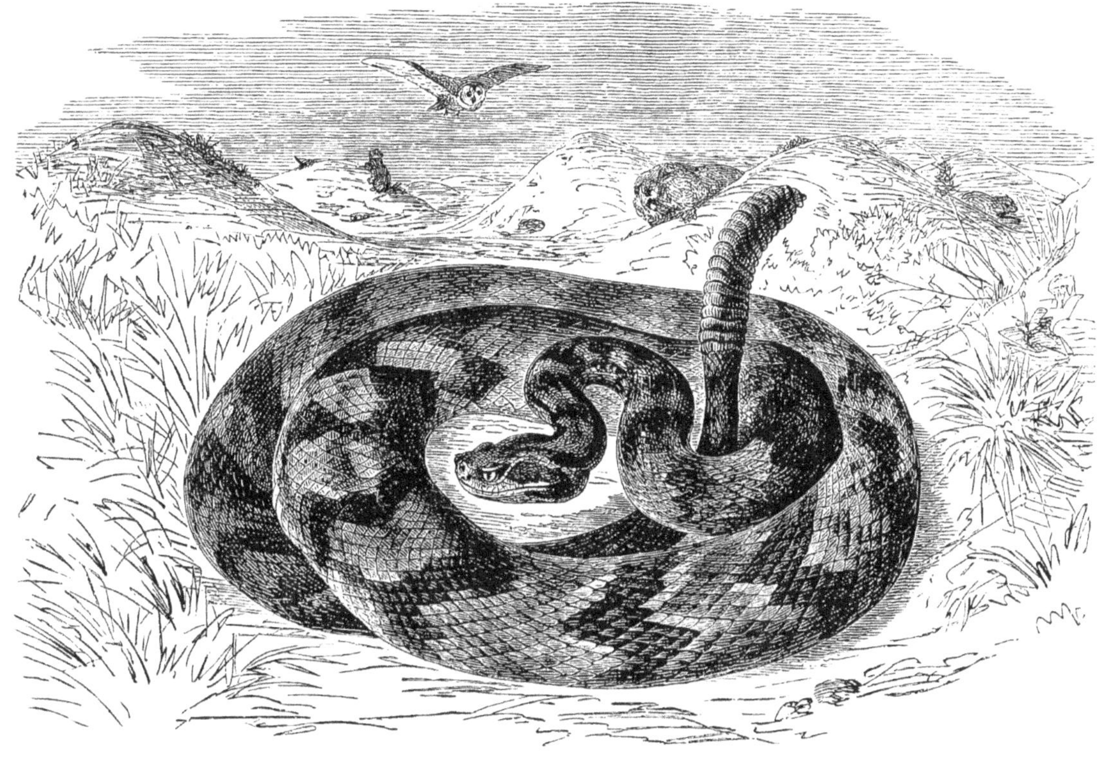

62

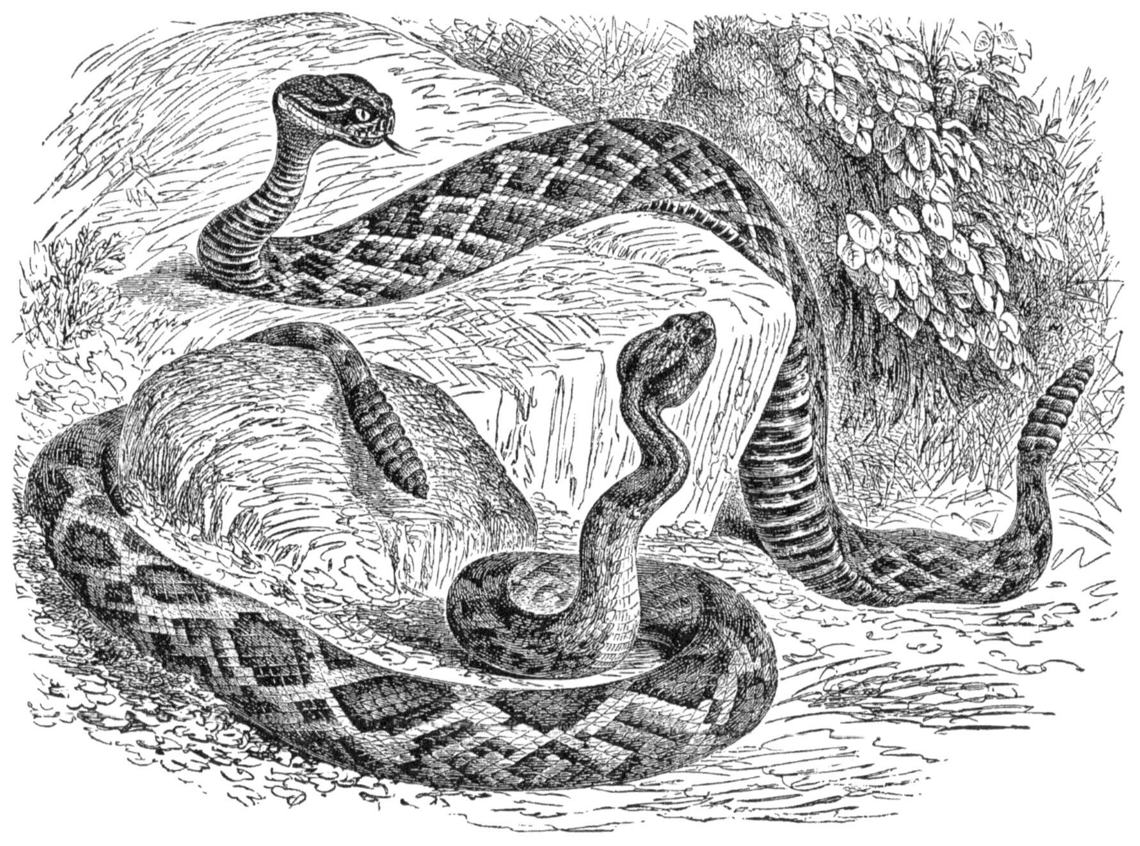

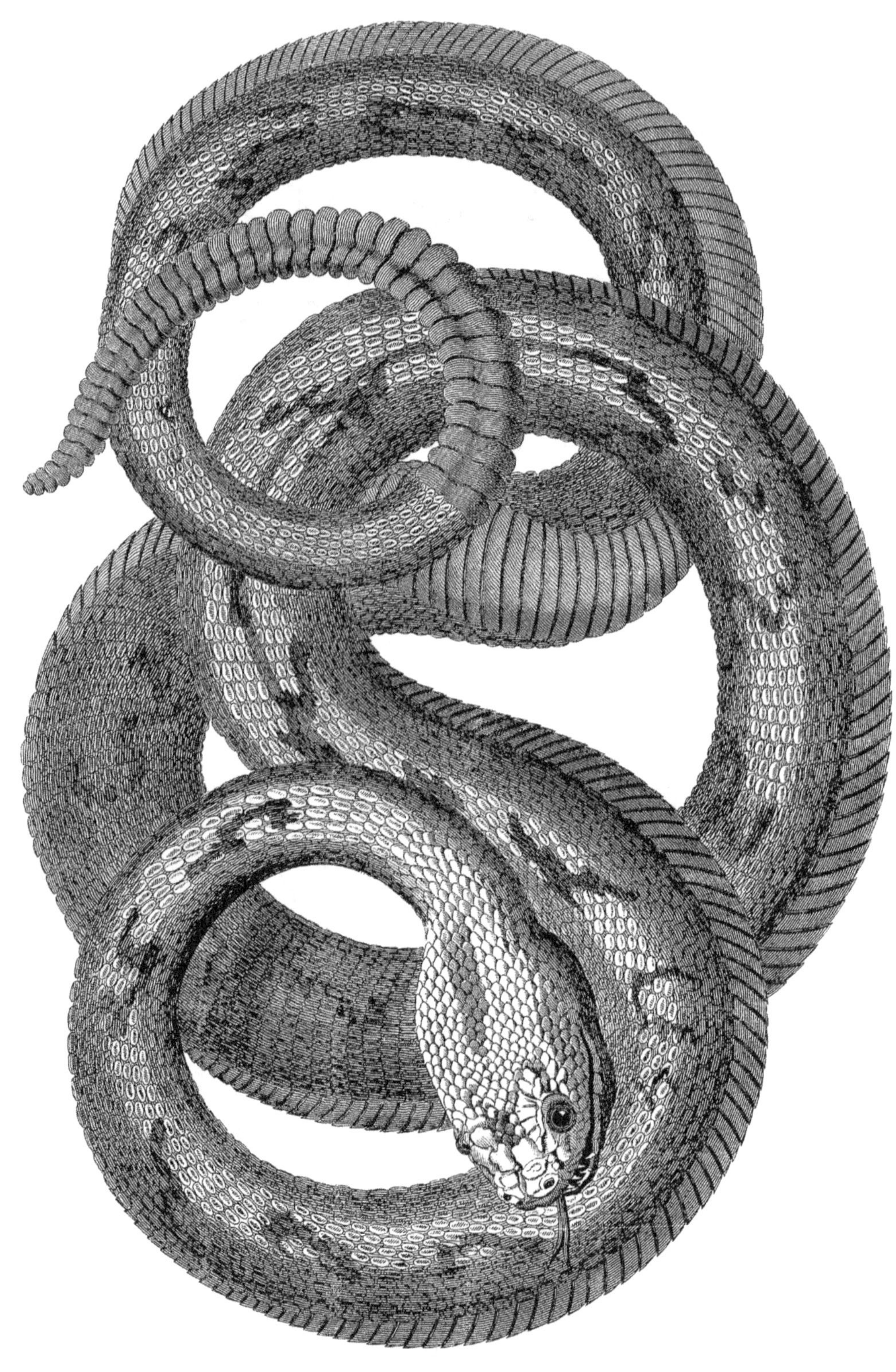

64

65

66

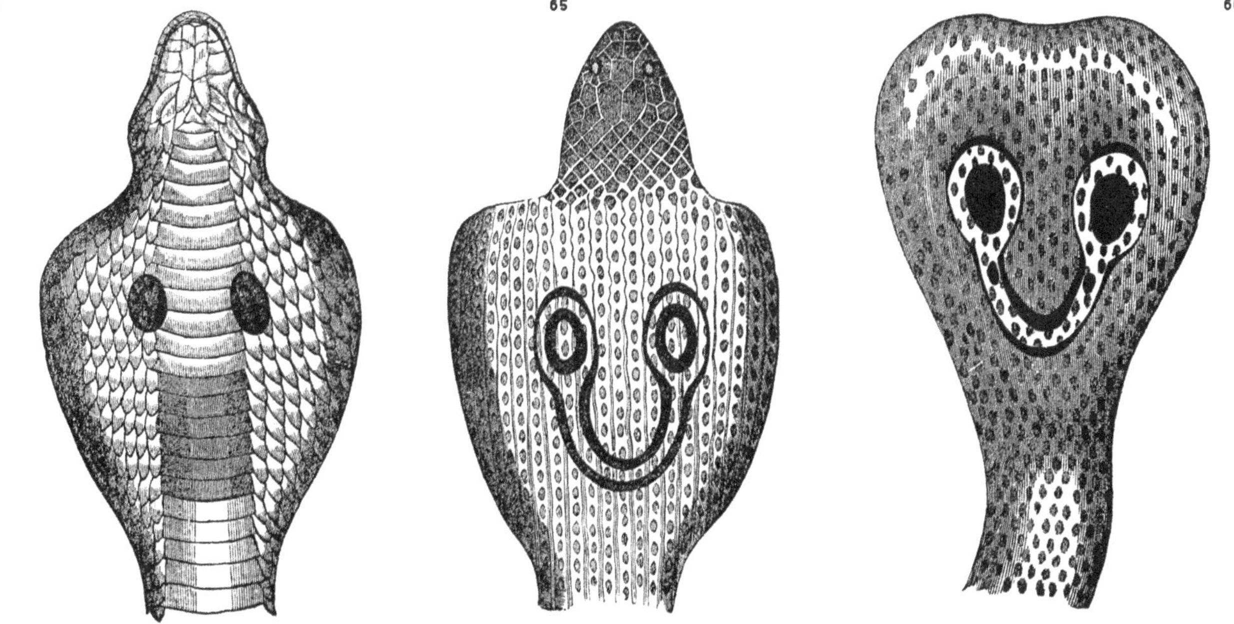

67

68

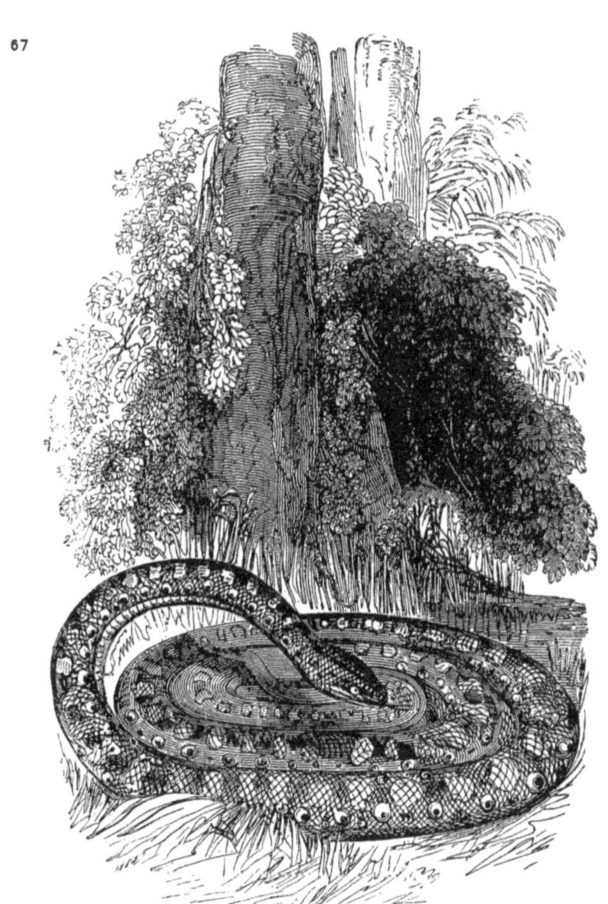

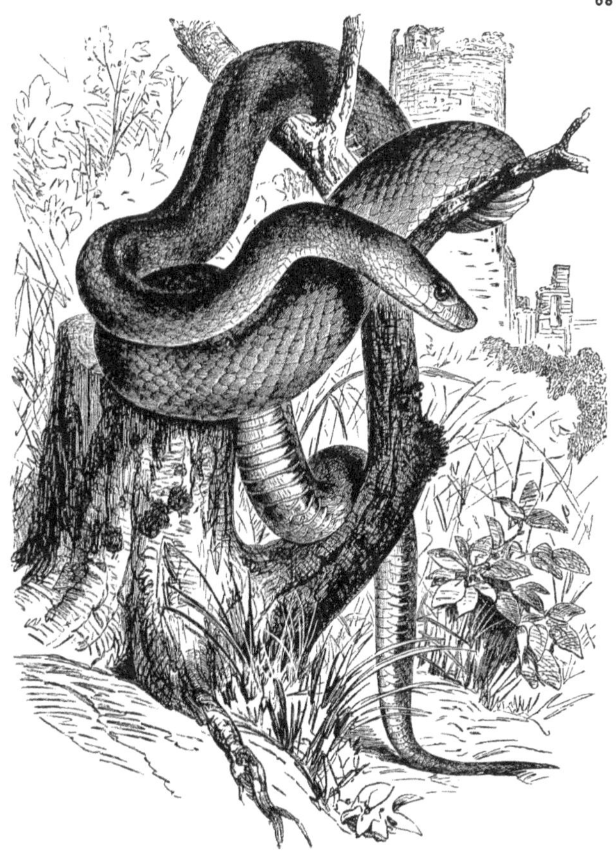

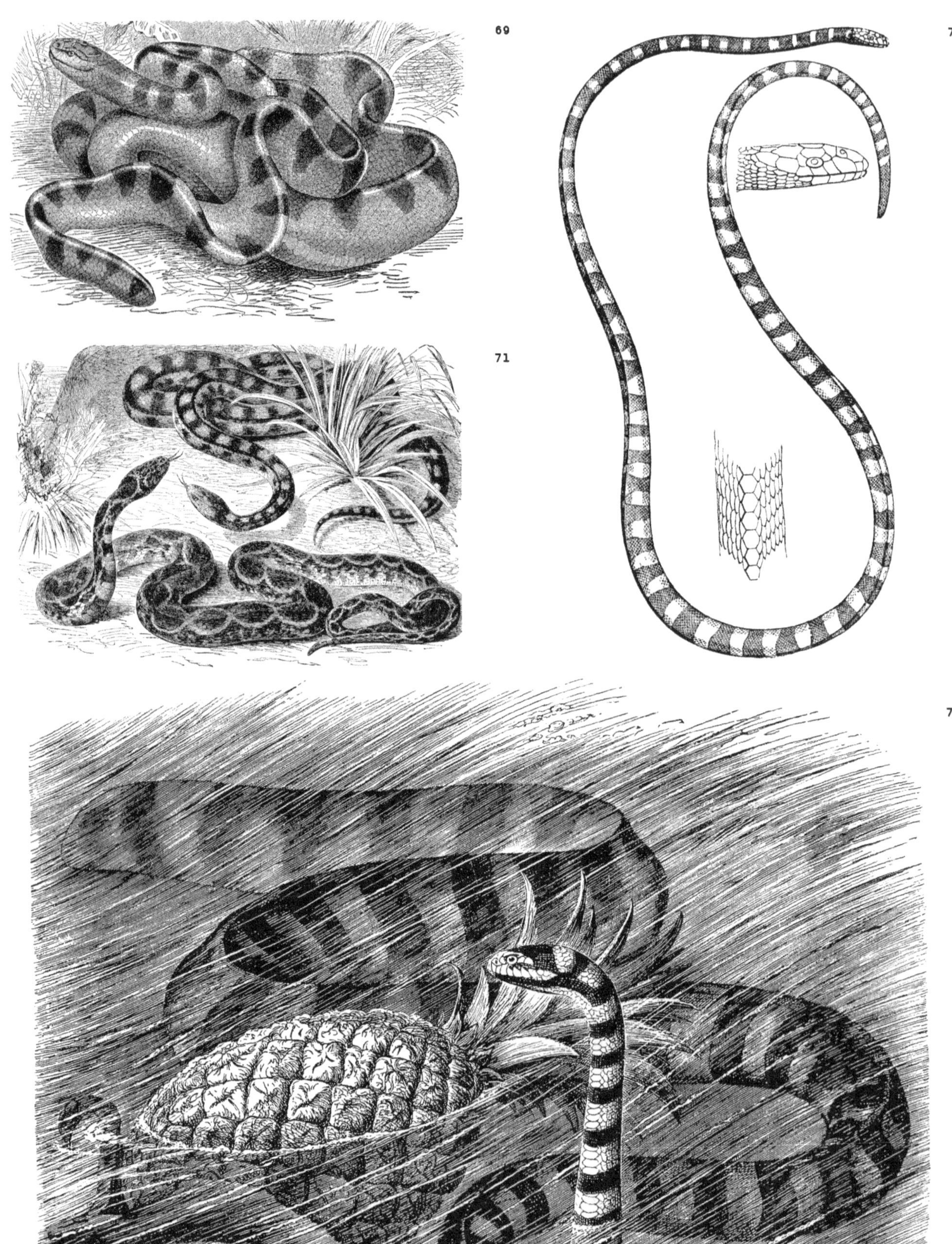

69

70

71

72

73

74

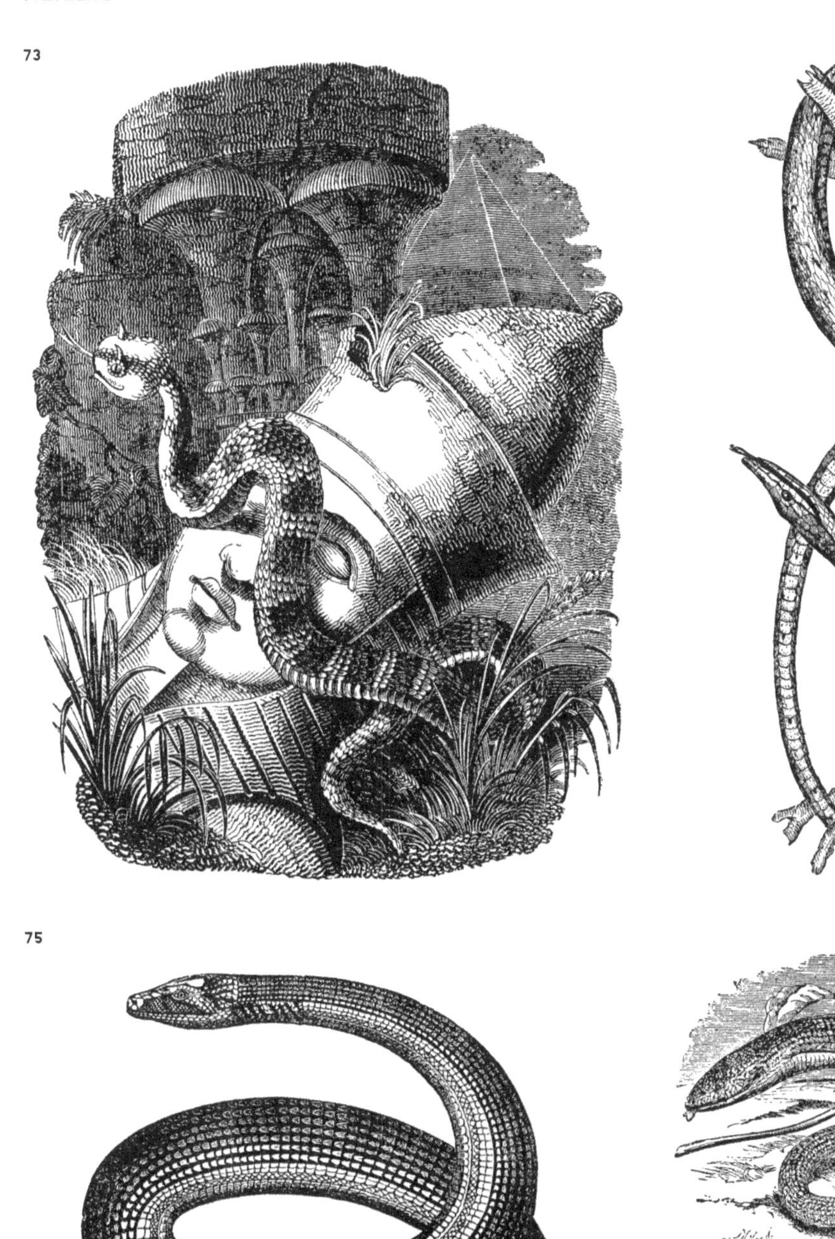

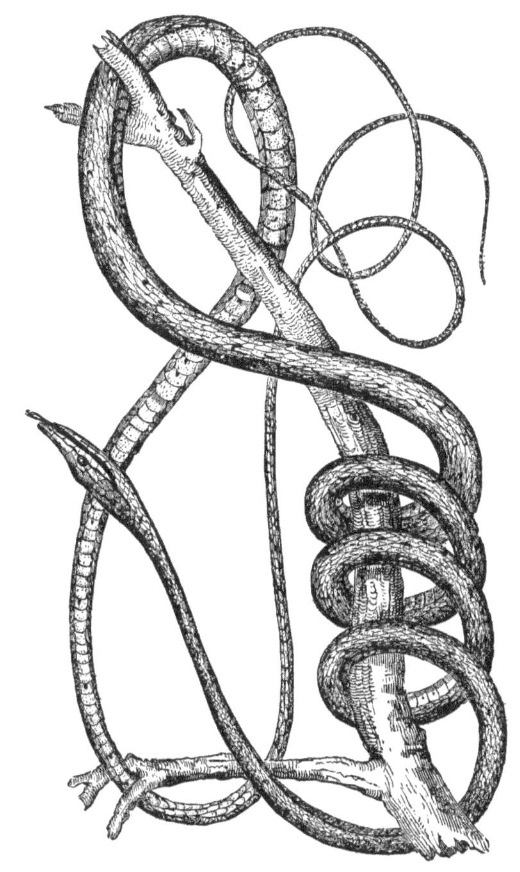

75

76

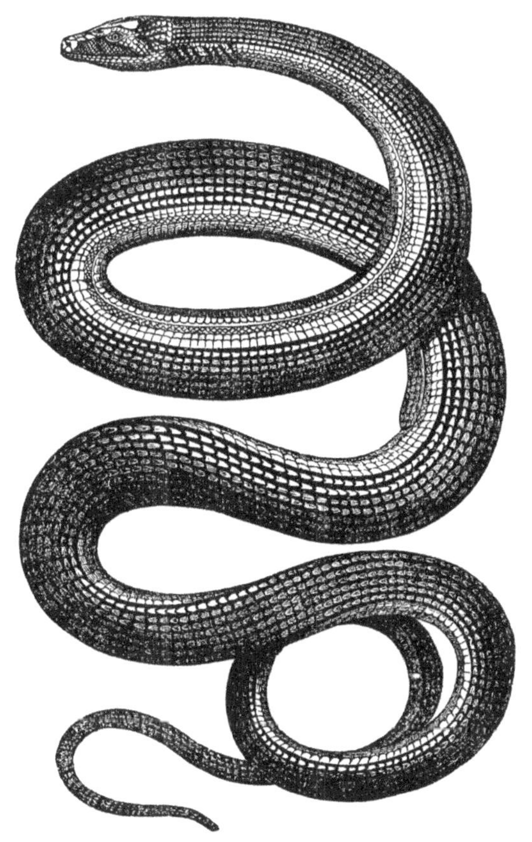

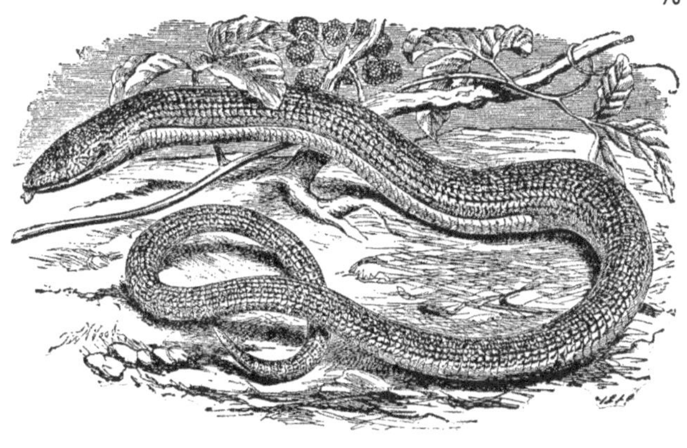

77

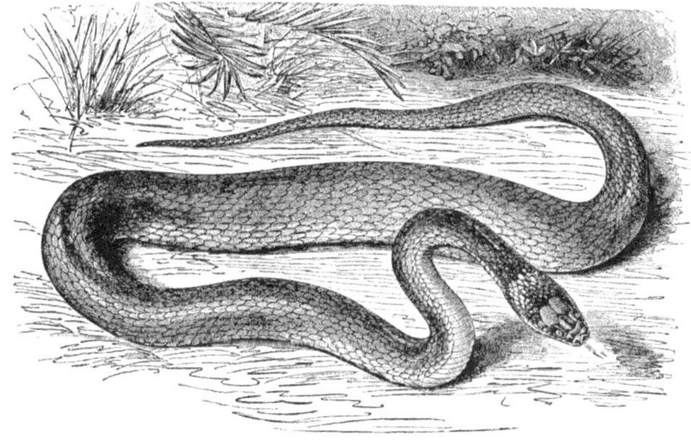

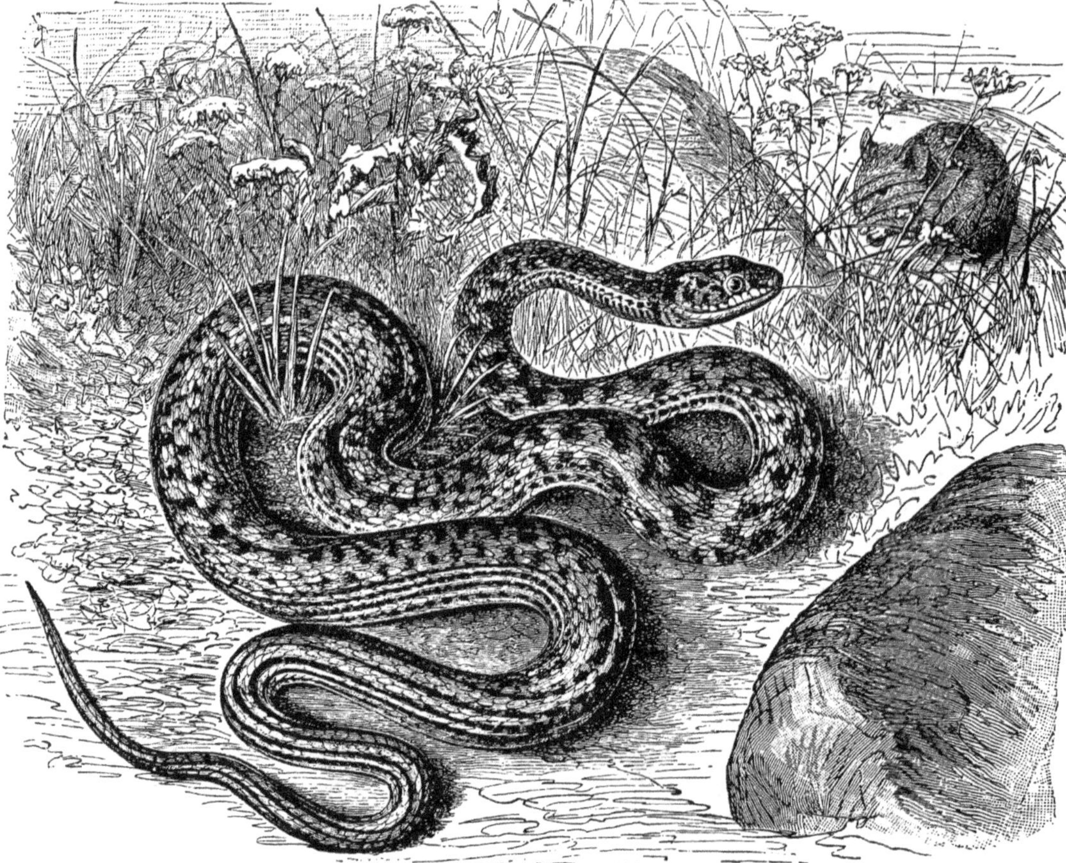

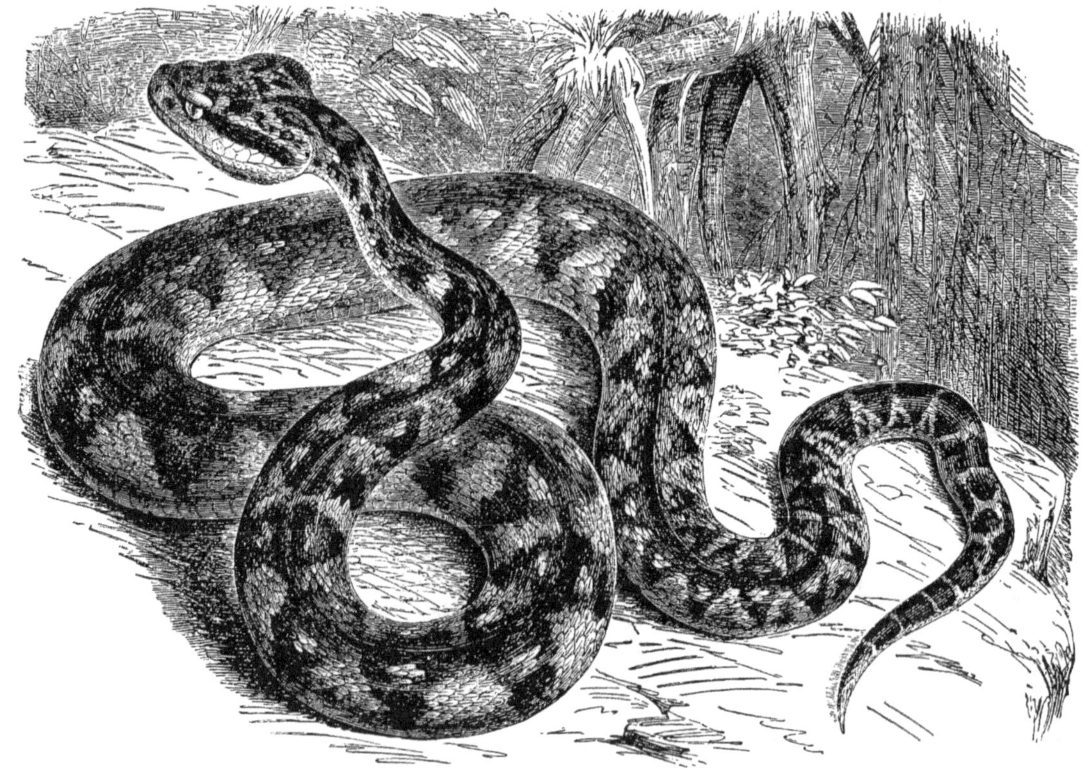

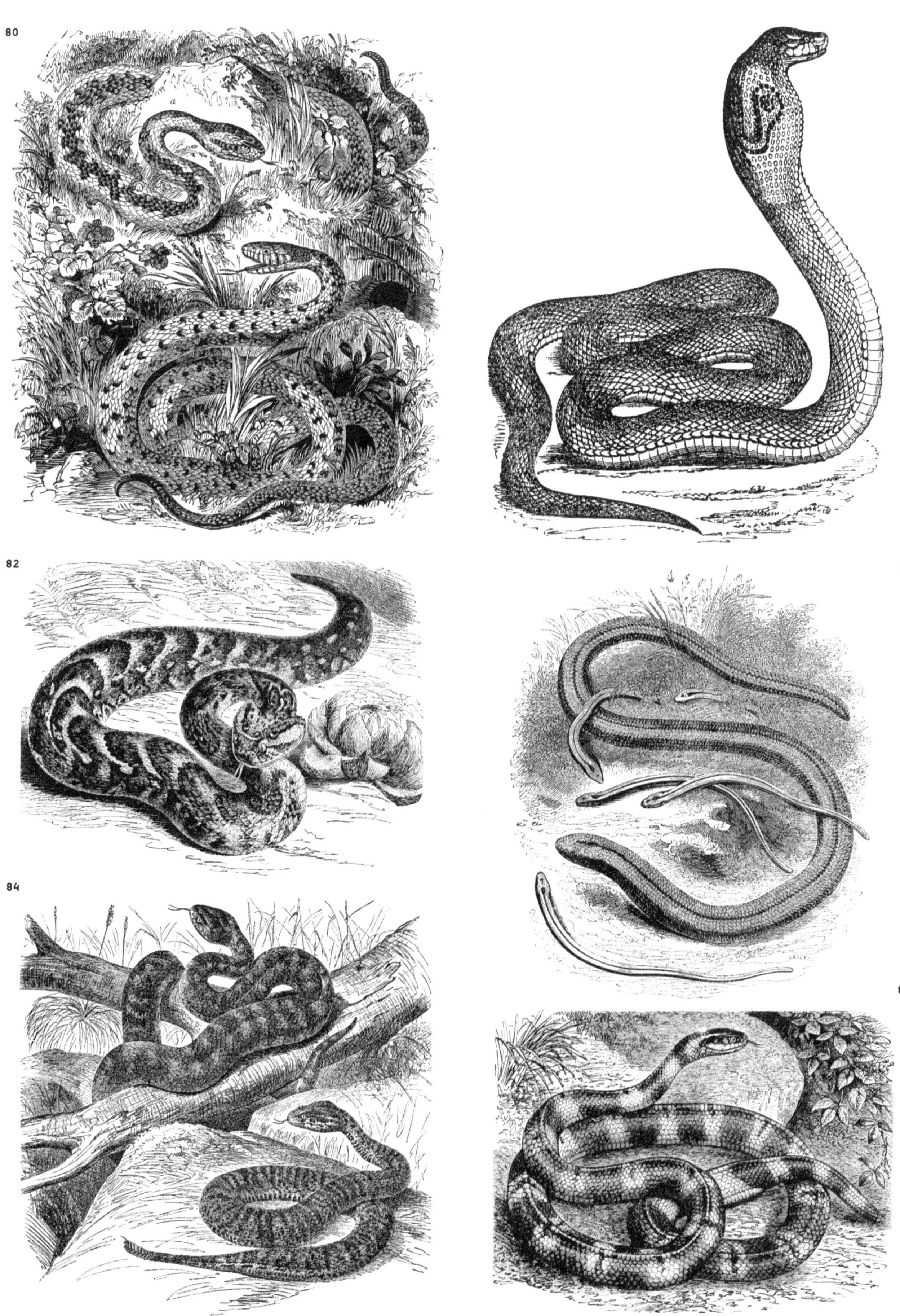

80
81
82
83
84
85
SNAKES & OTHER REPTILES

86

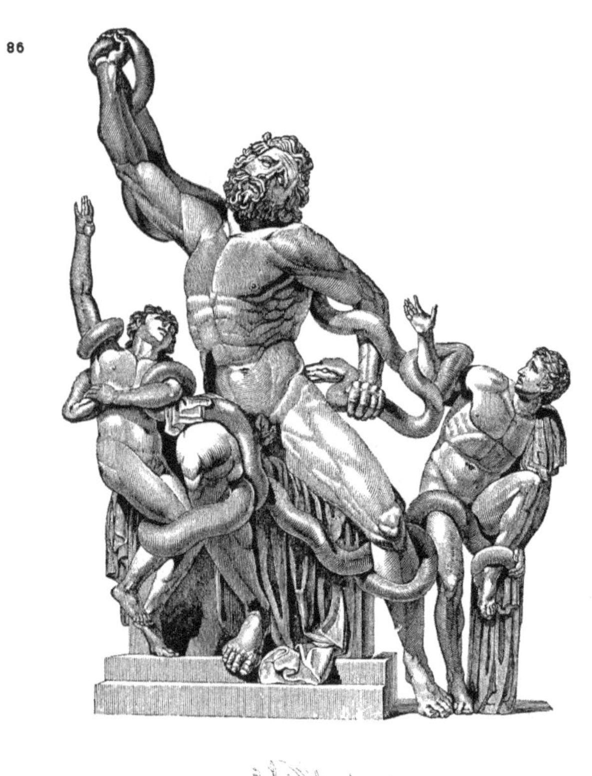

87

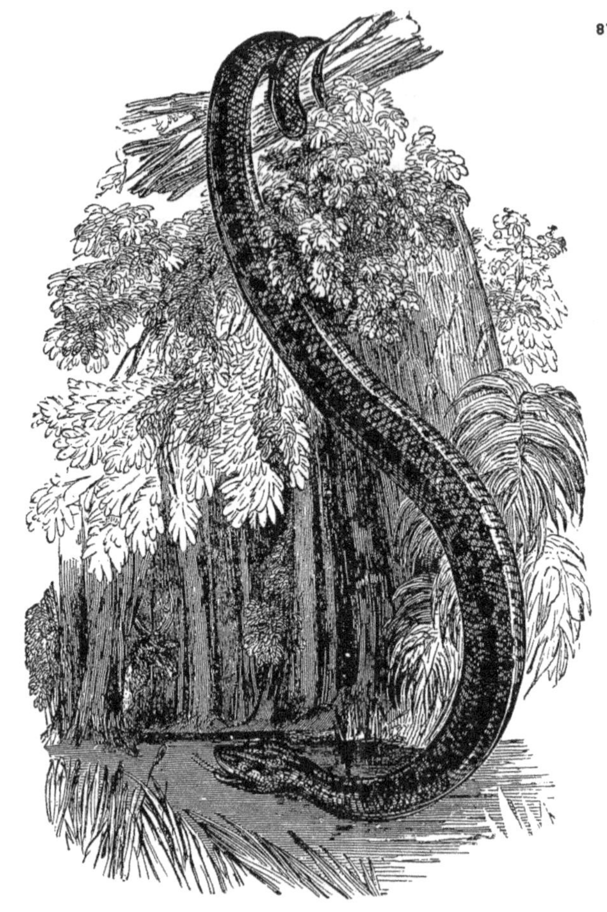

88

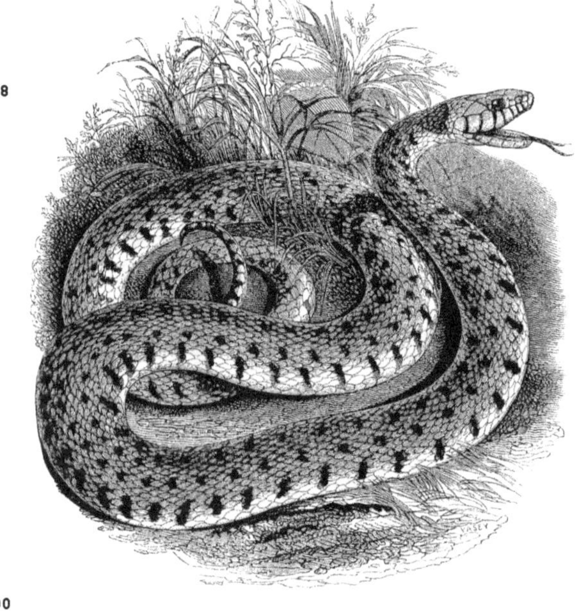

89

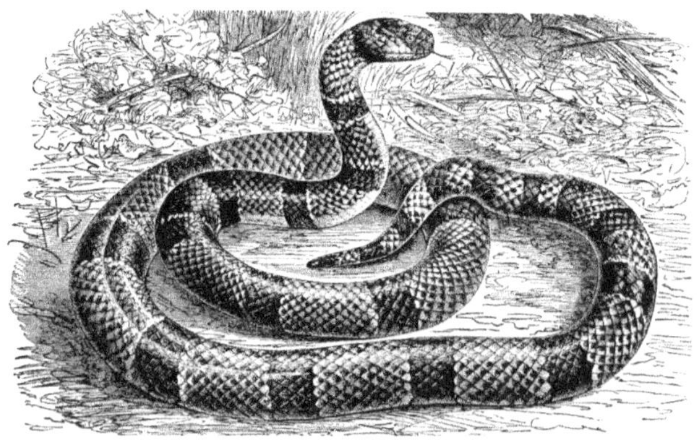

90

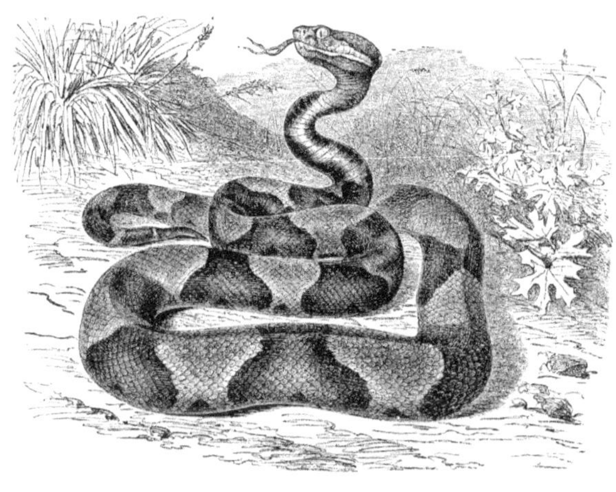

91

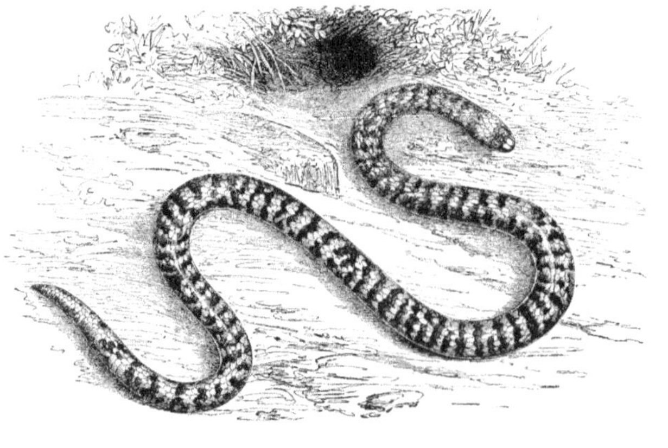

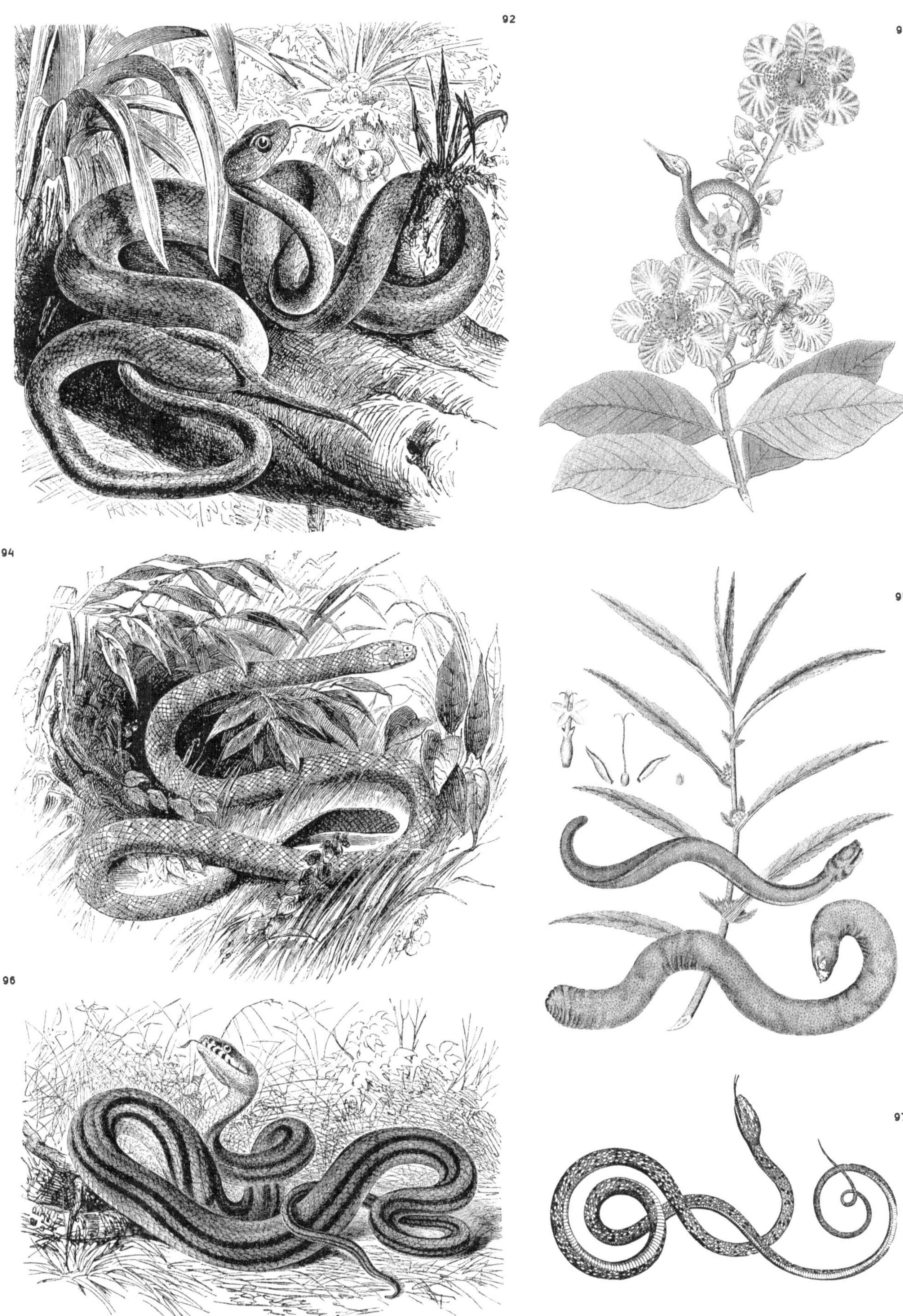

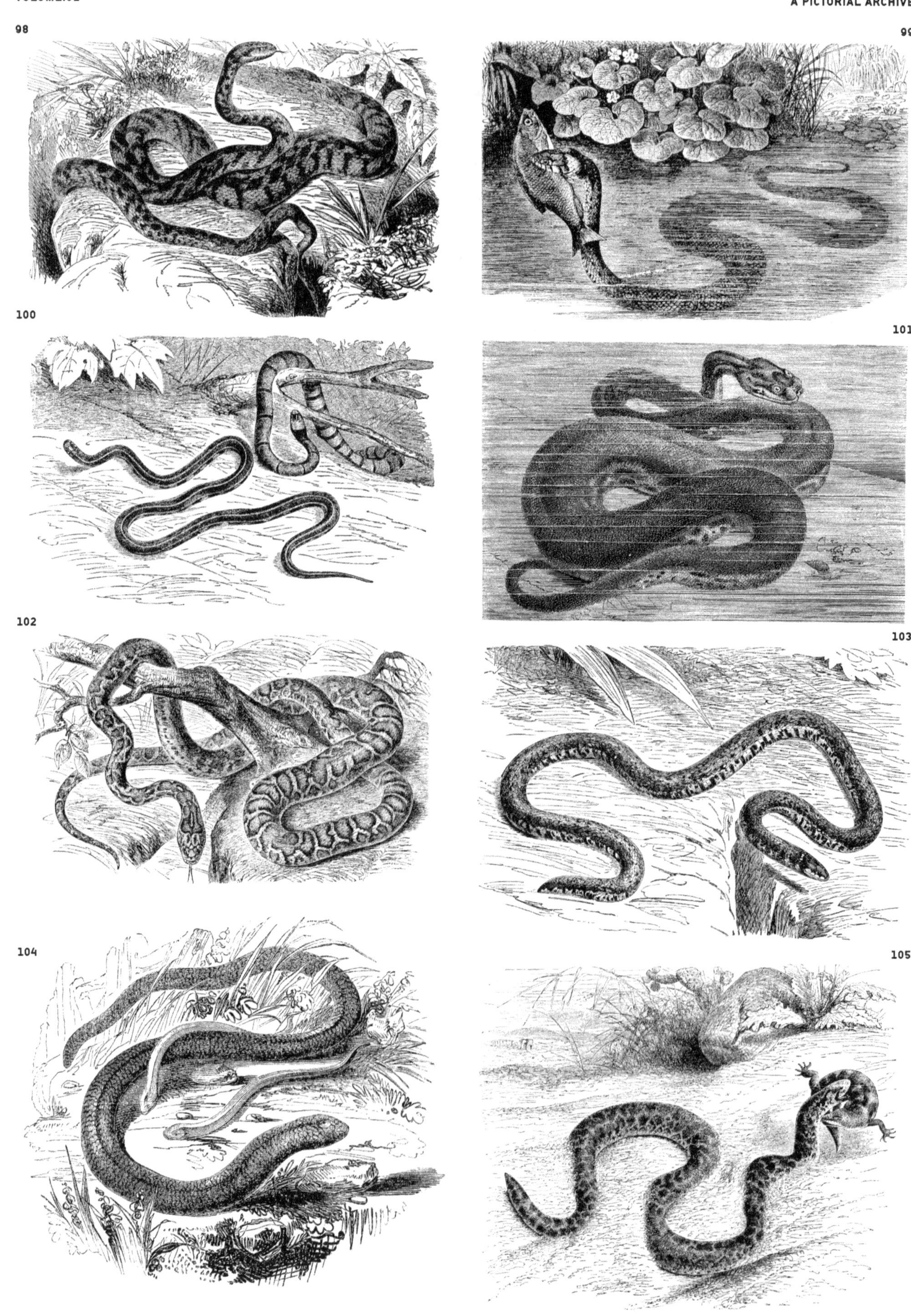

98

99

100

101

102

103

104

105

106

107

108

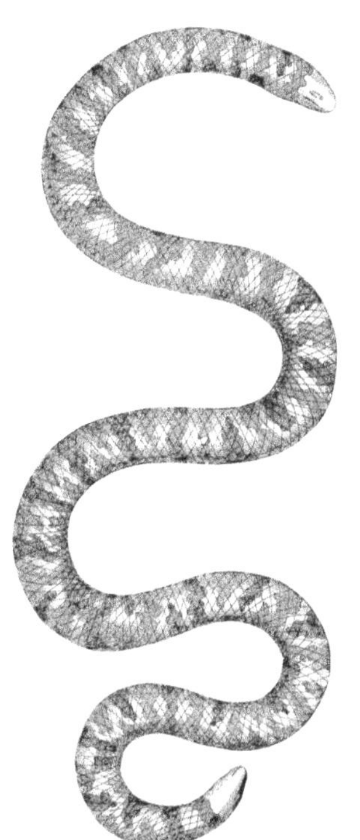

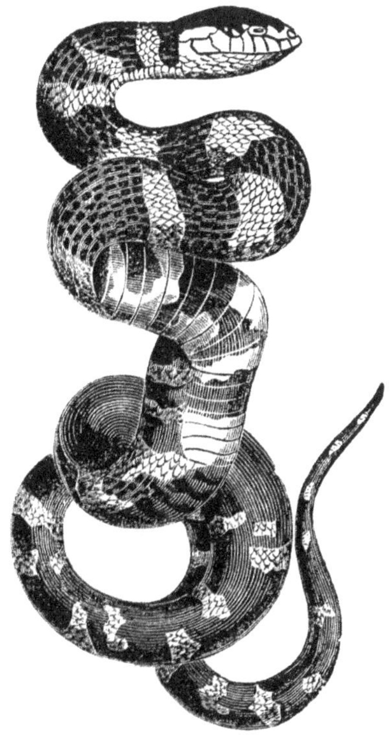

109

110

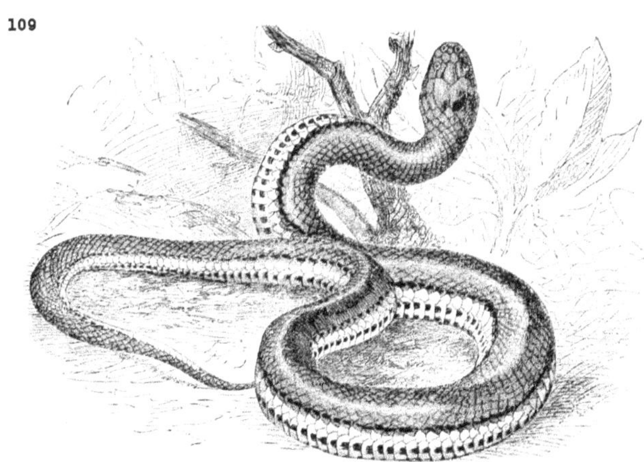

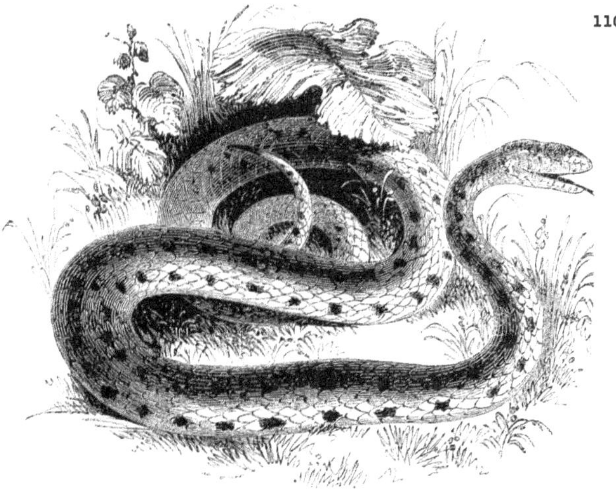

111

112

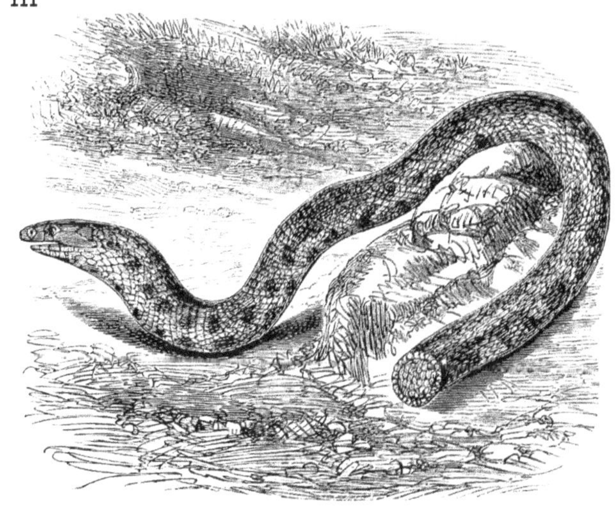

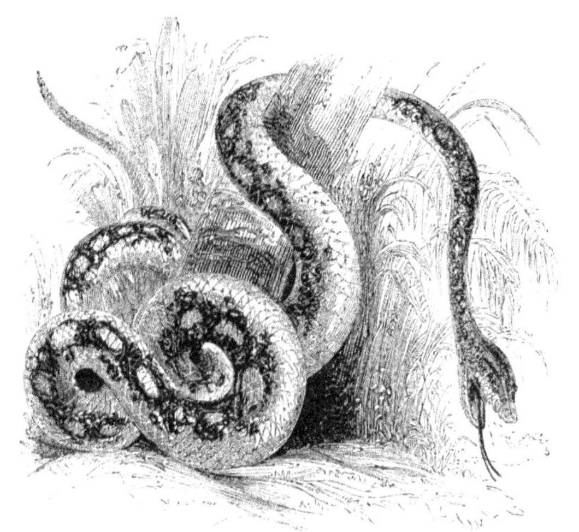

113

115

116

114

117

119

118

120

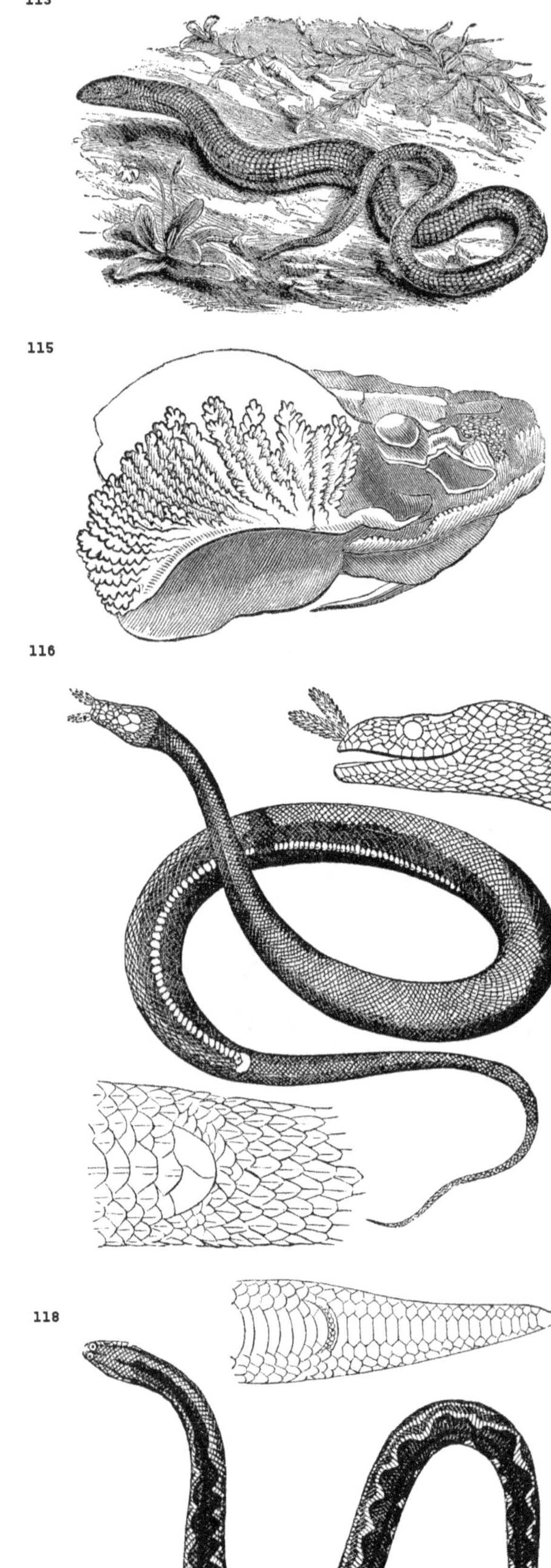

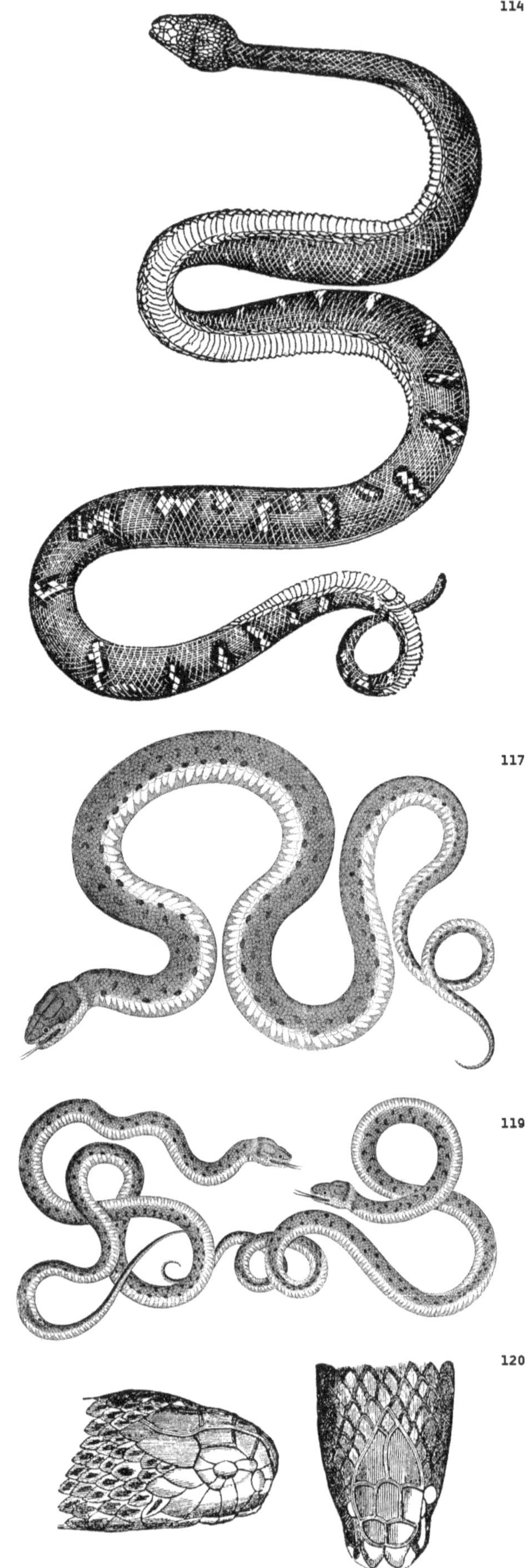

121

122

123

124

125

126

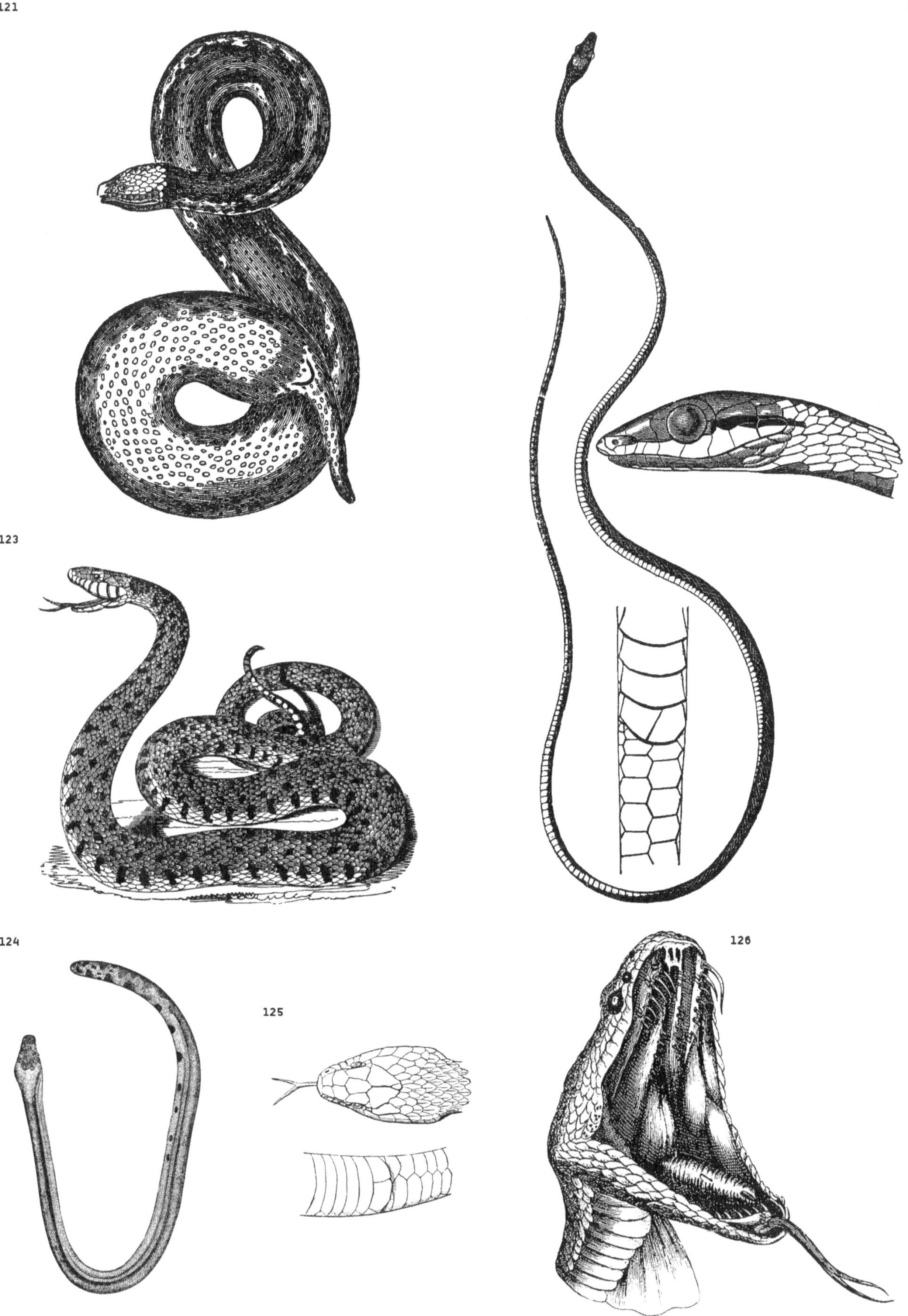

127

128

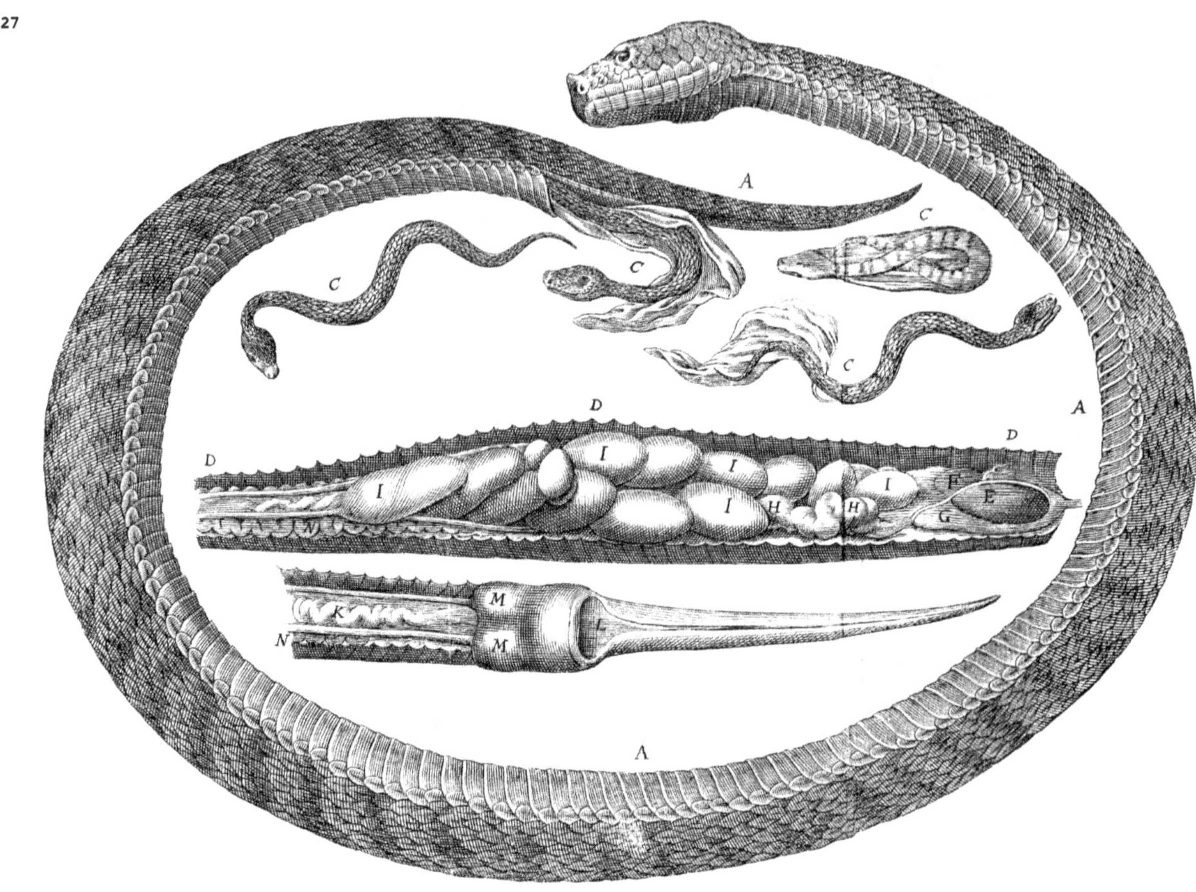

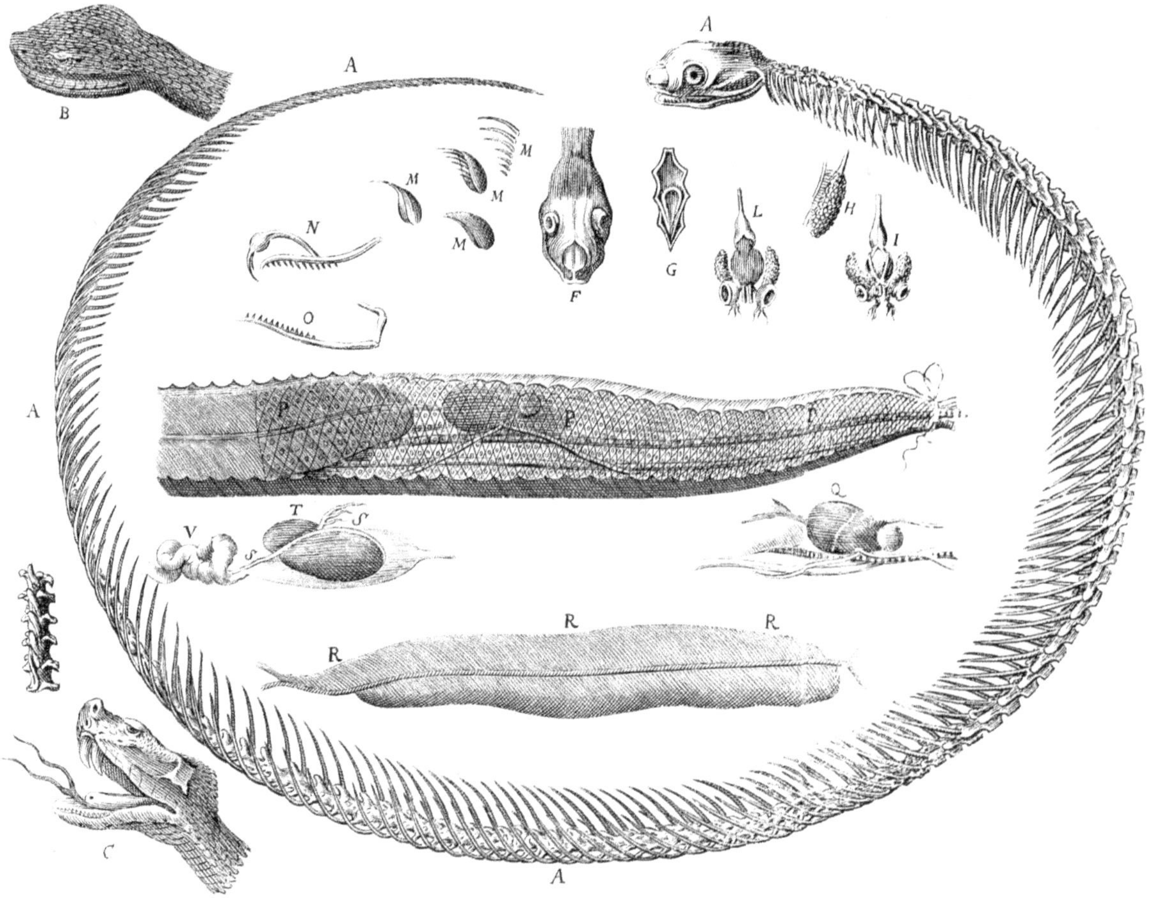

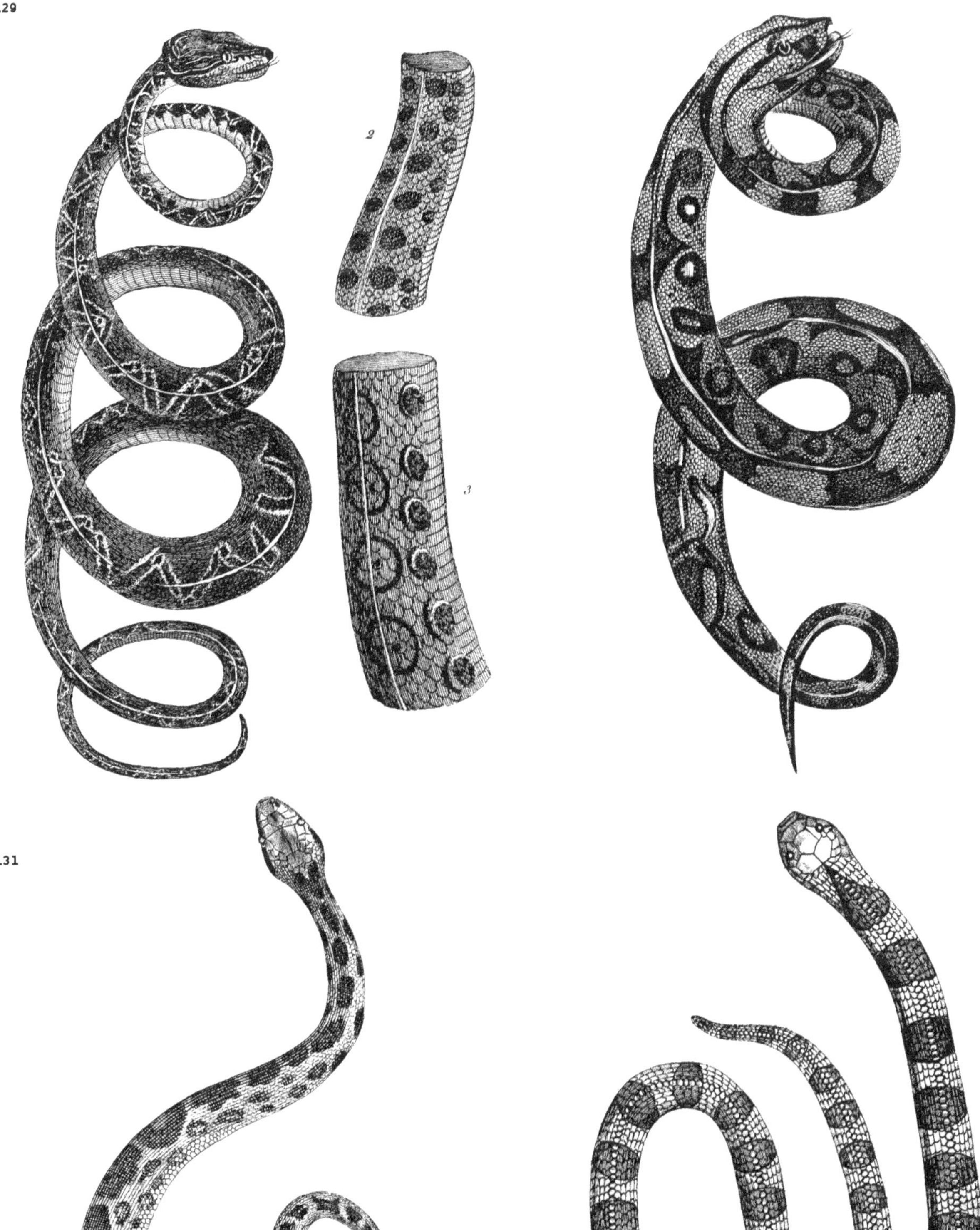

133

134

135

136

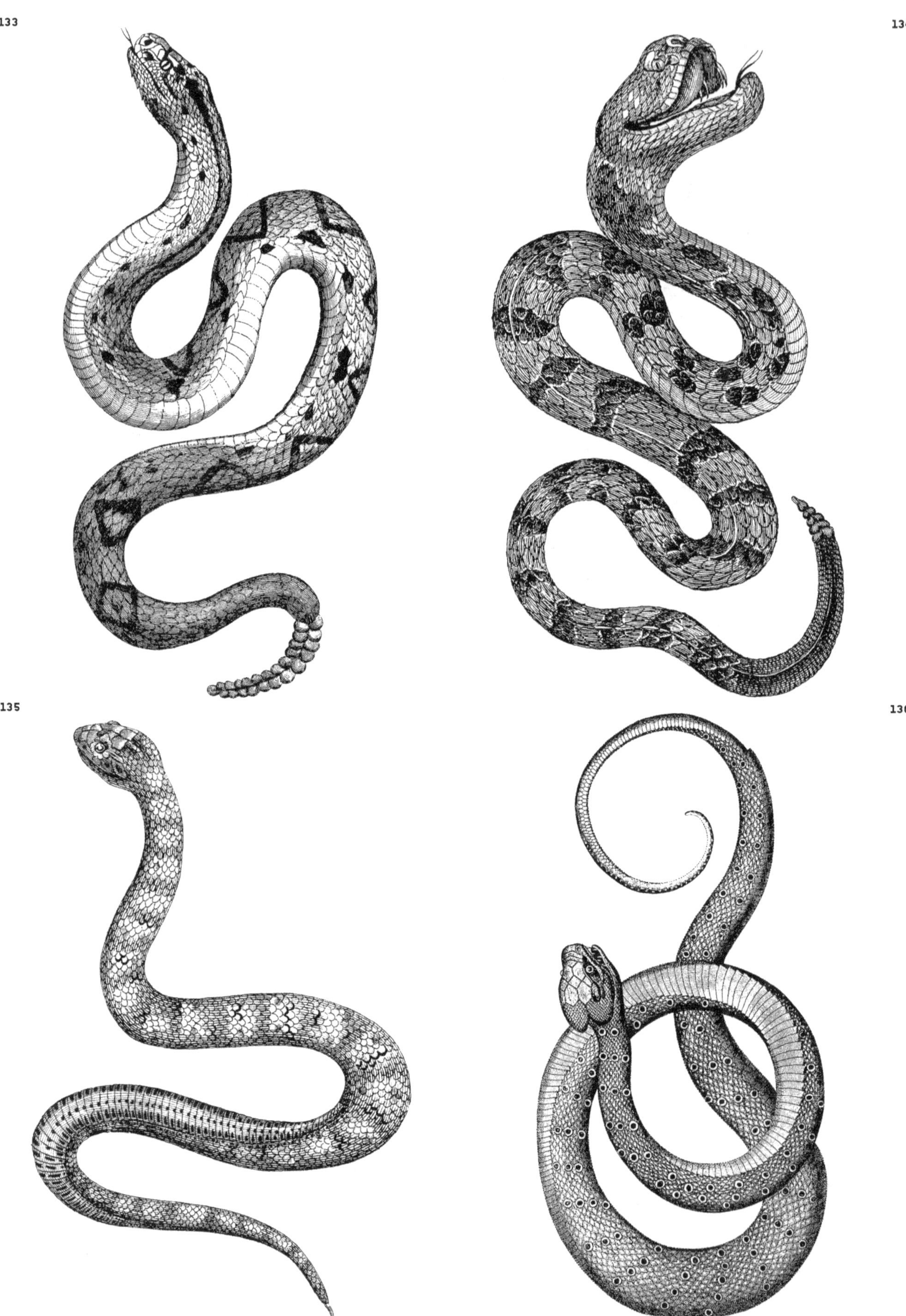

137

138

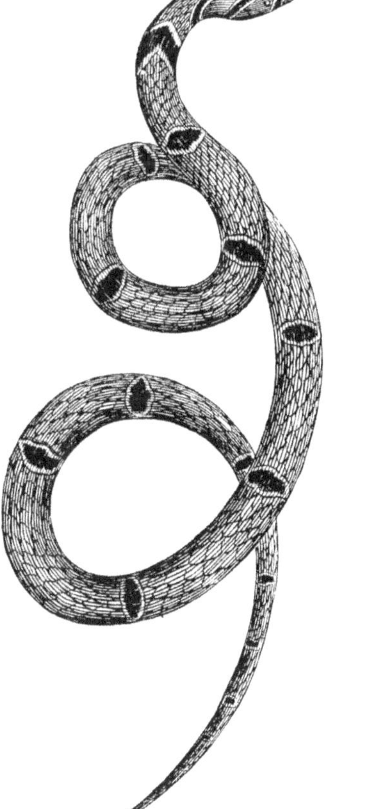

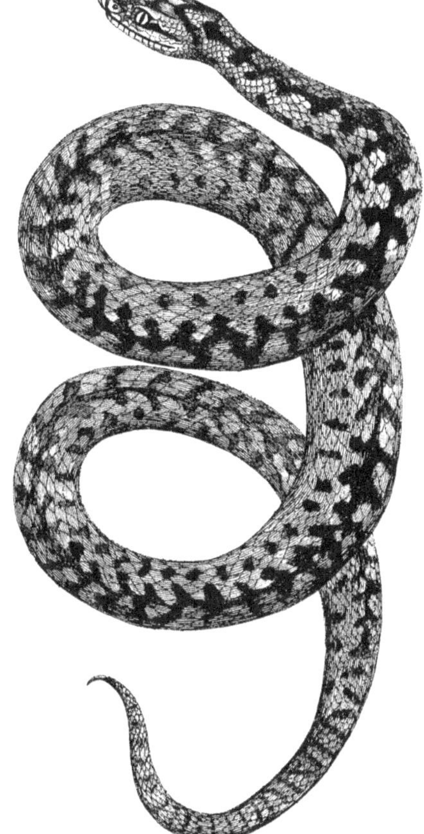

139

140

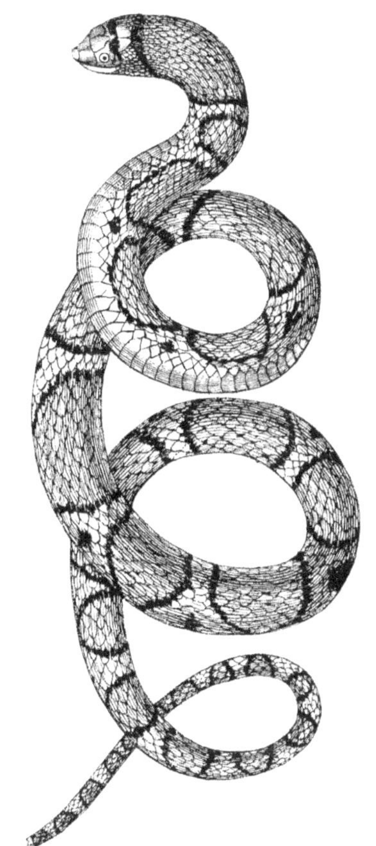

141

142

143

144

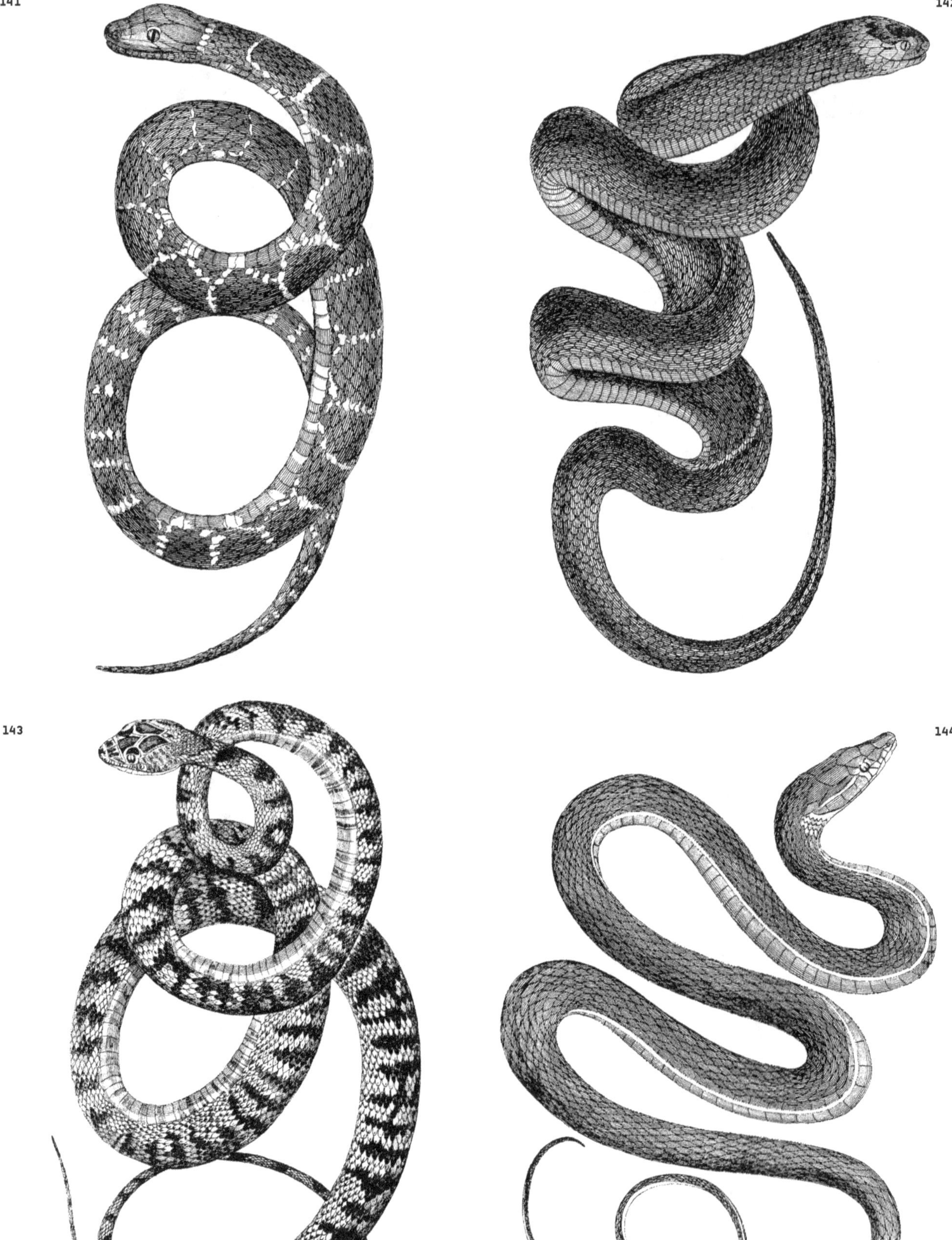

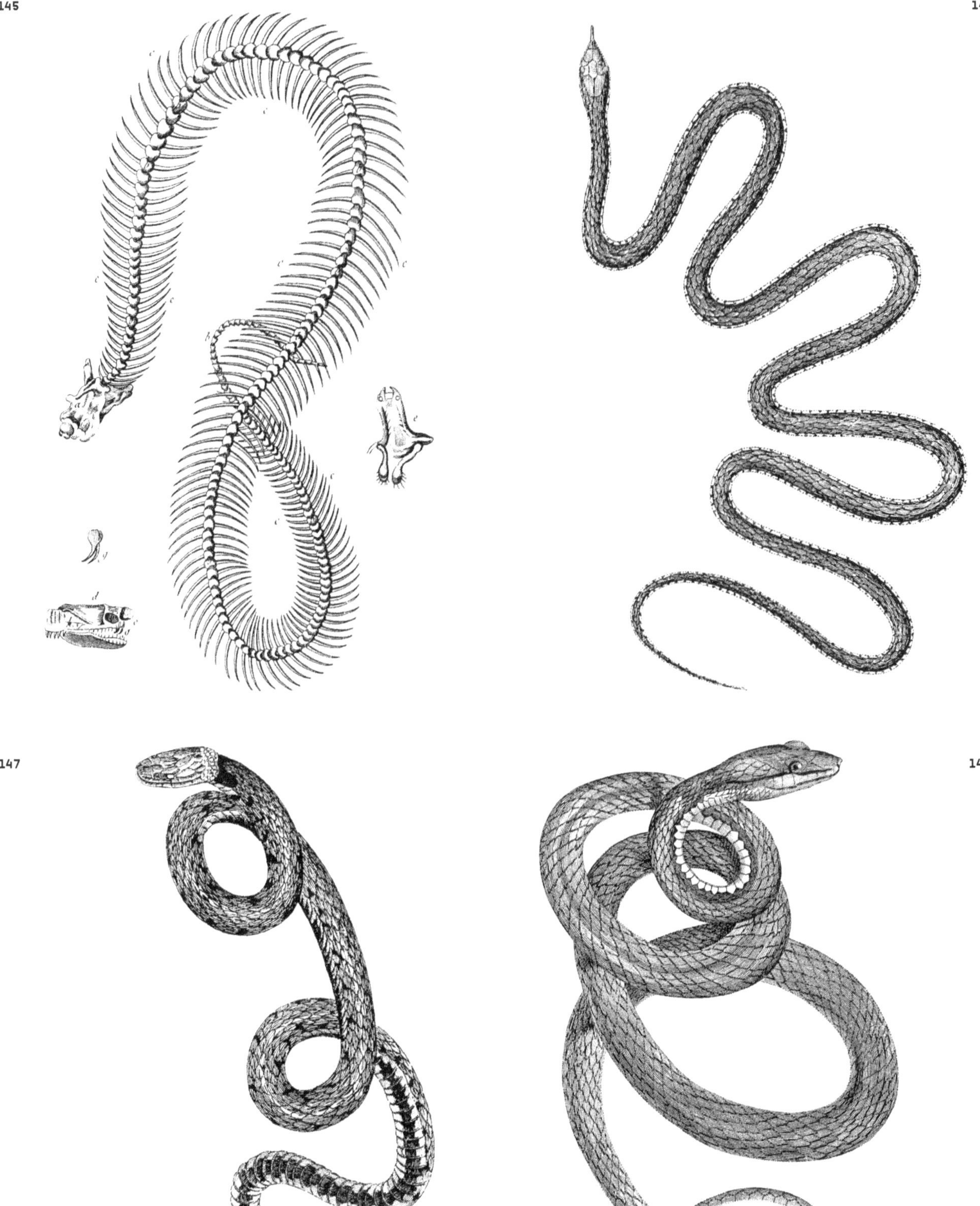

147

148

149

150

151

152

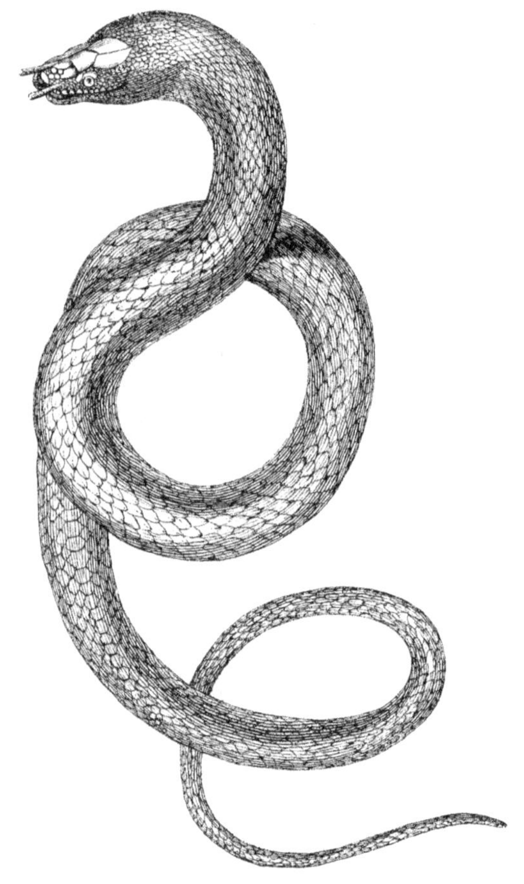

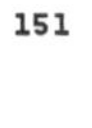

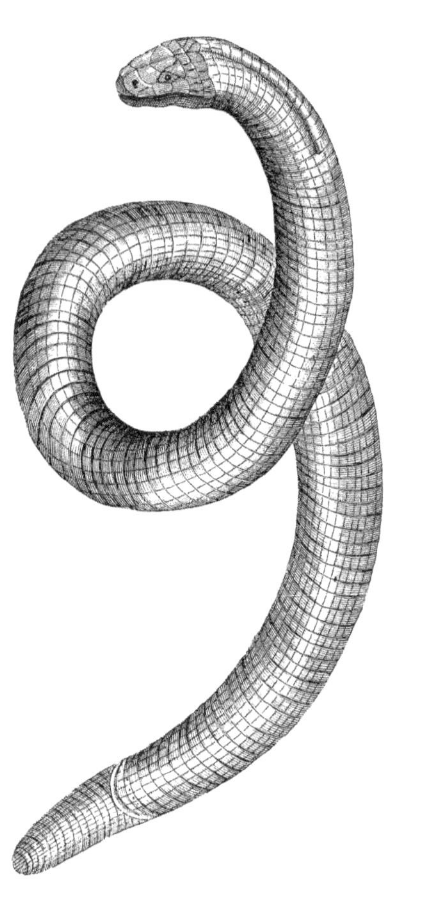

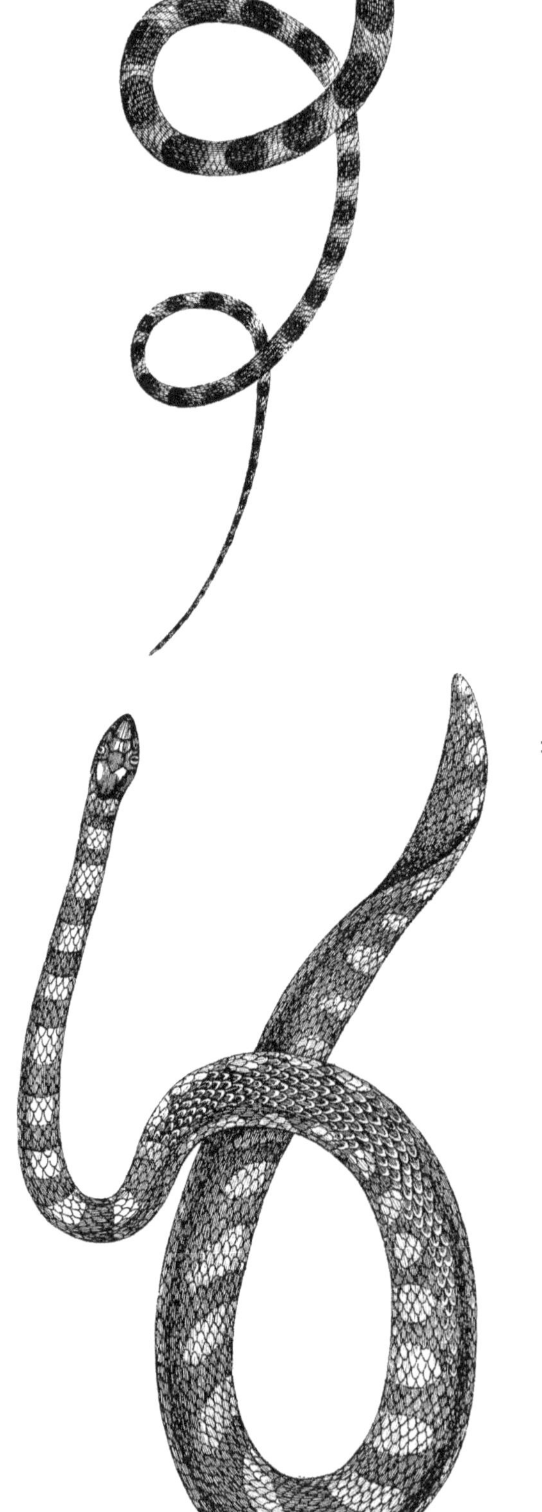

153

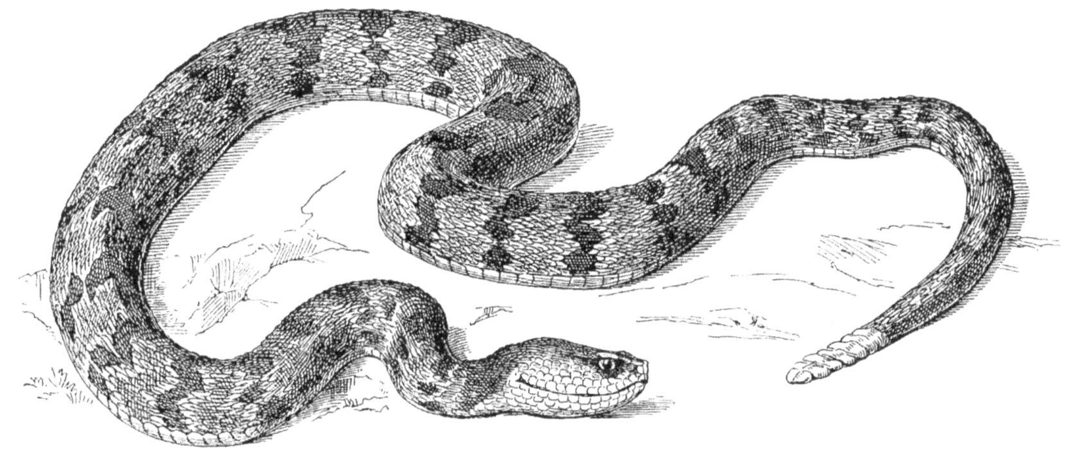

154

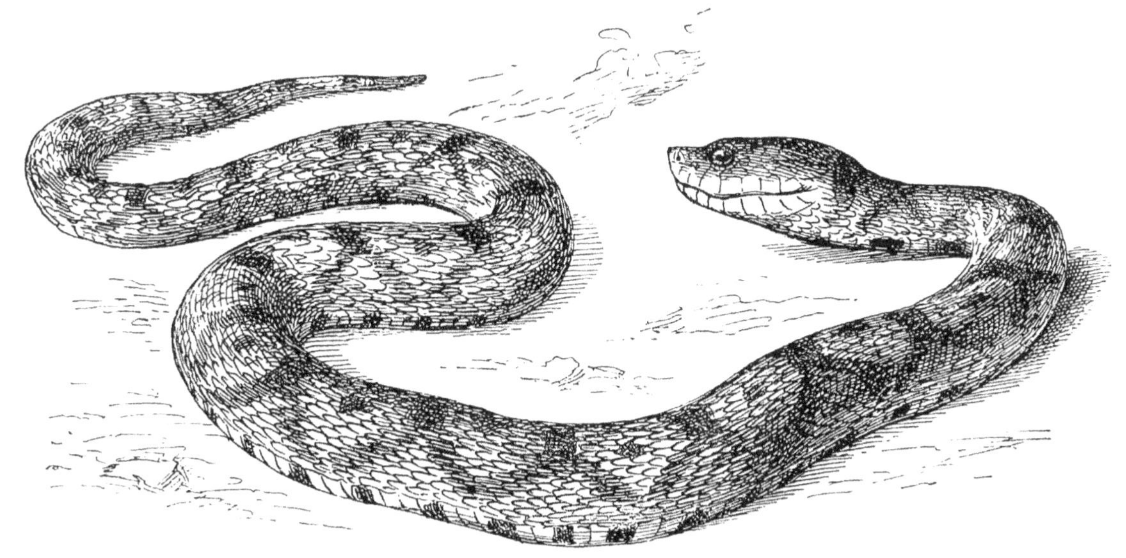

155

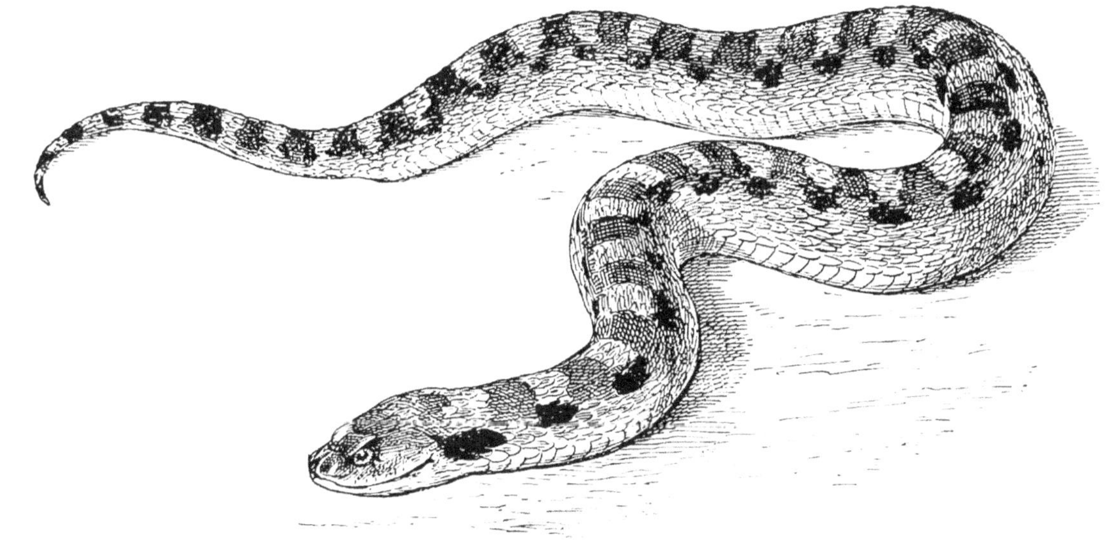

156

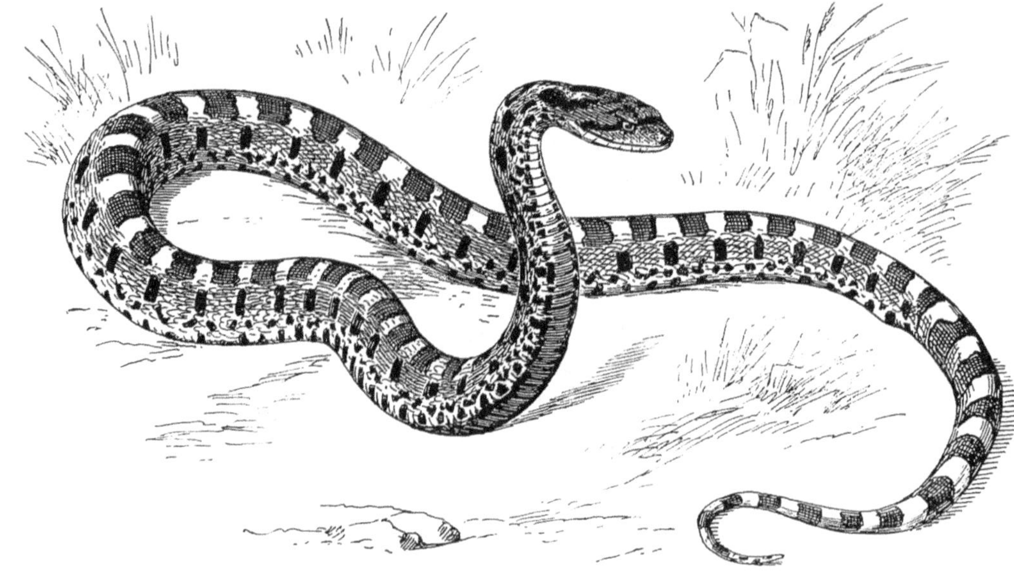

157

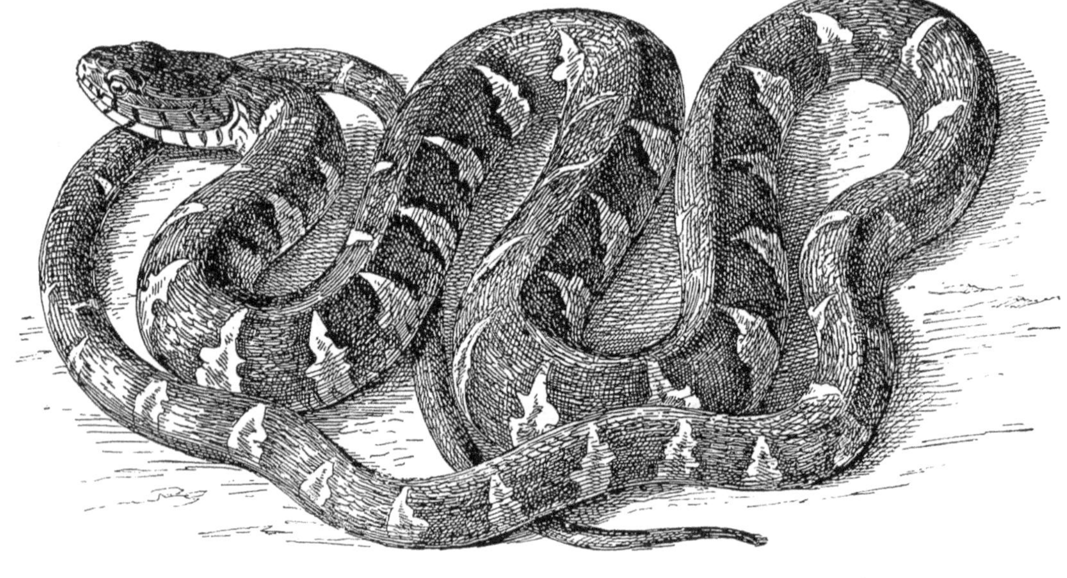

158

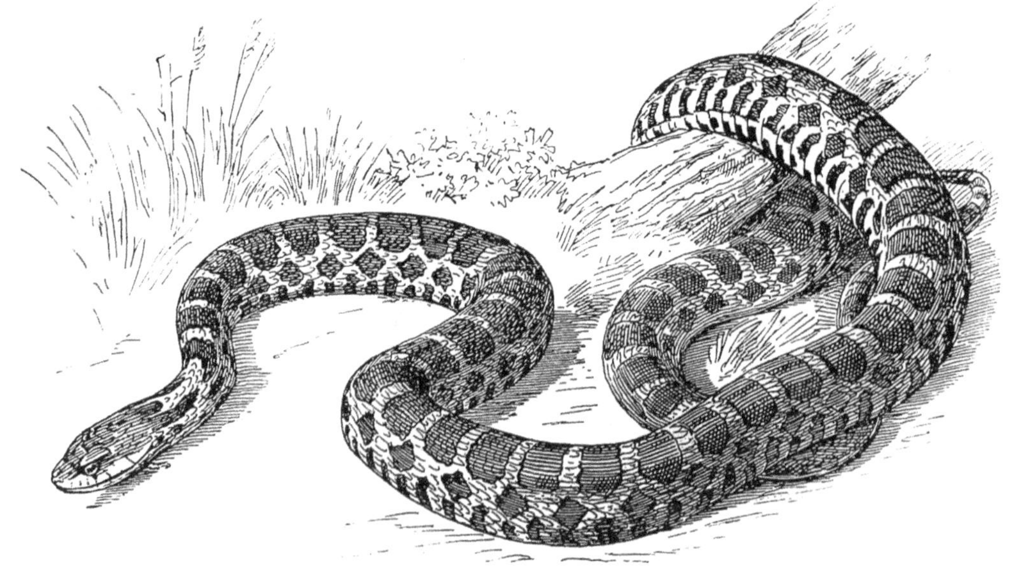

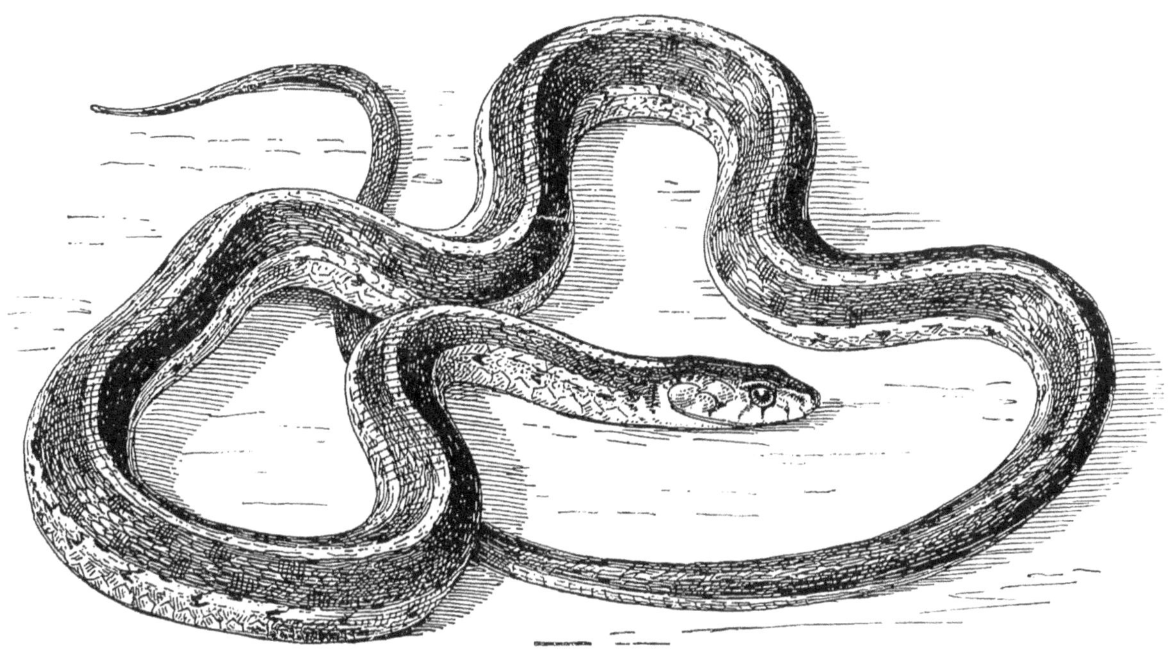

160

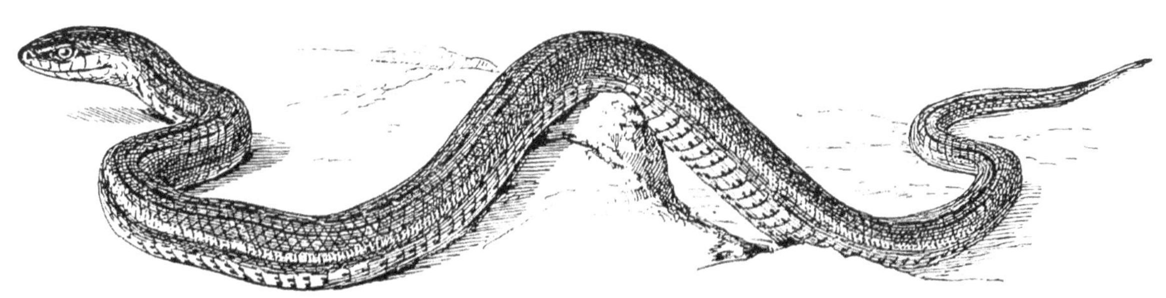

161

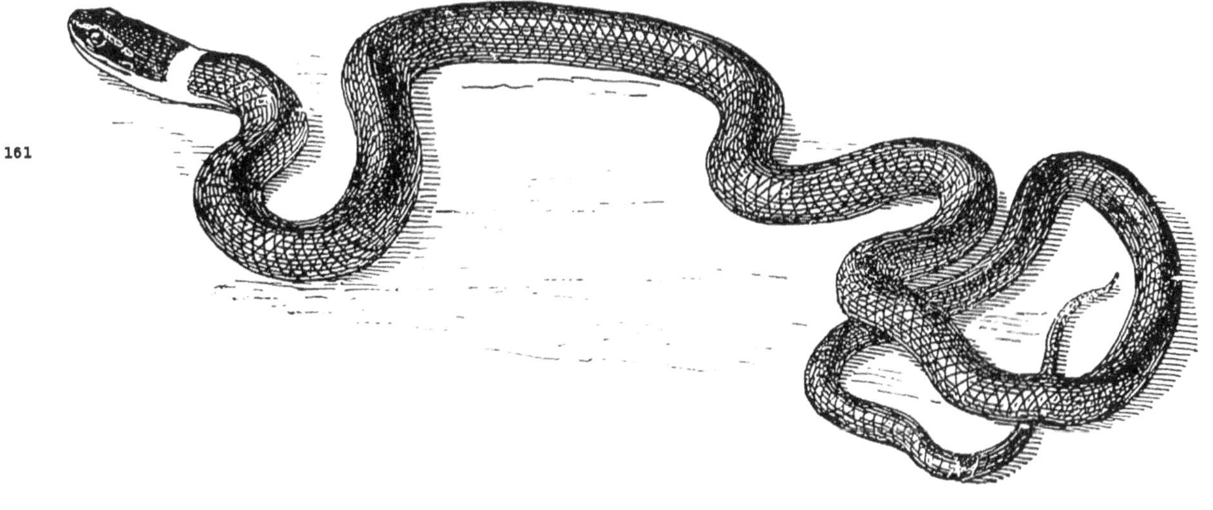

162

163

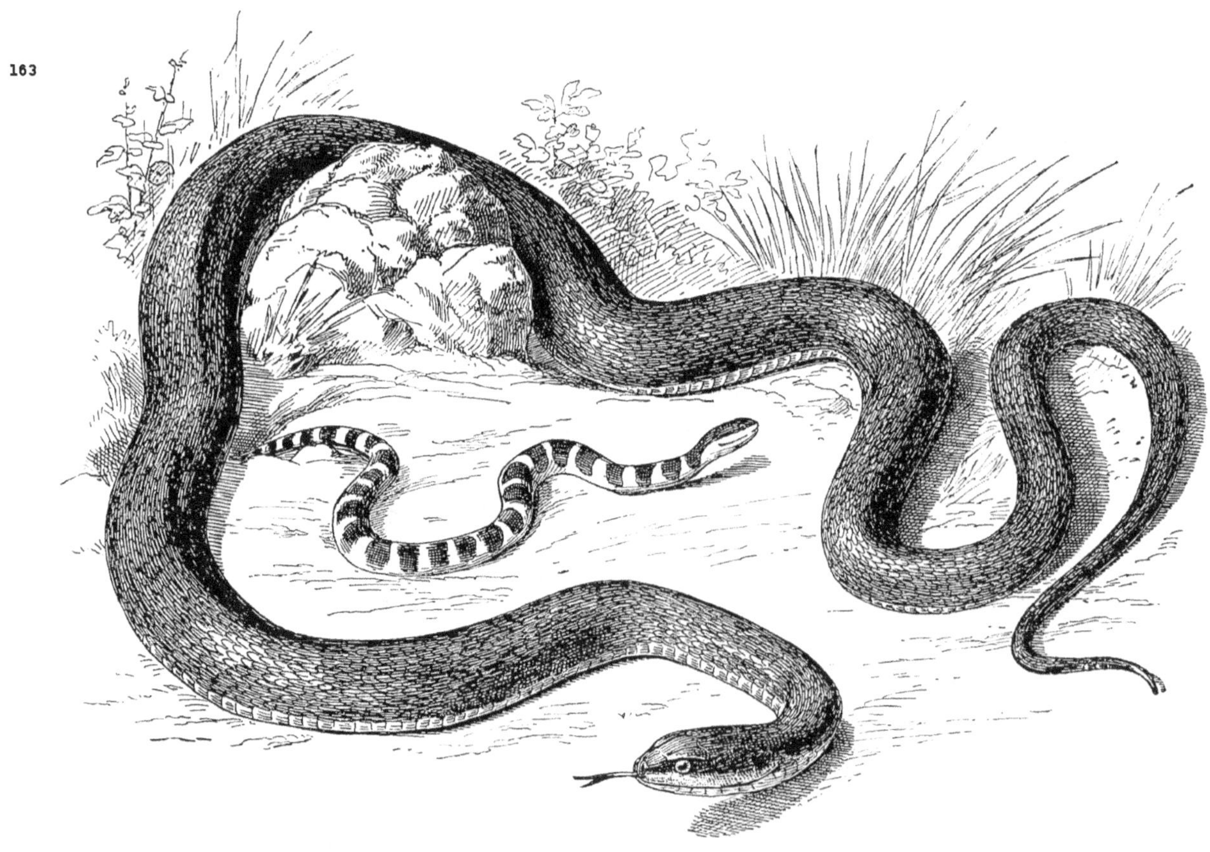

164

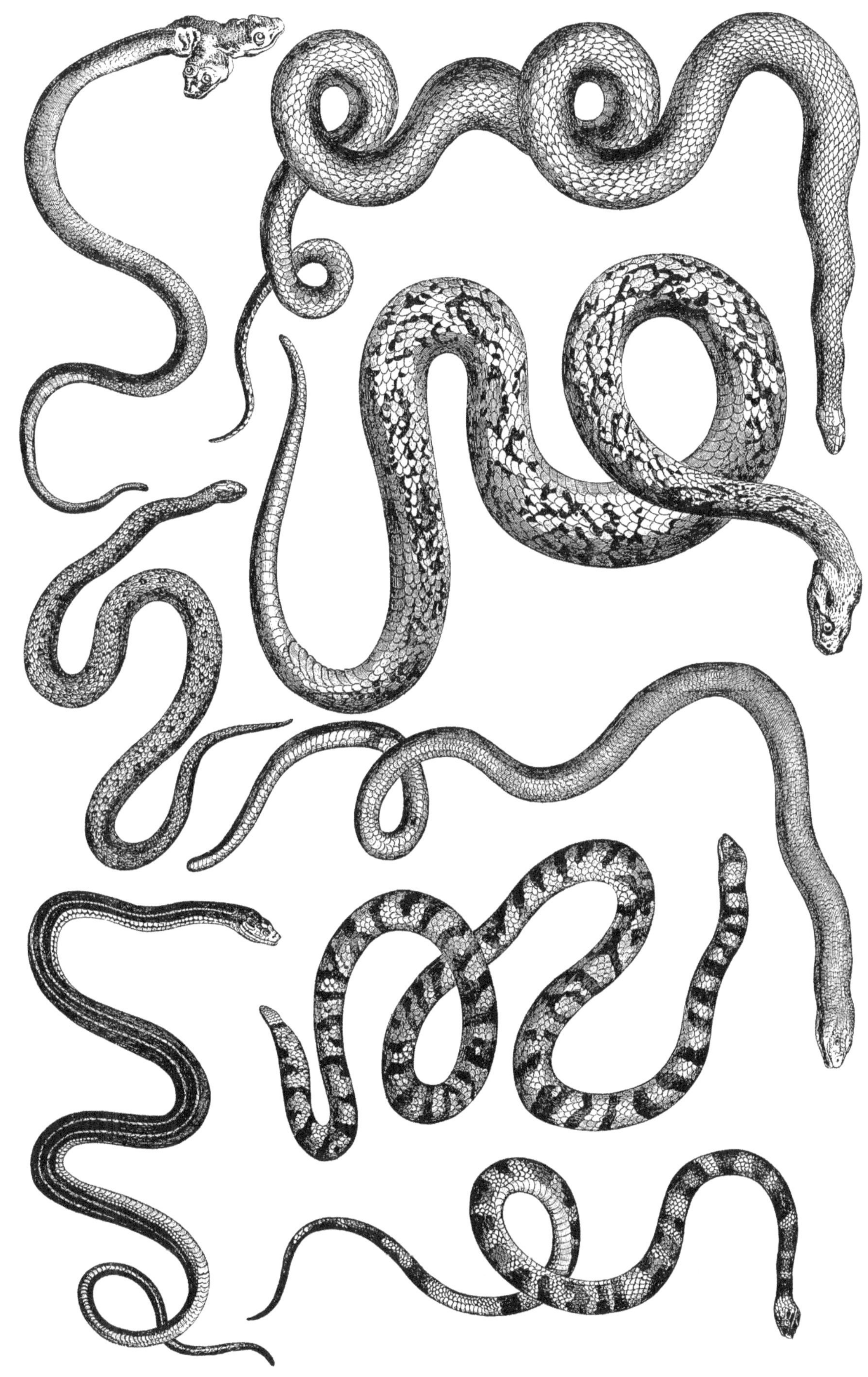

165

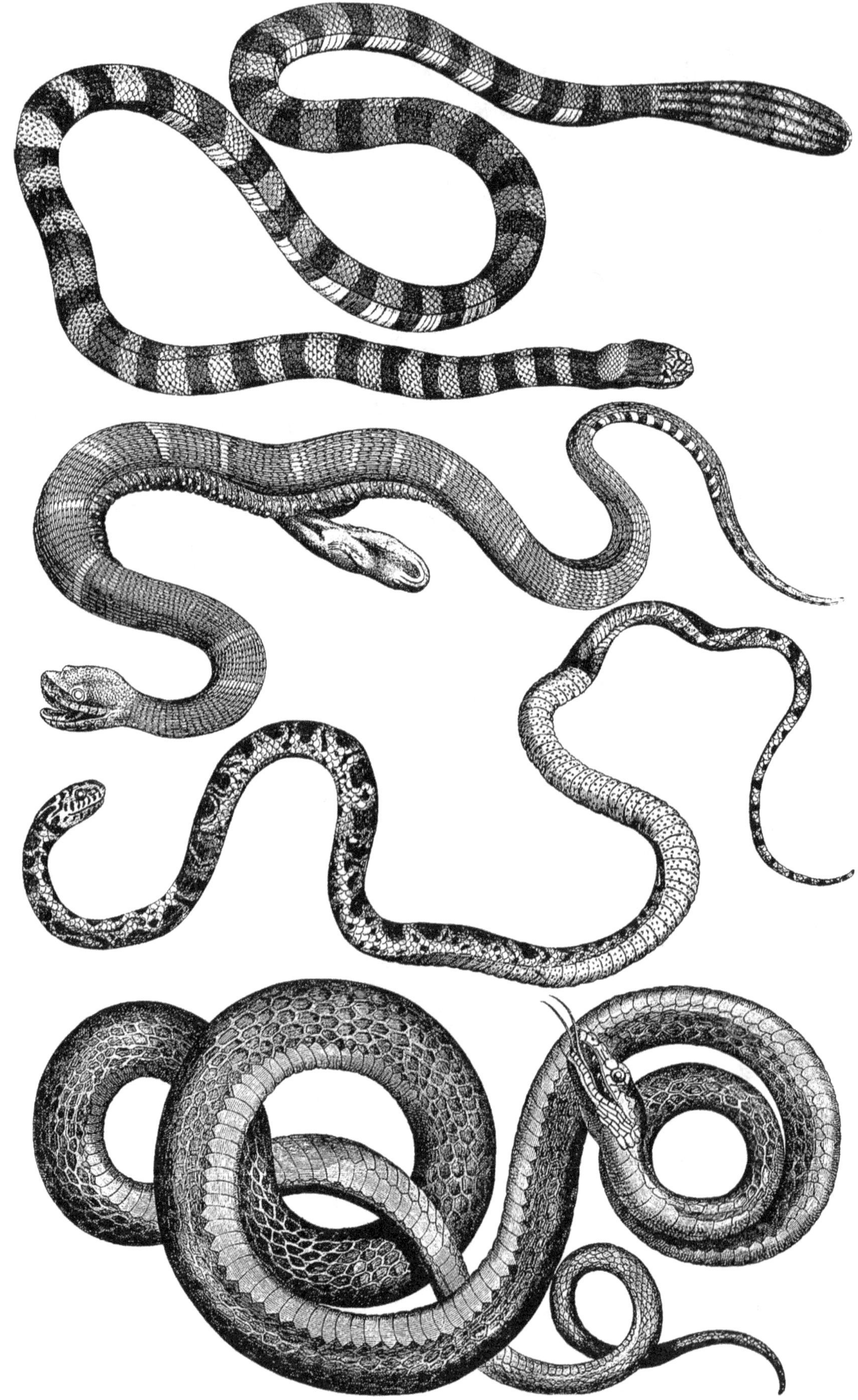

166

167

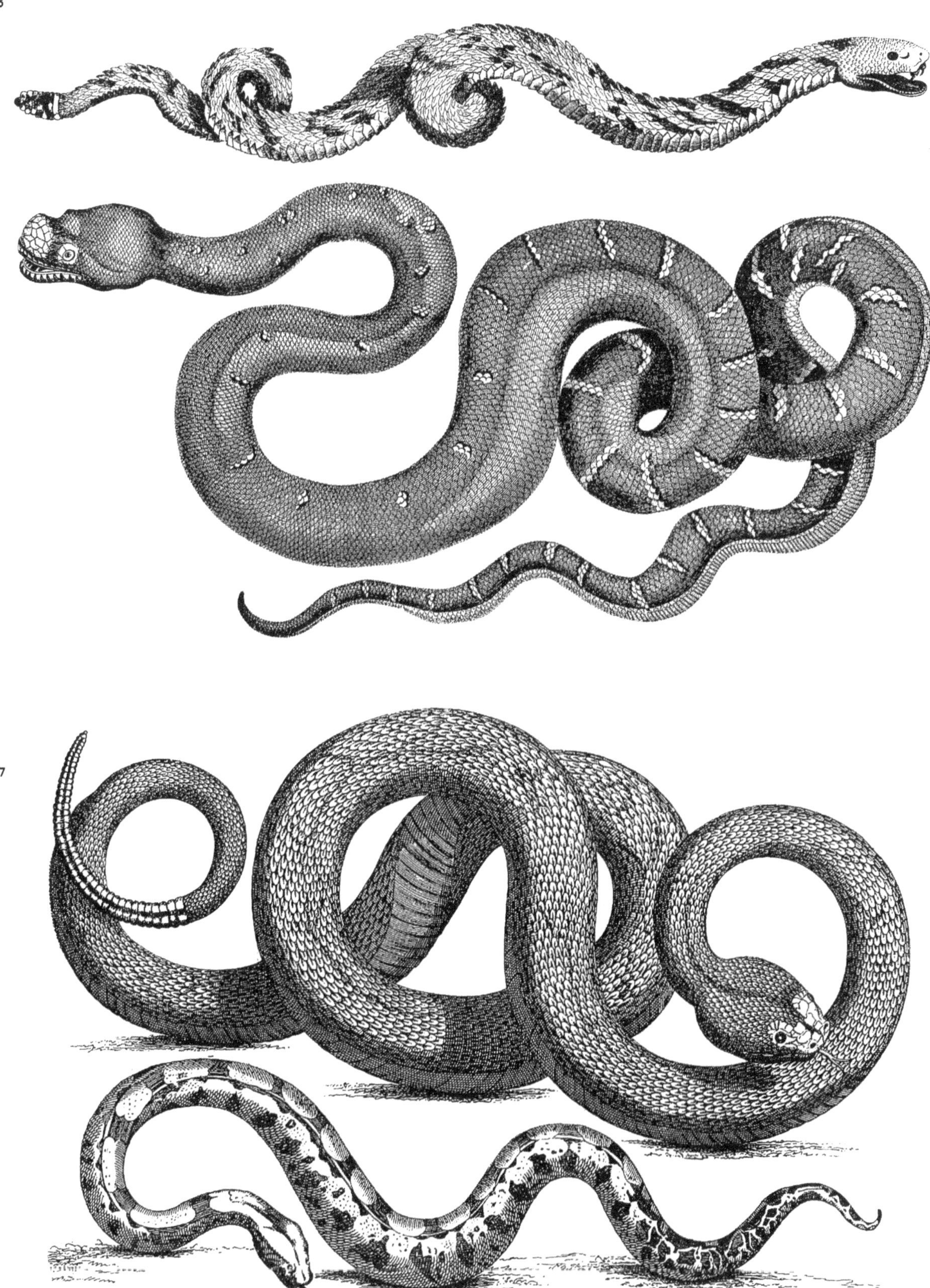

168

169

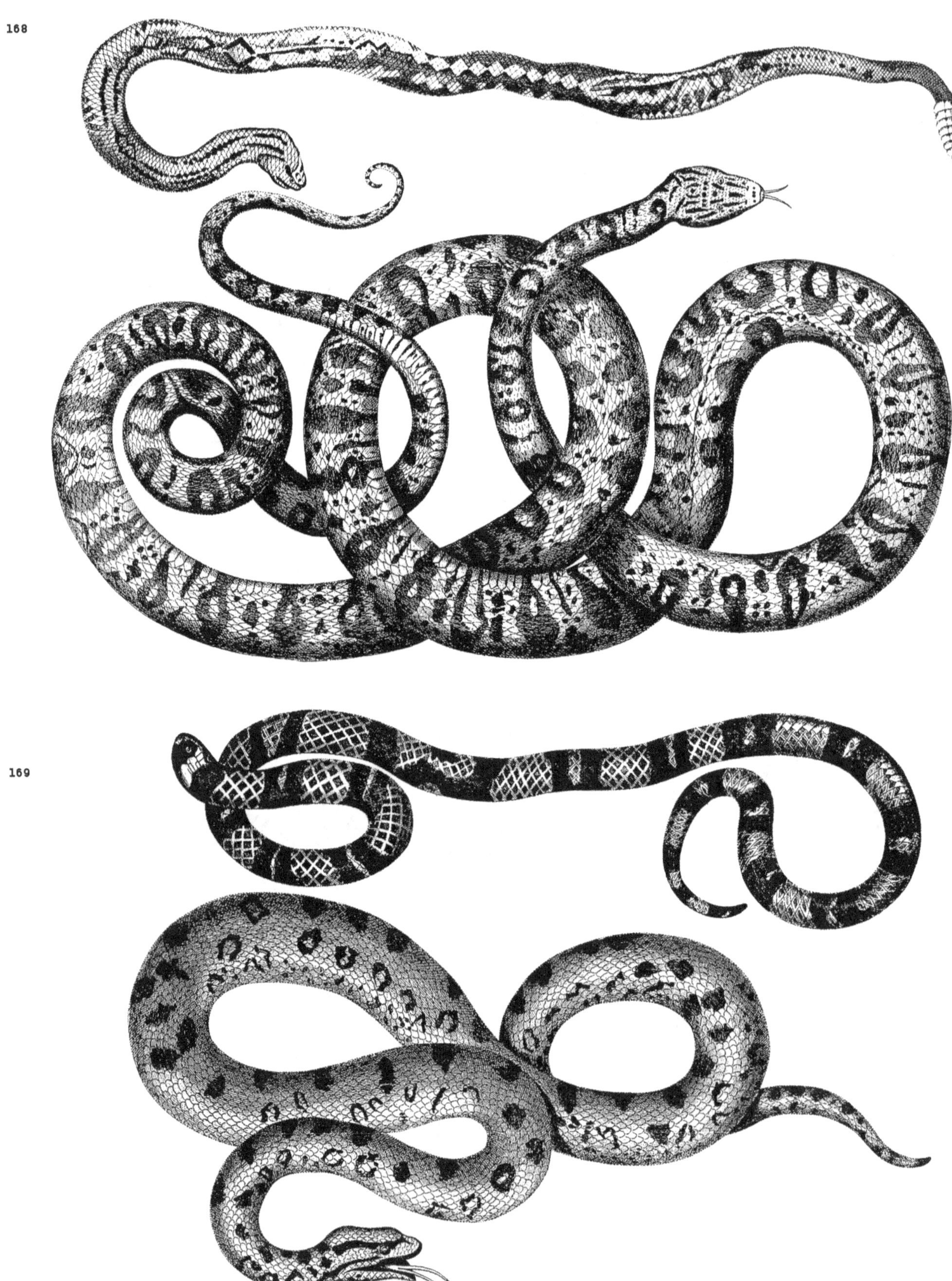

170

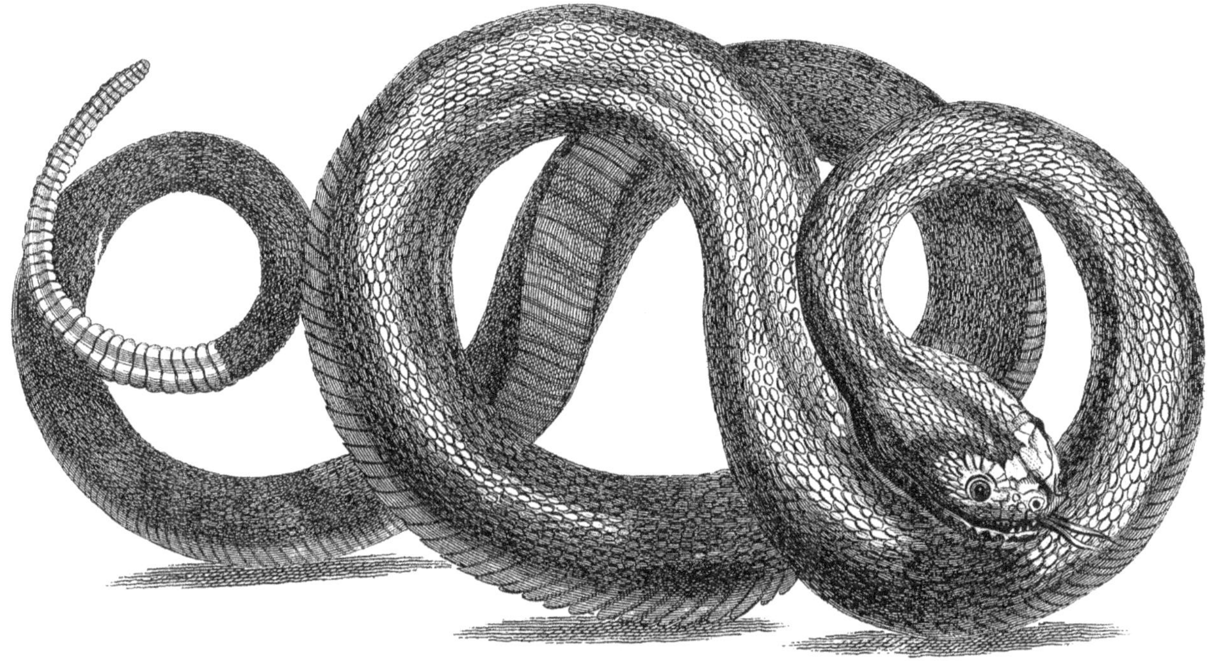

171

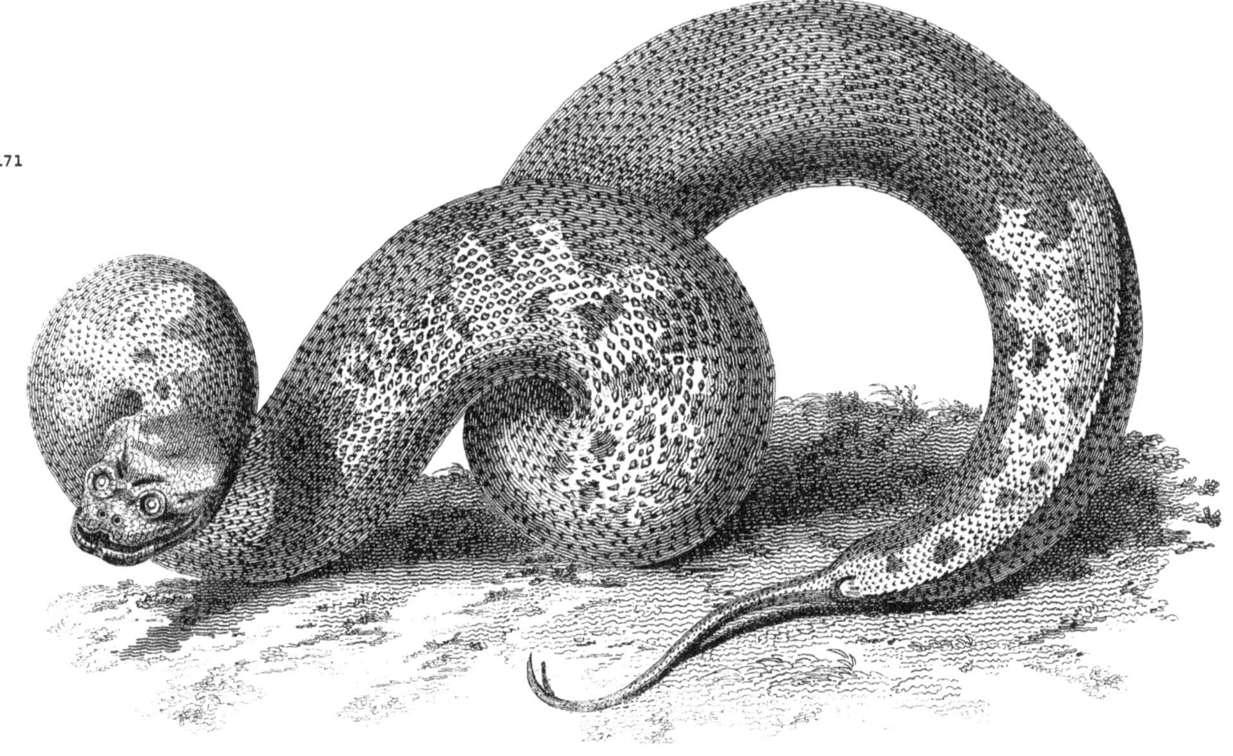

172

173

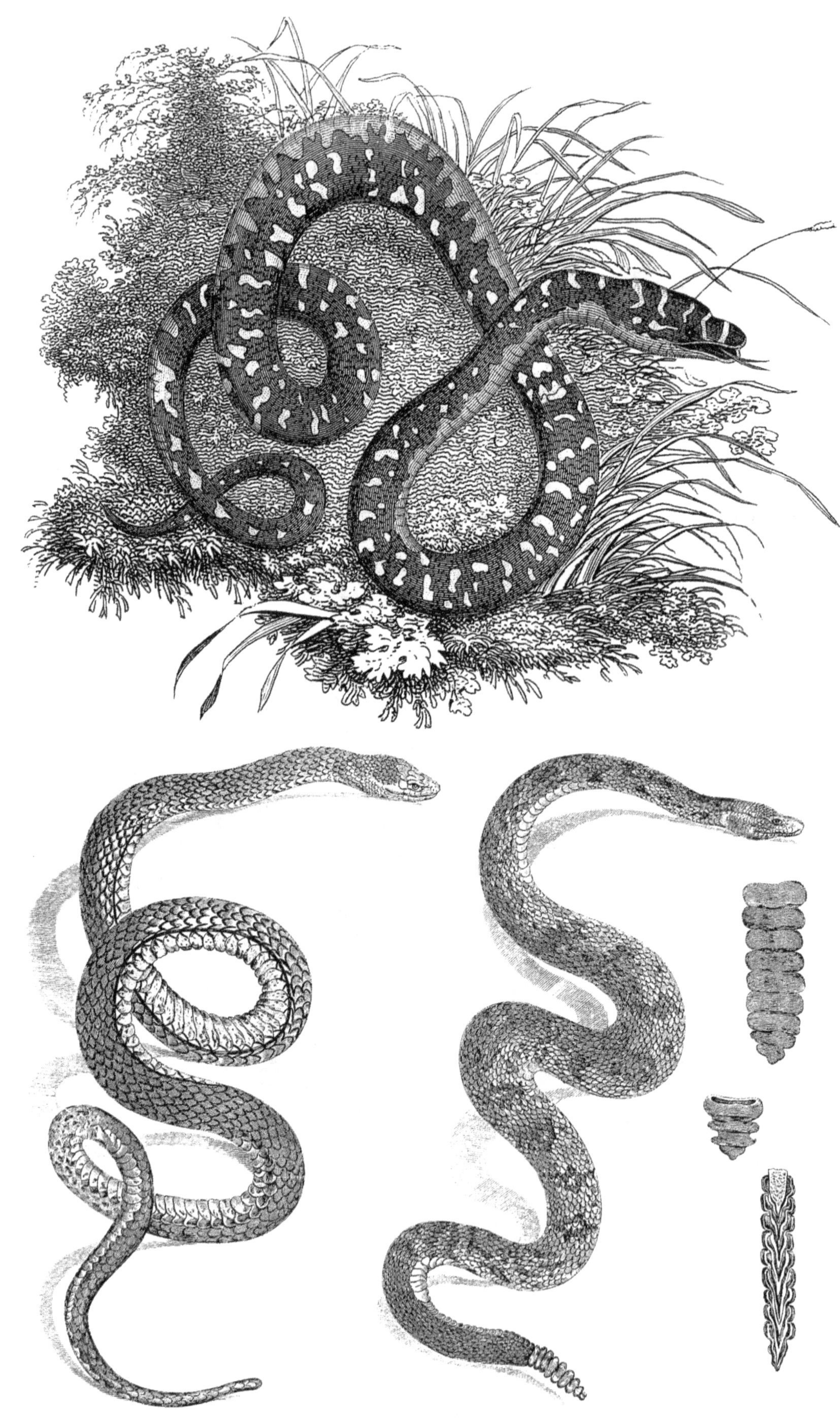

174

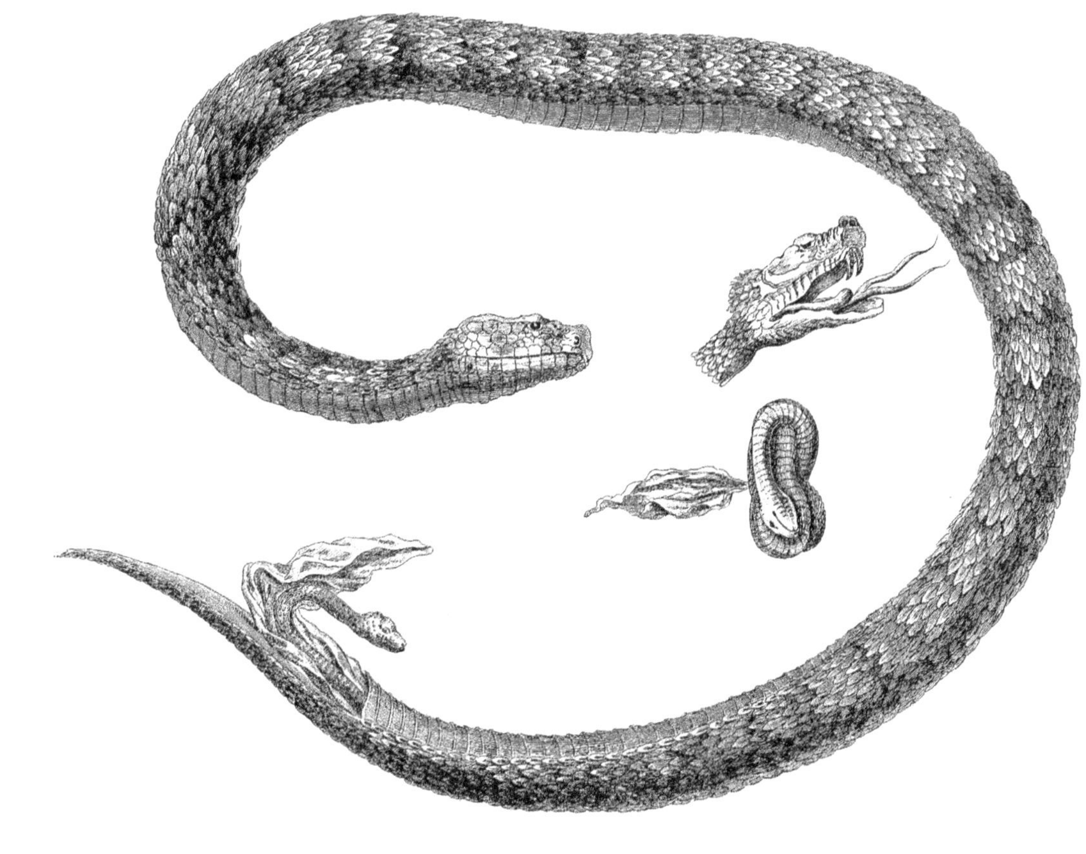

175

176

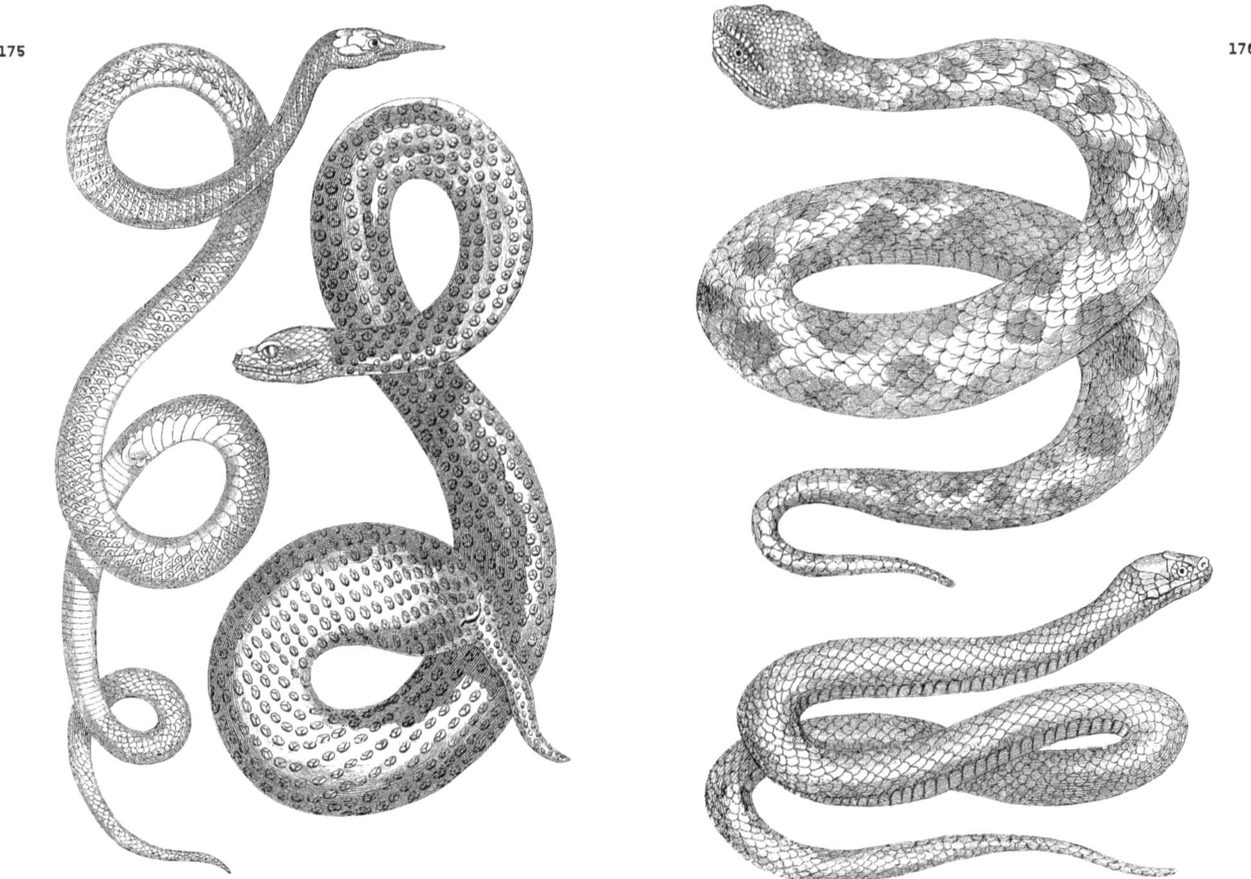

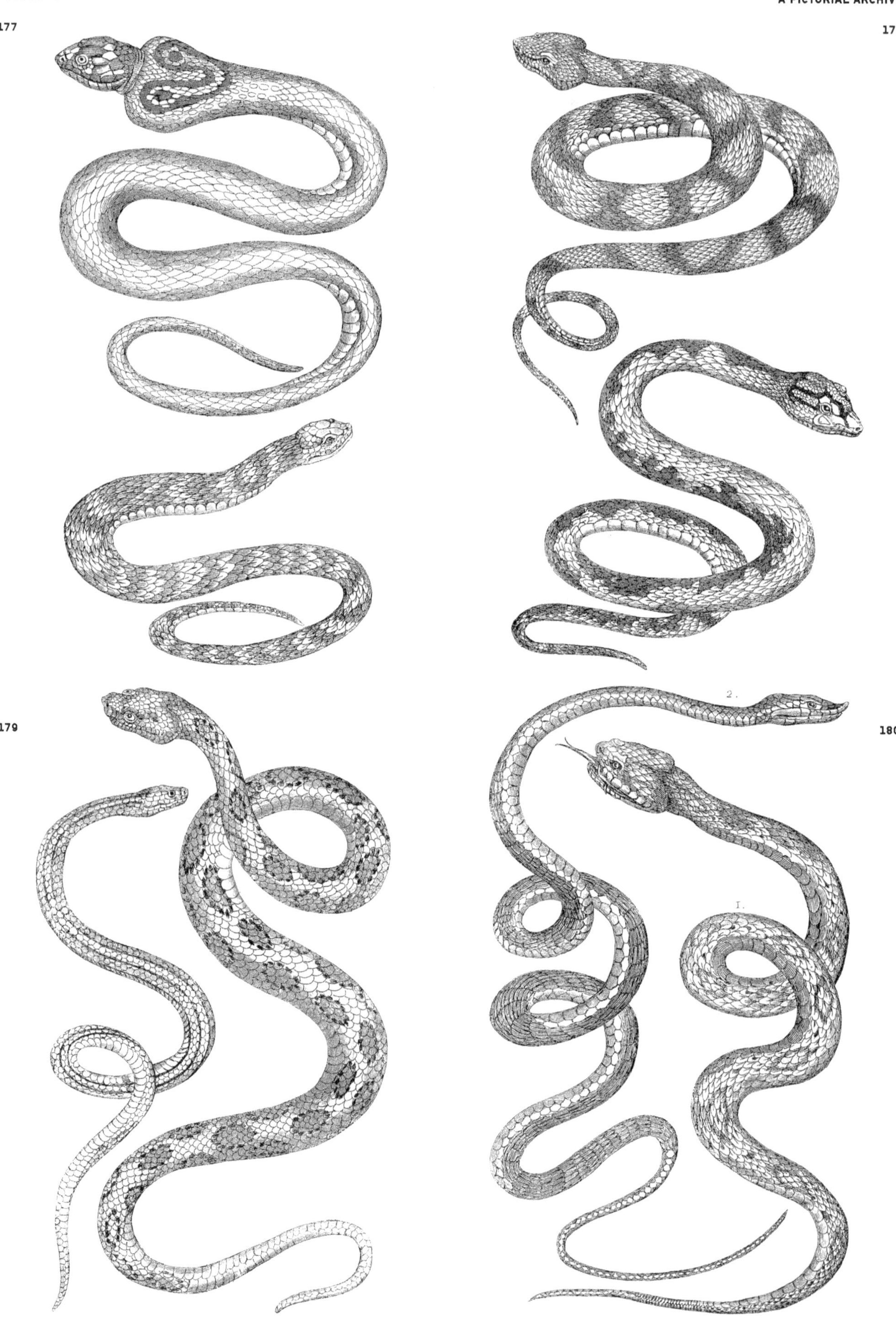

181

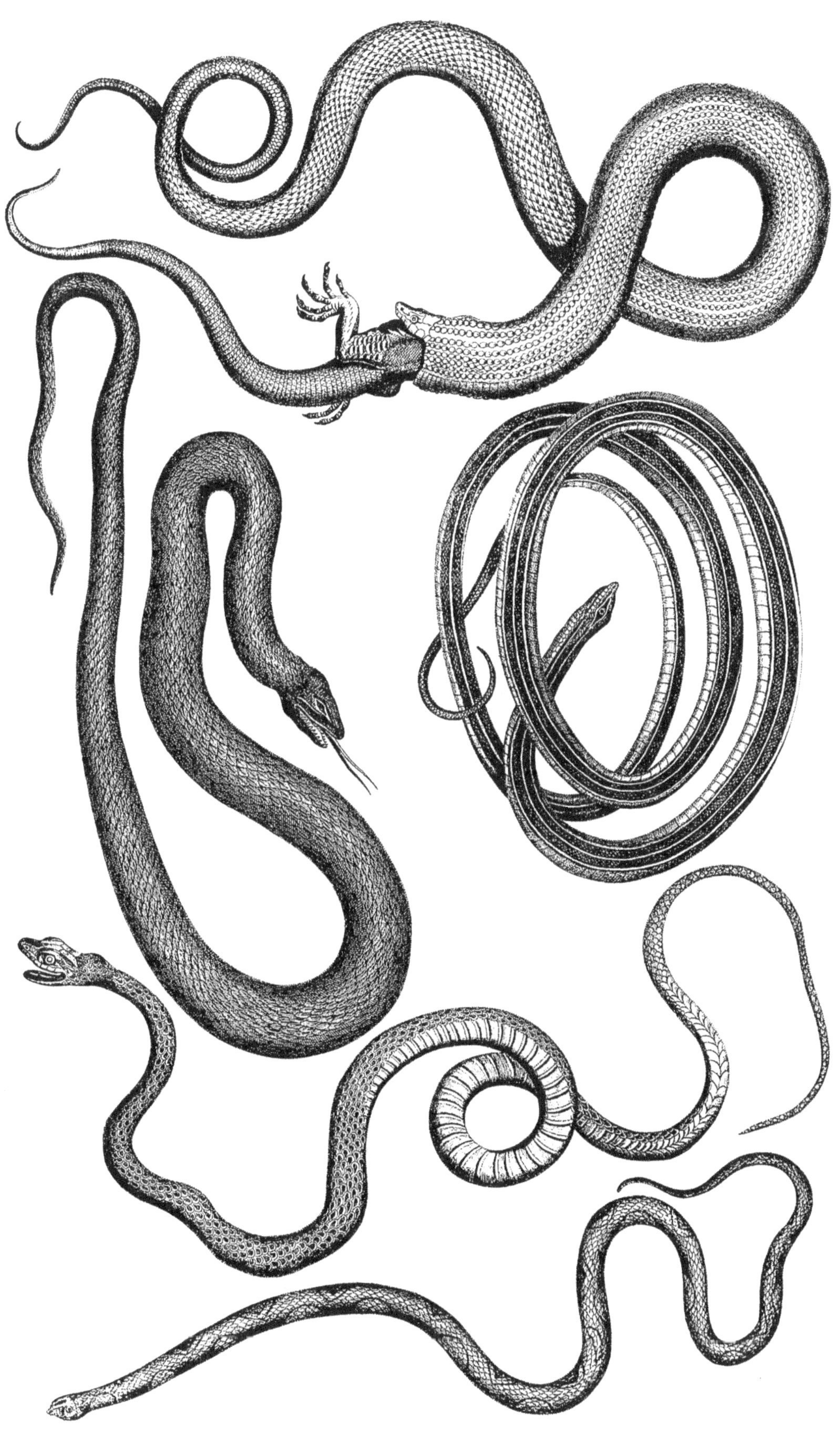

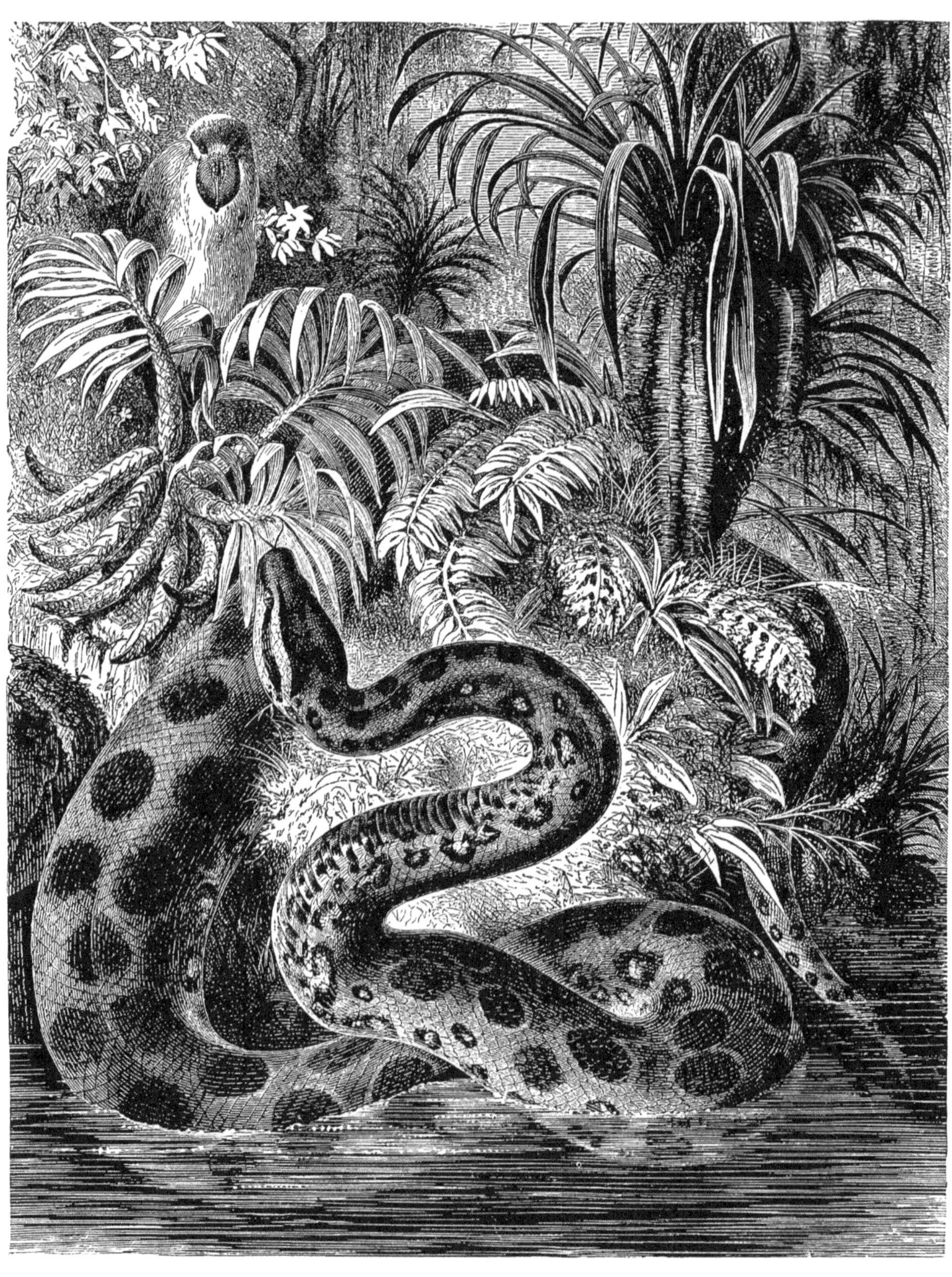

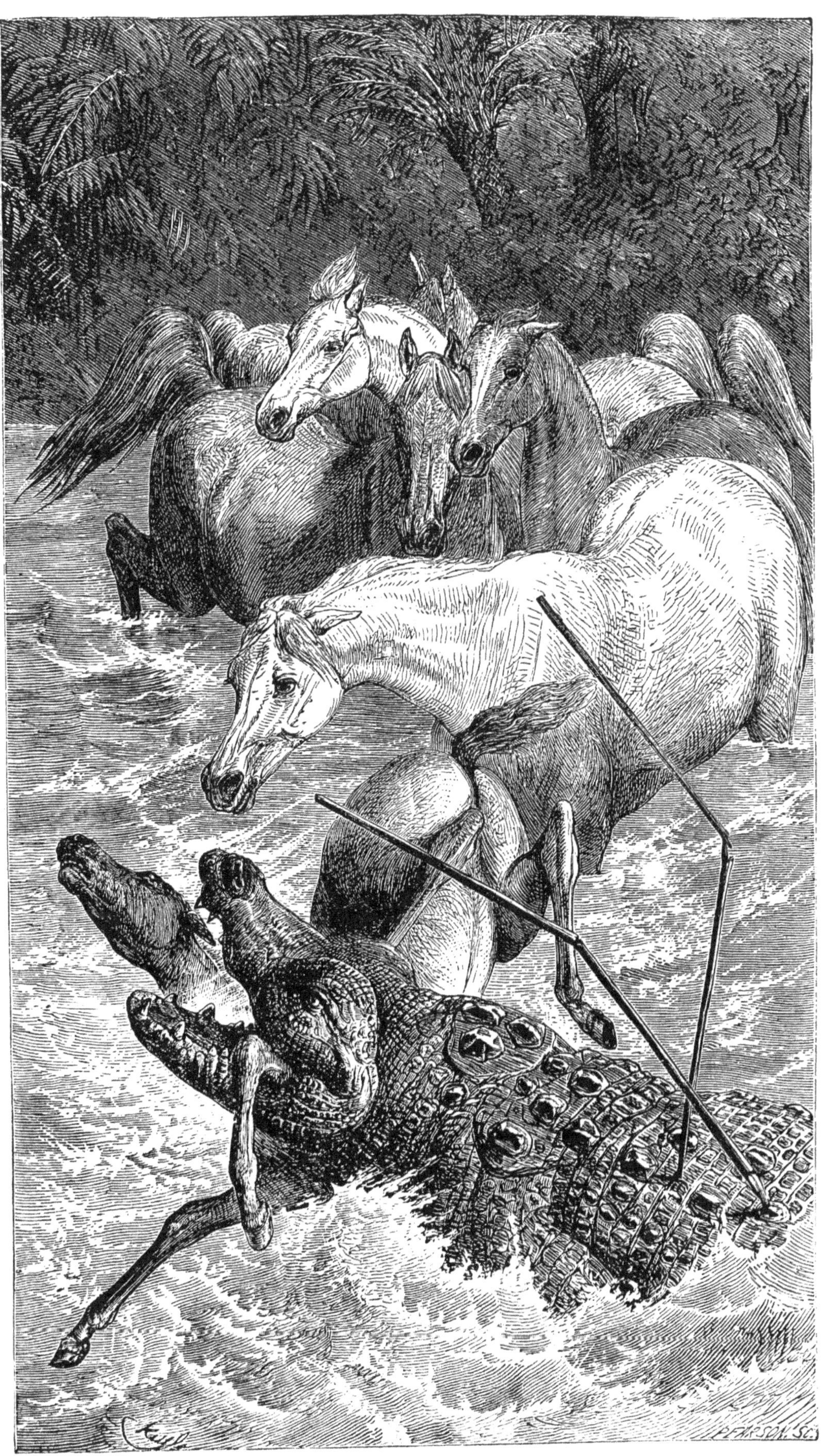

CROCODILIA

184

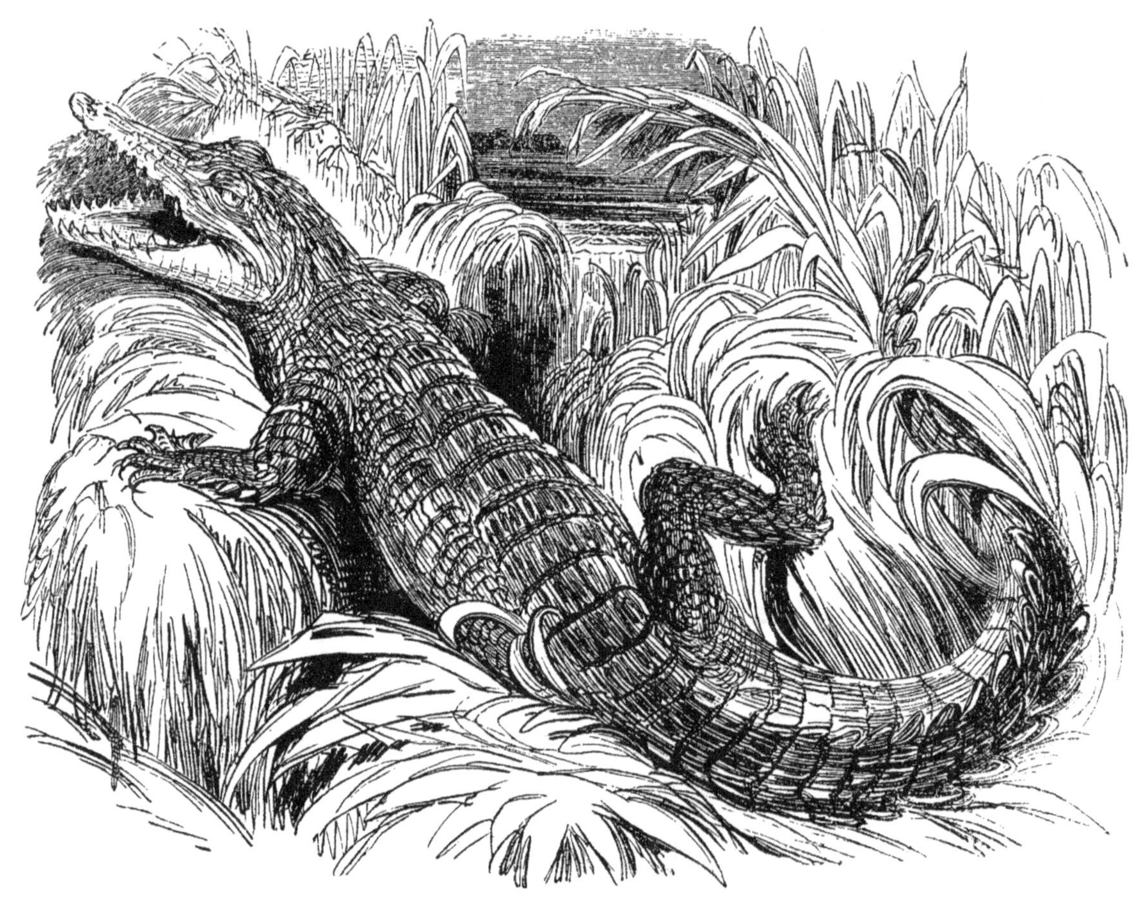

185

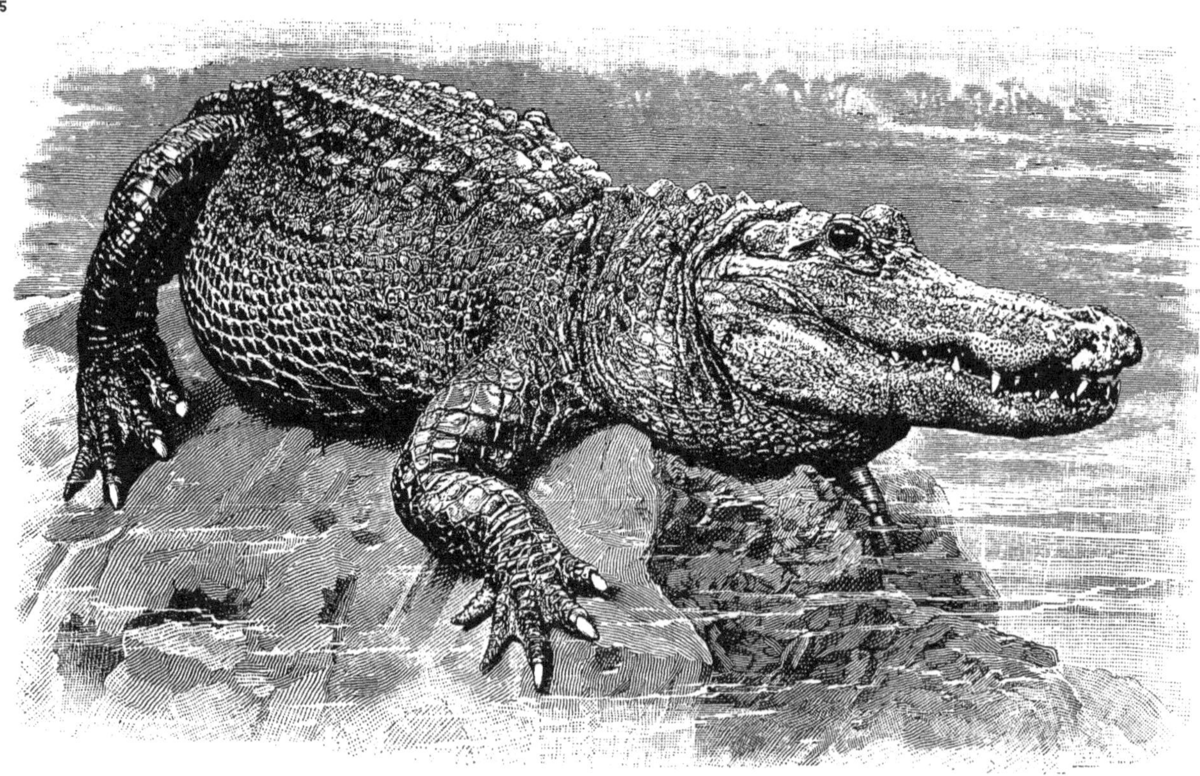

CROCODILIA

186

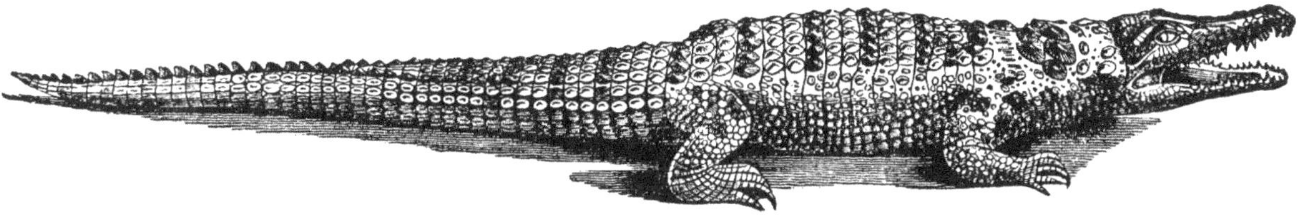

187

188

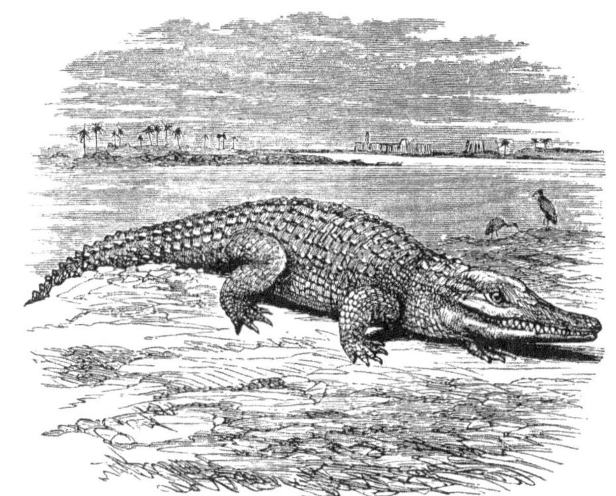

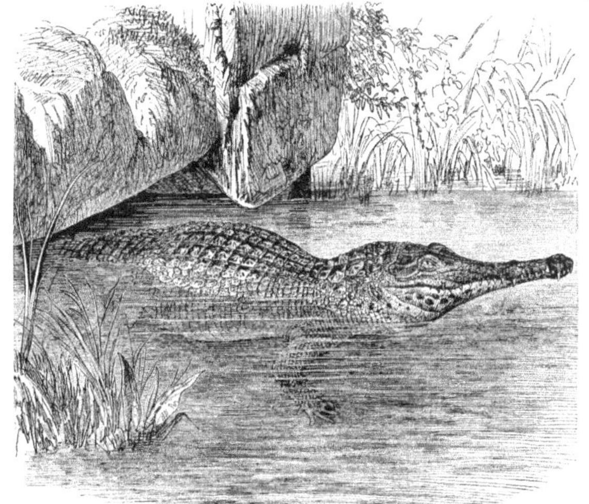

189

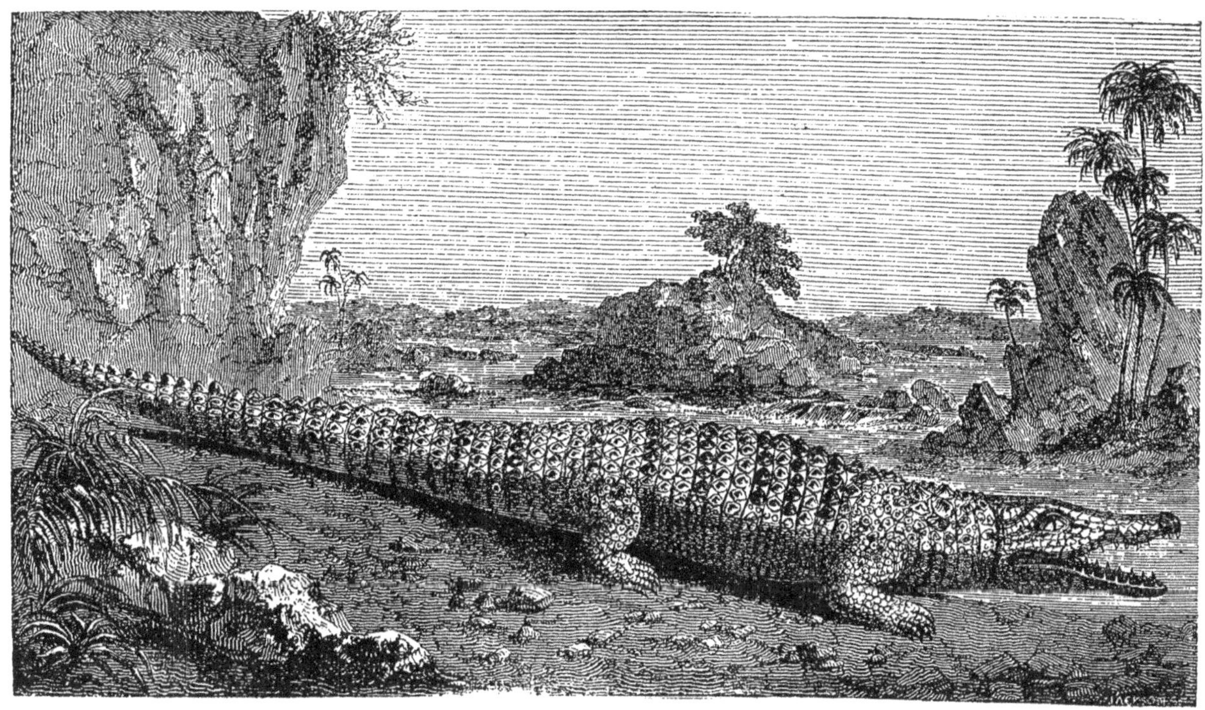

190

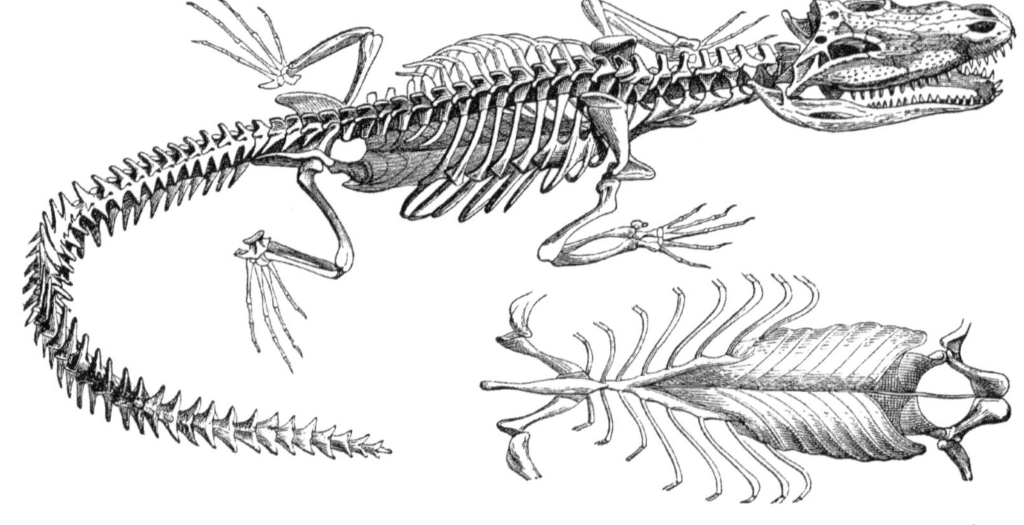

191

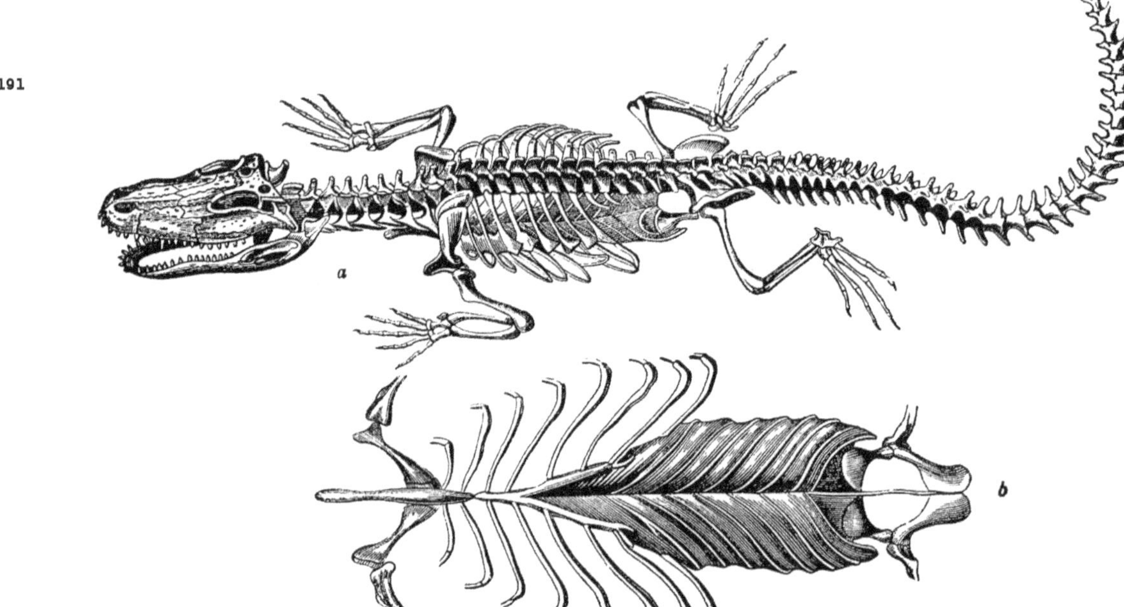

192

193

194

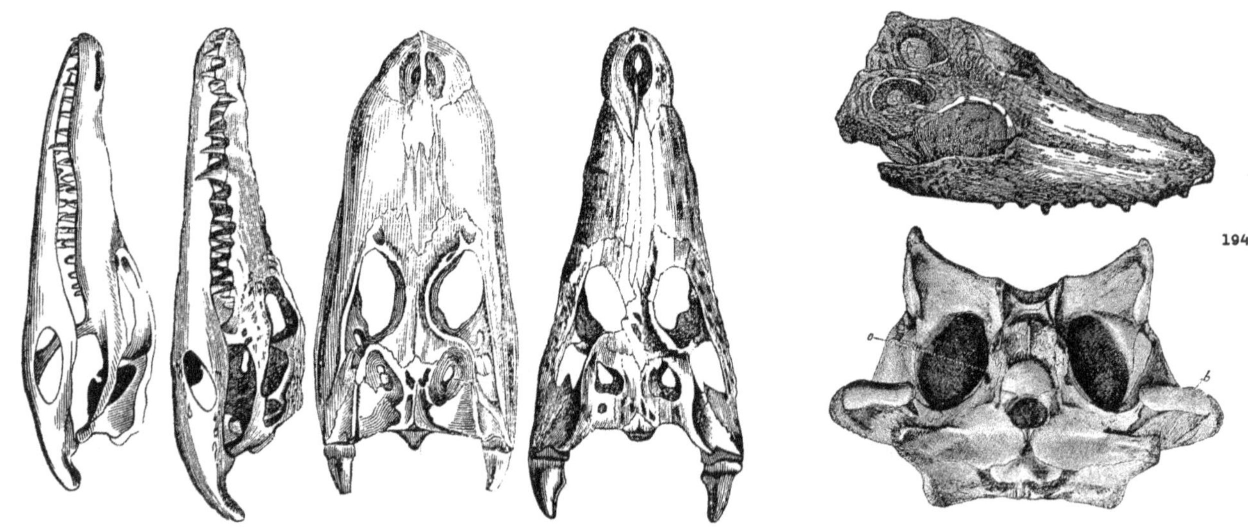

195

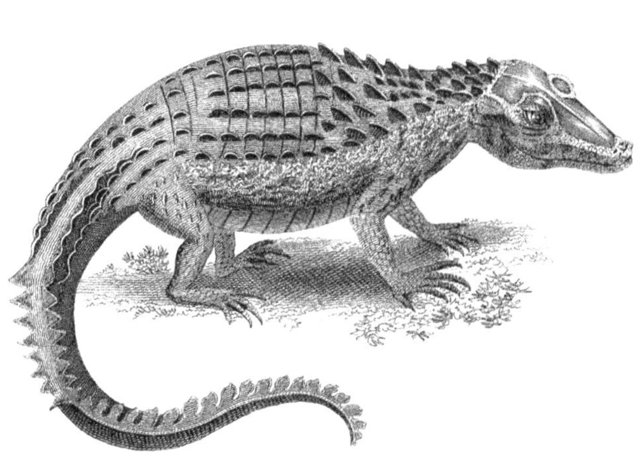

196

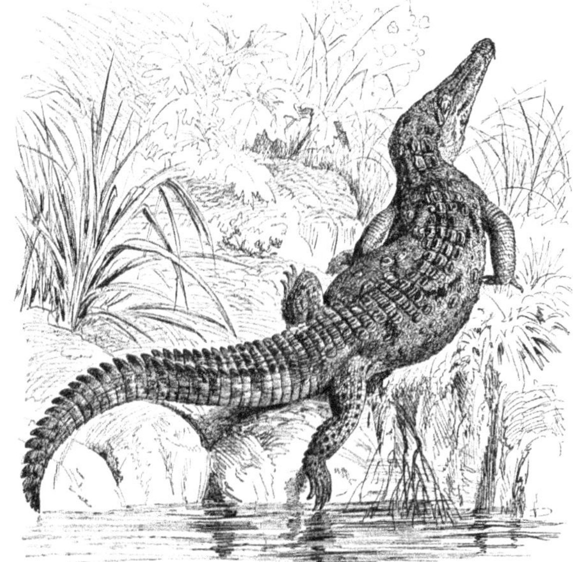

197

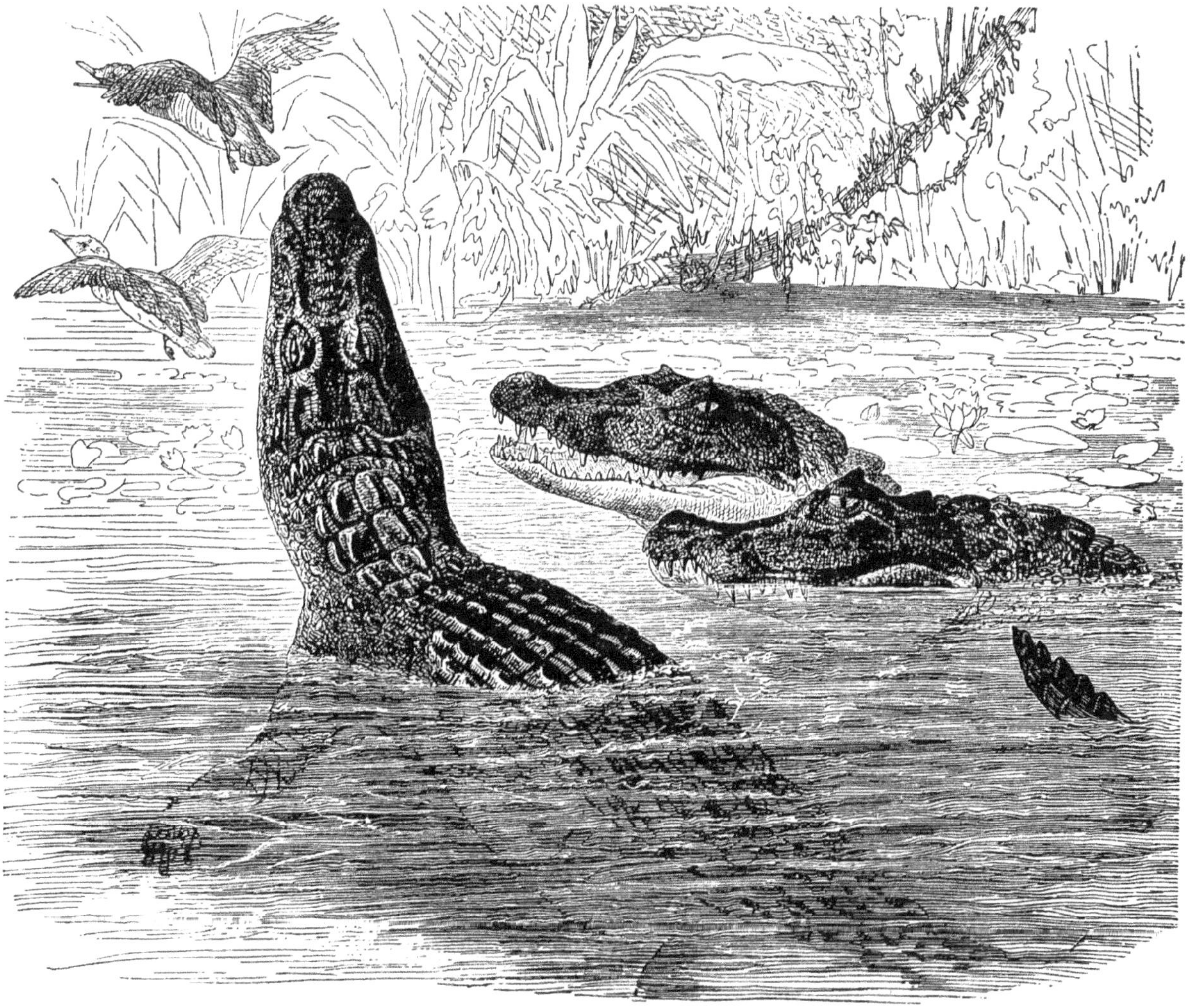

CROCODILIA

198

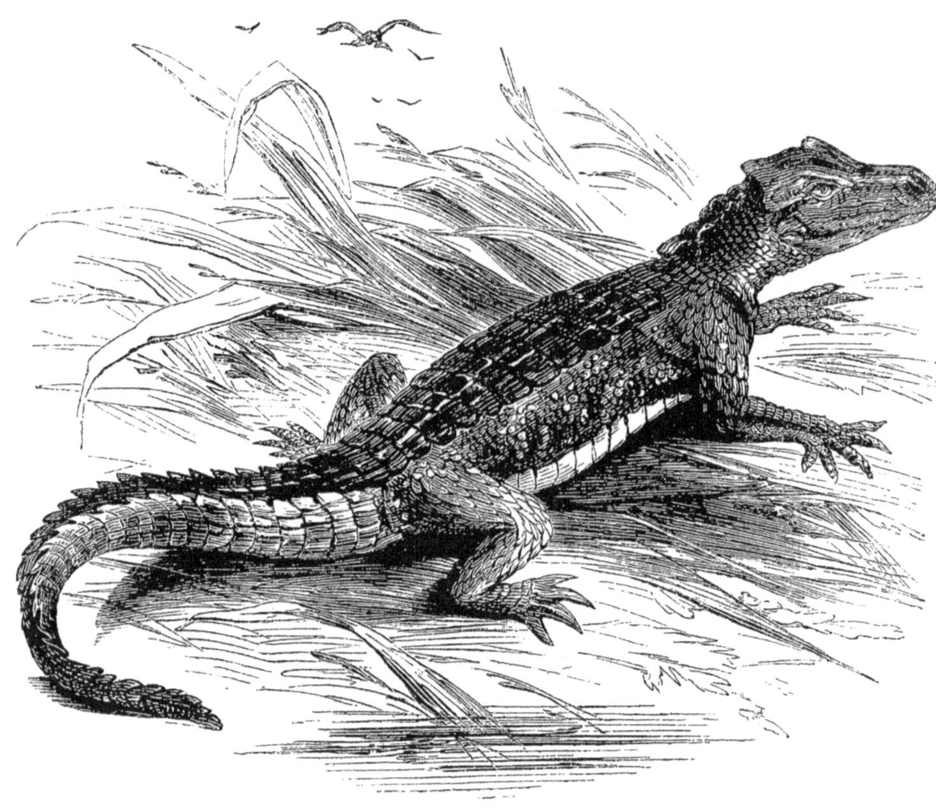

199

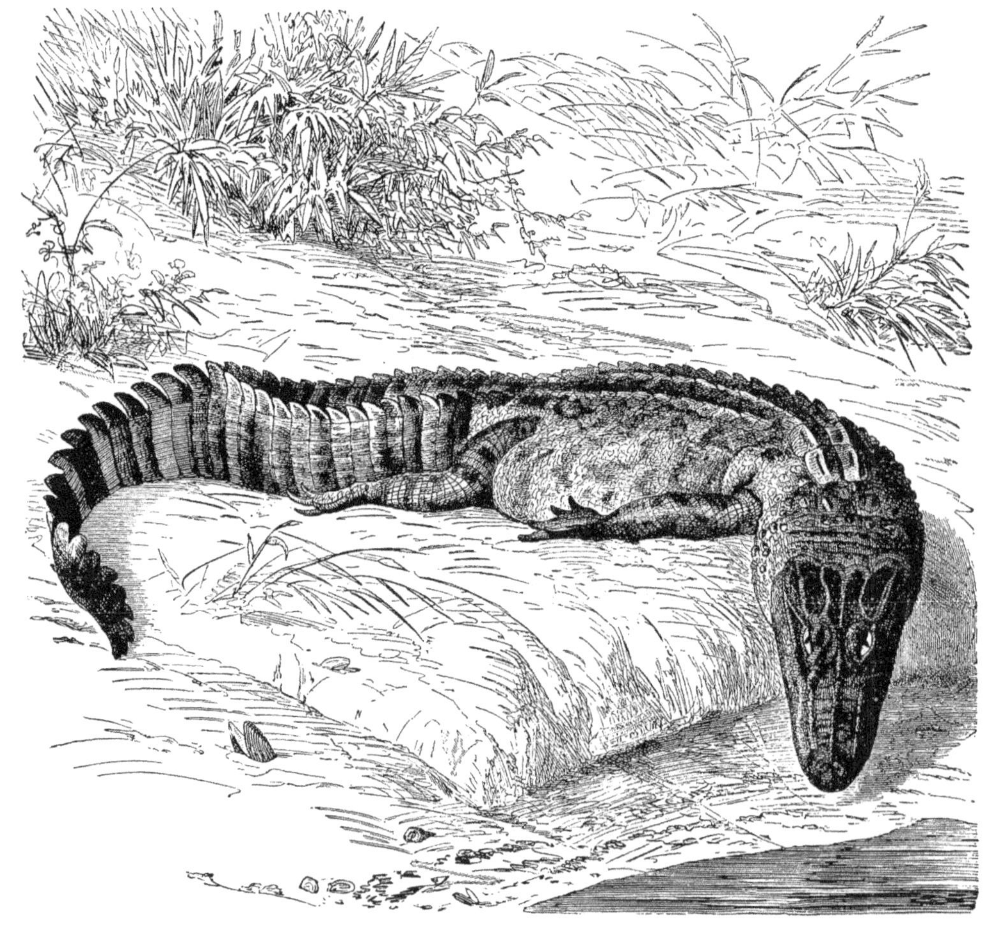

200

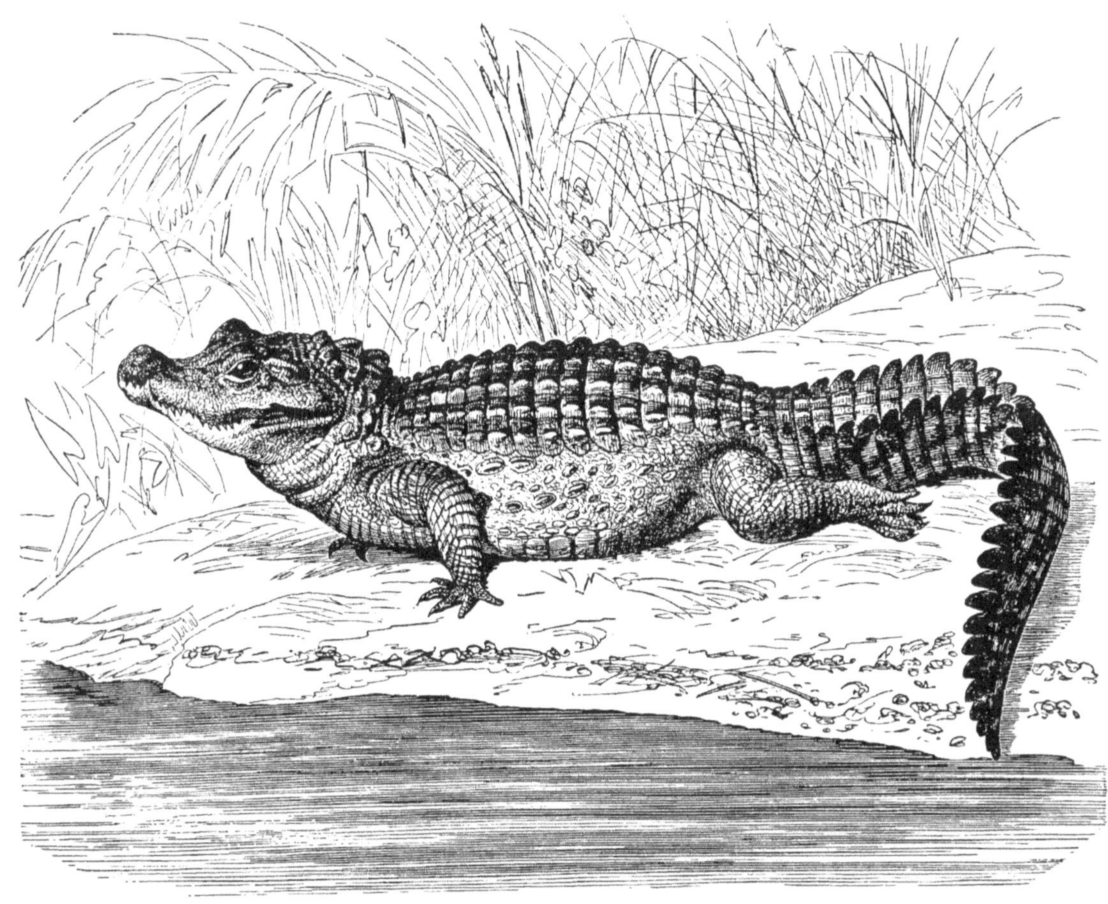

201

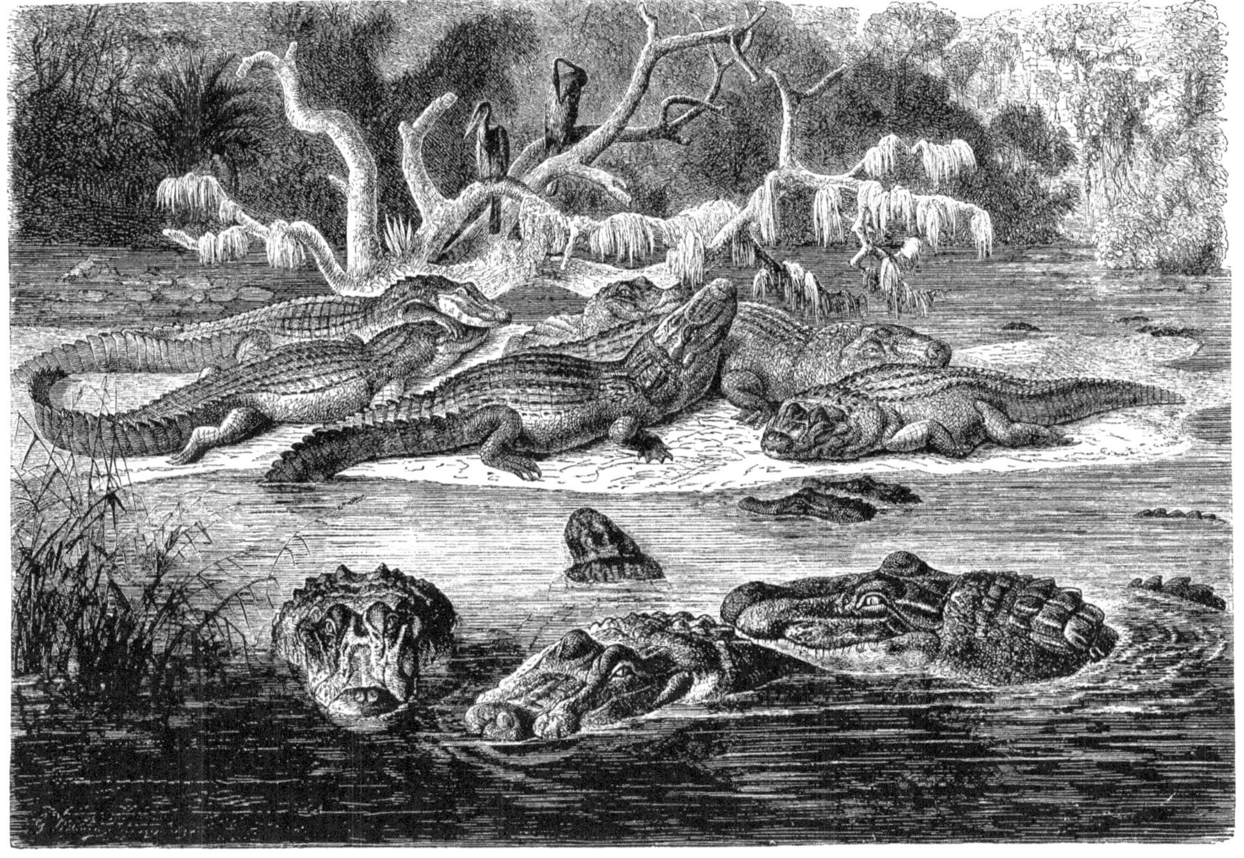

CROCODILIA

202

203

204

205

207

206

208

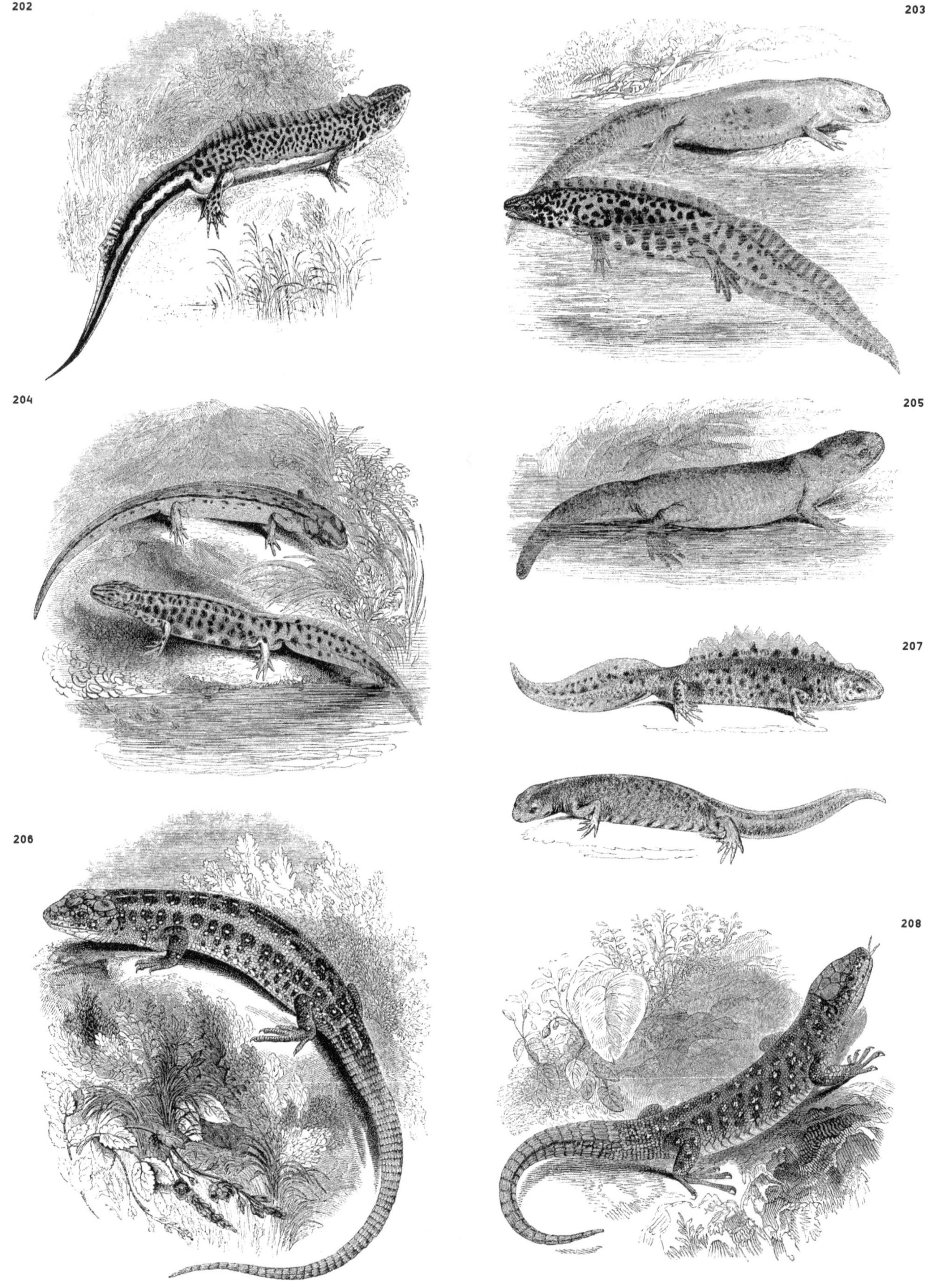

209

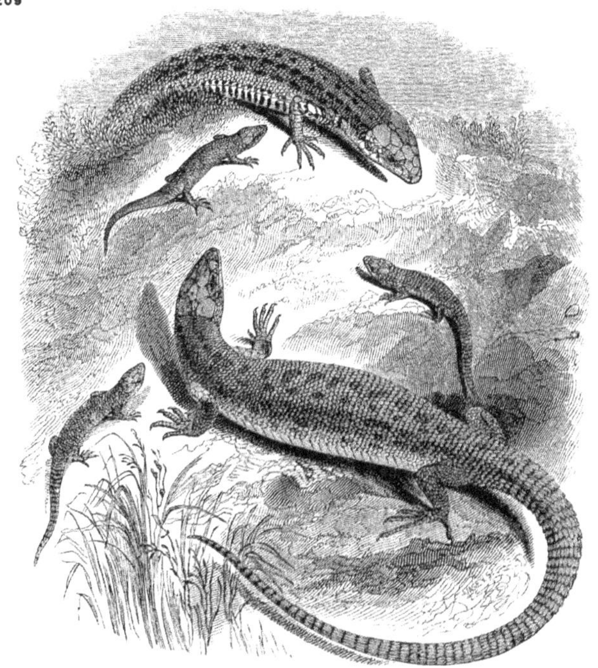

210

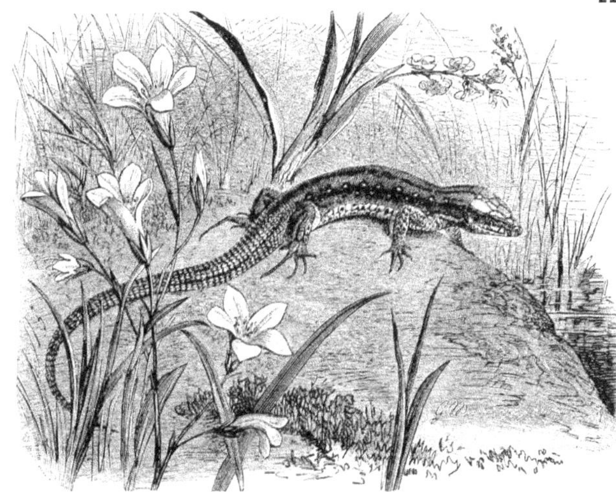

212

211

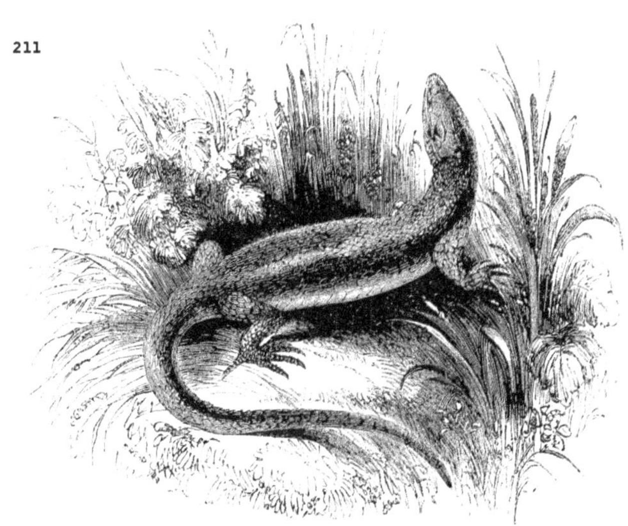

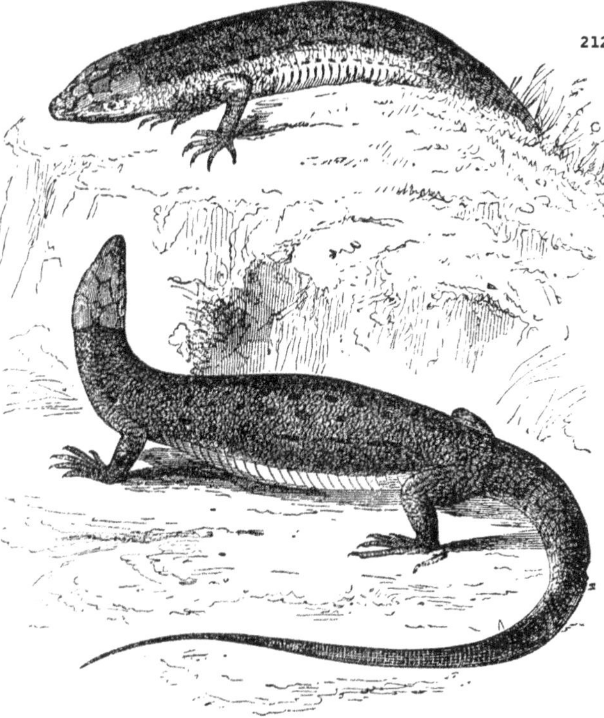

213

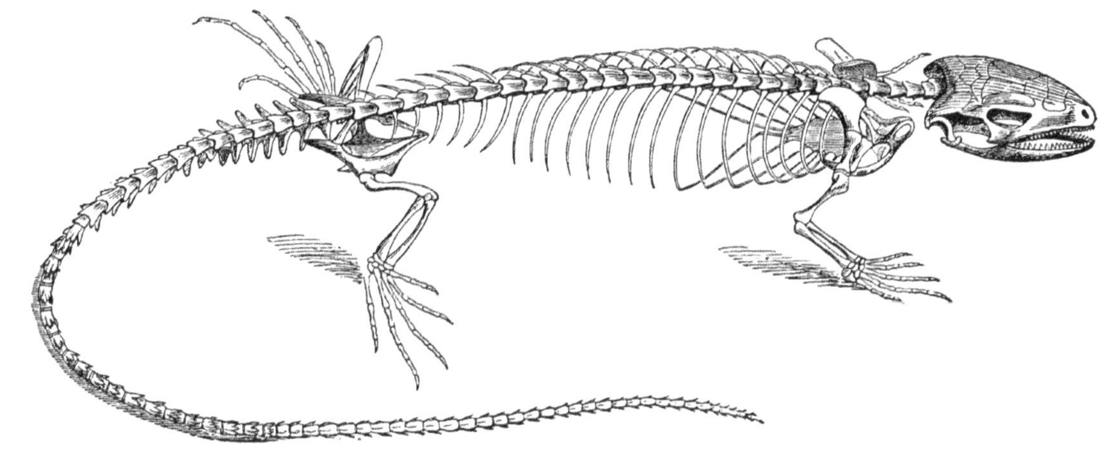

214

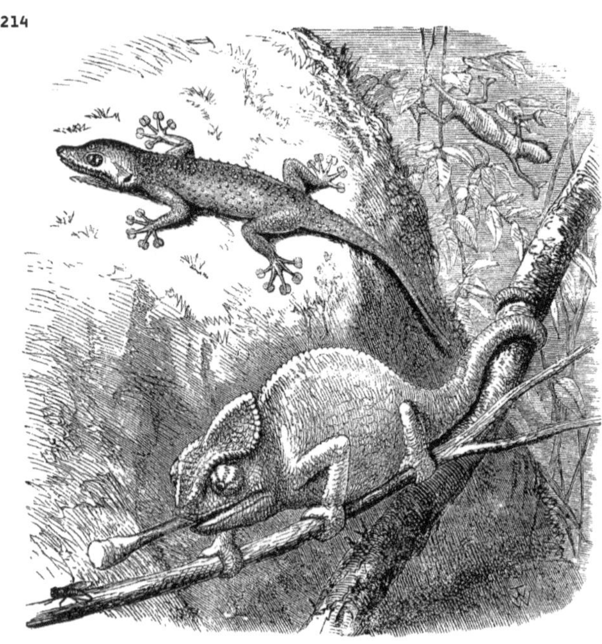

215

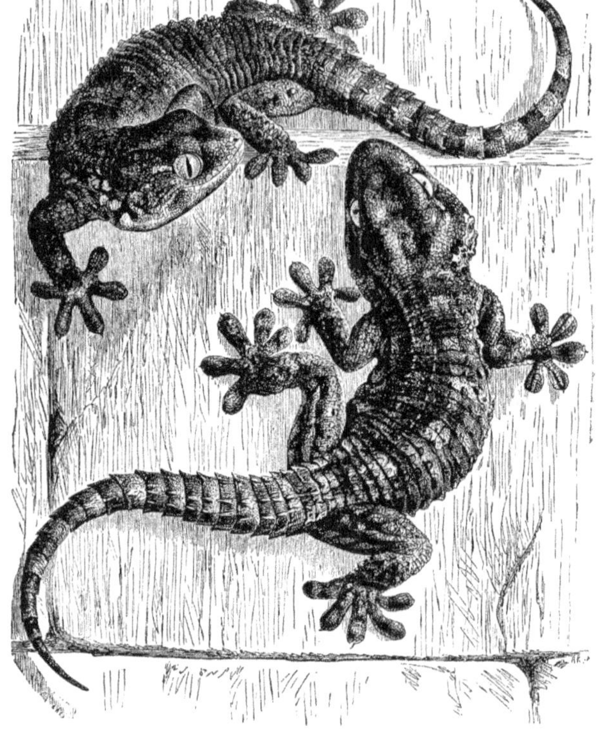

216

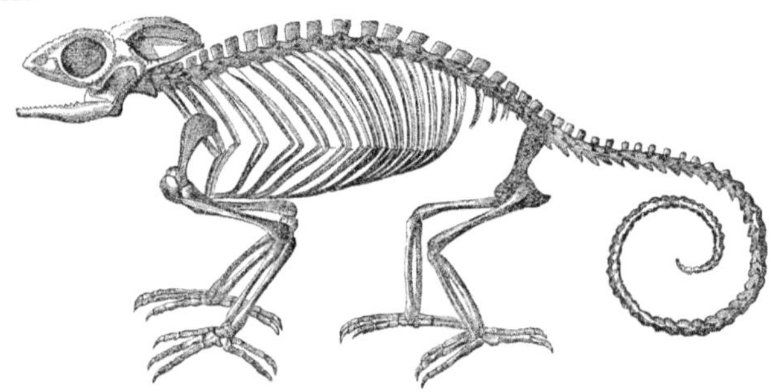

217

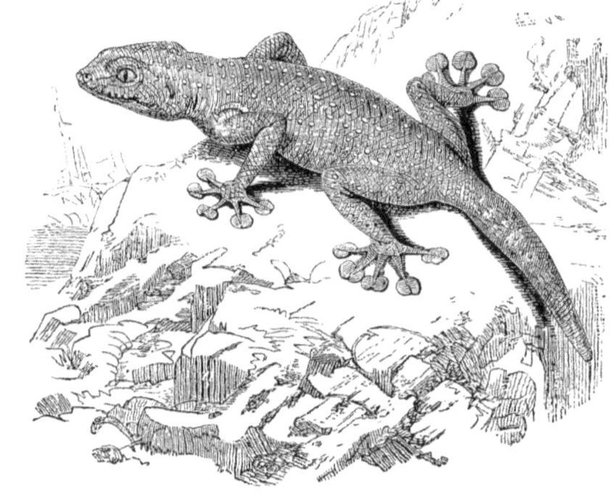

218

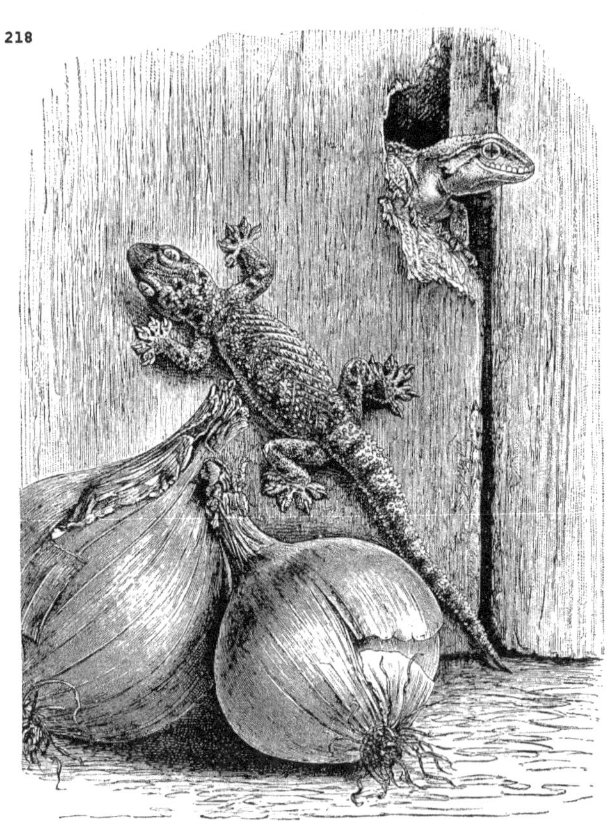

219

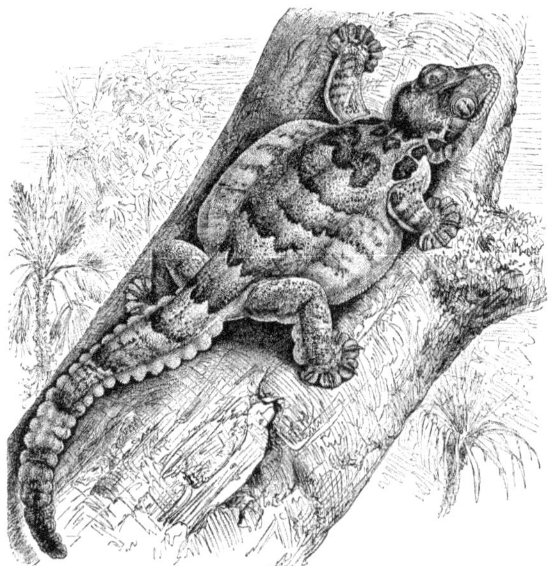

220

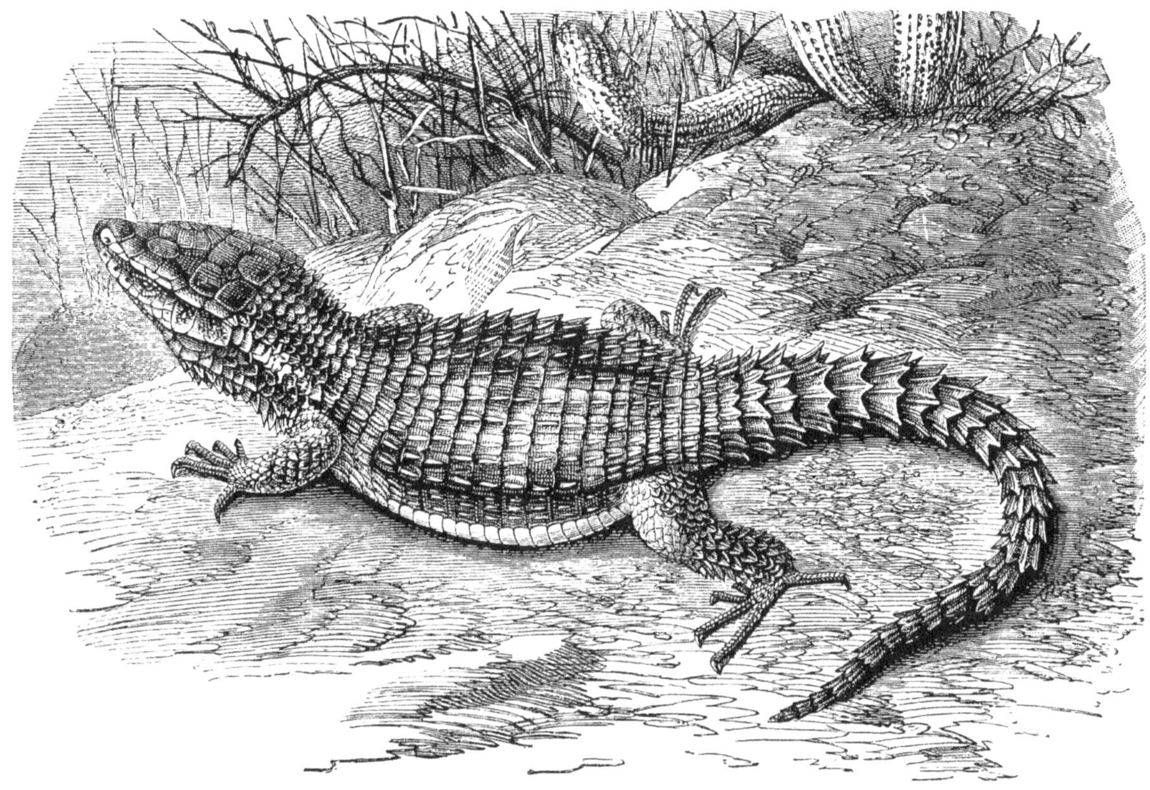

221

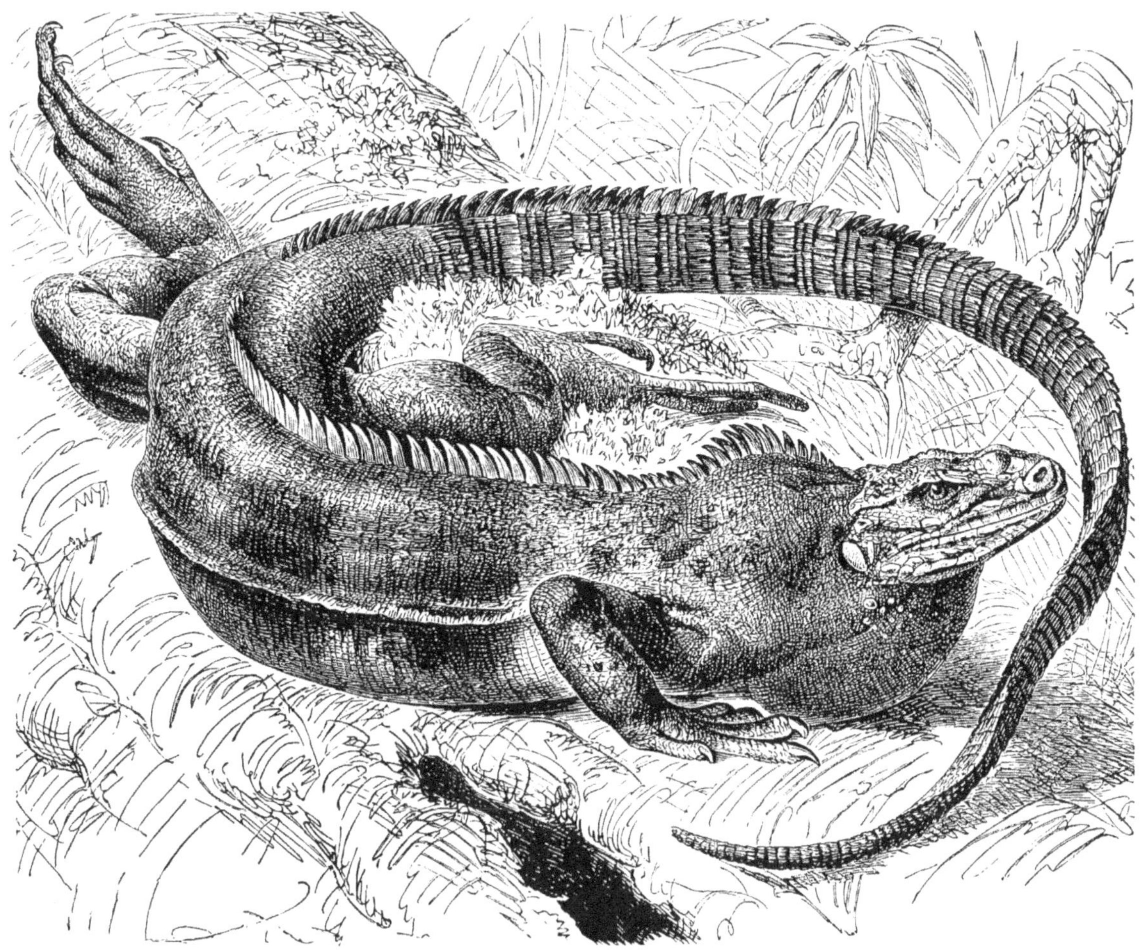

LIZARDS

222

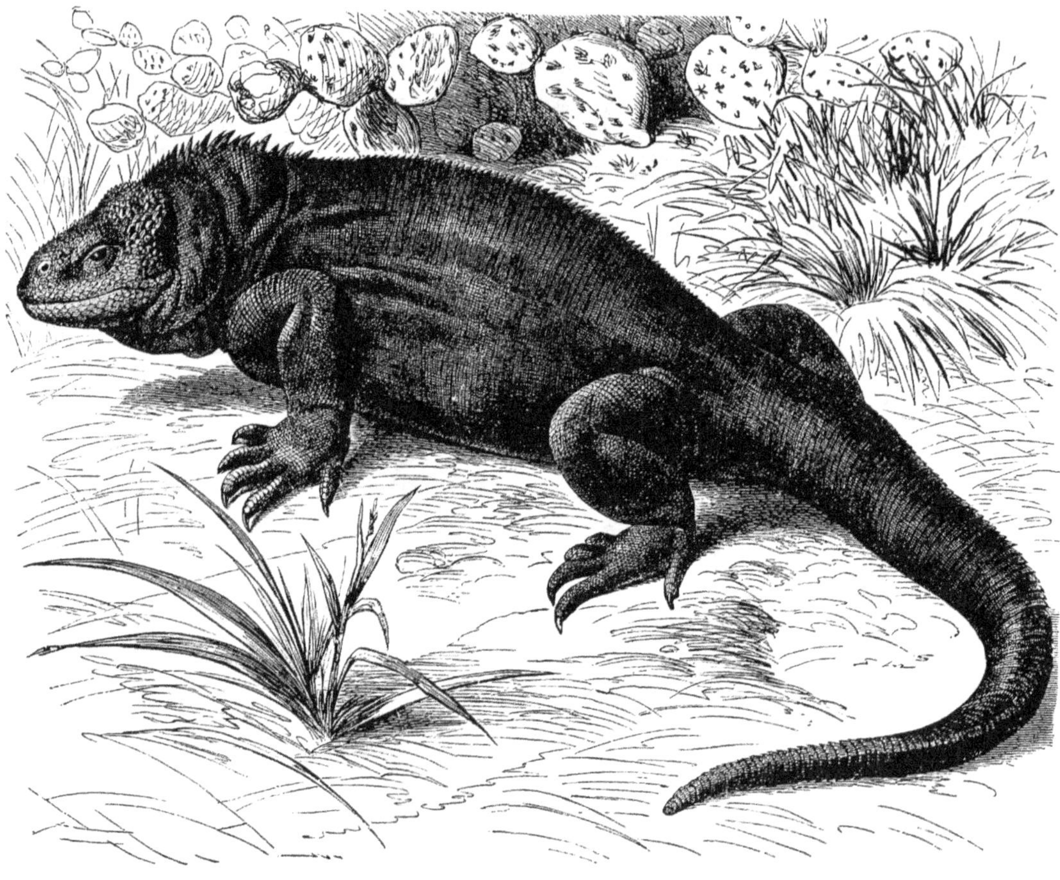

223

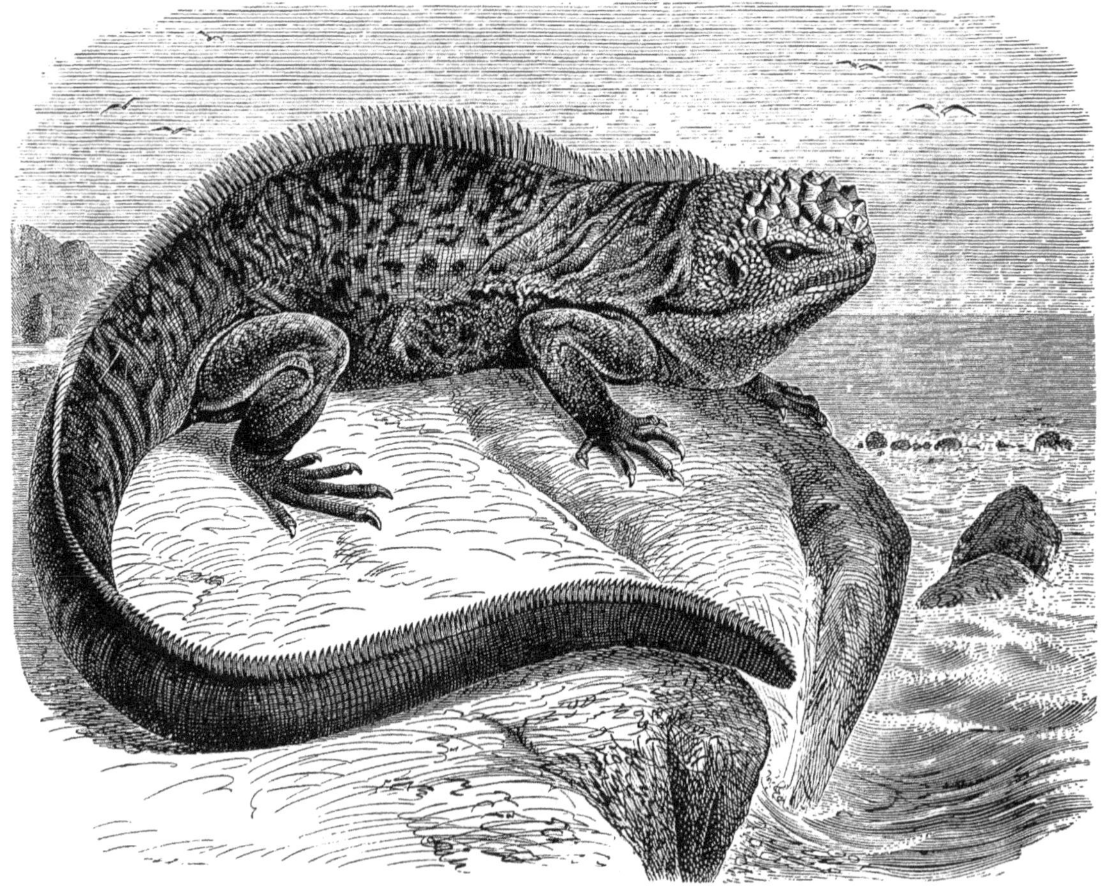

224

225

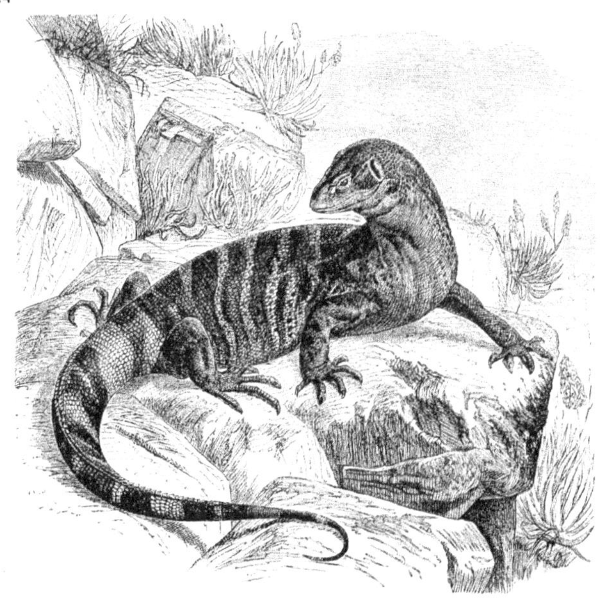

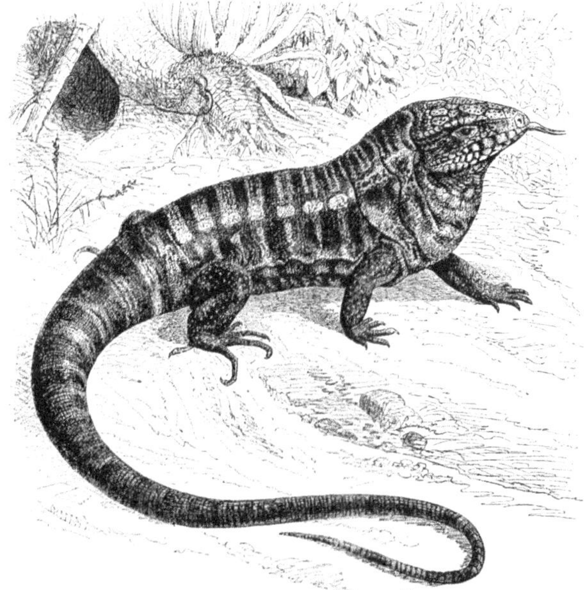

226

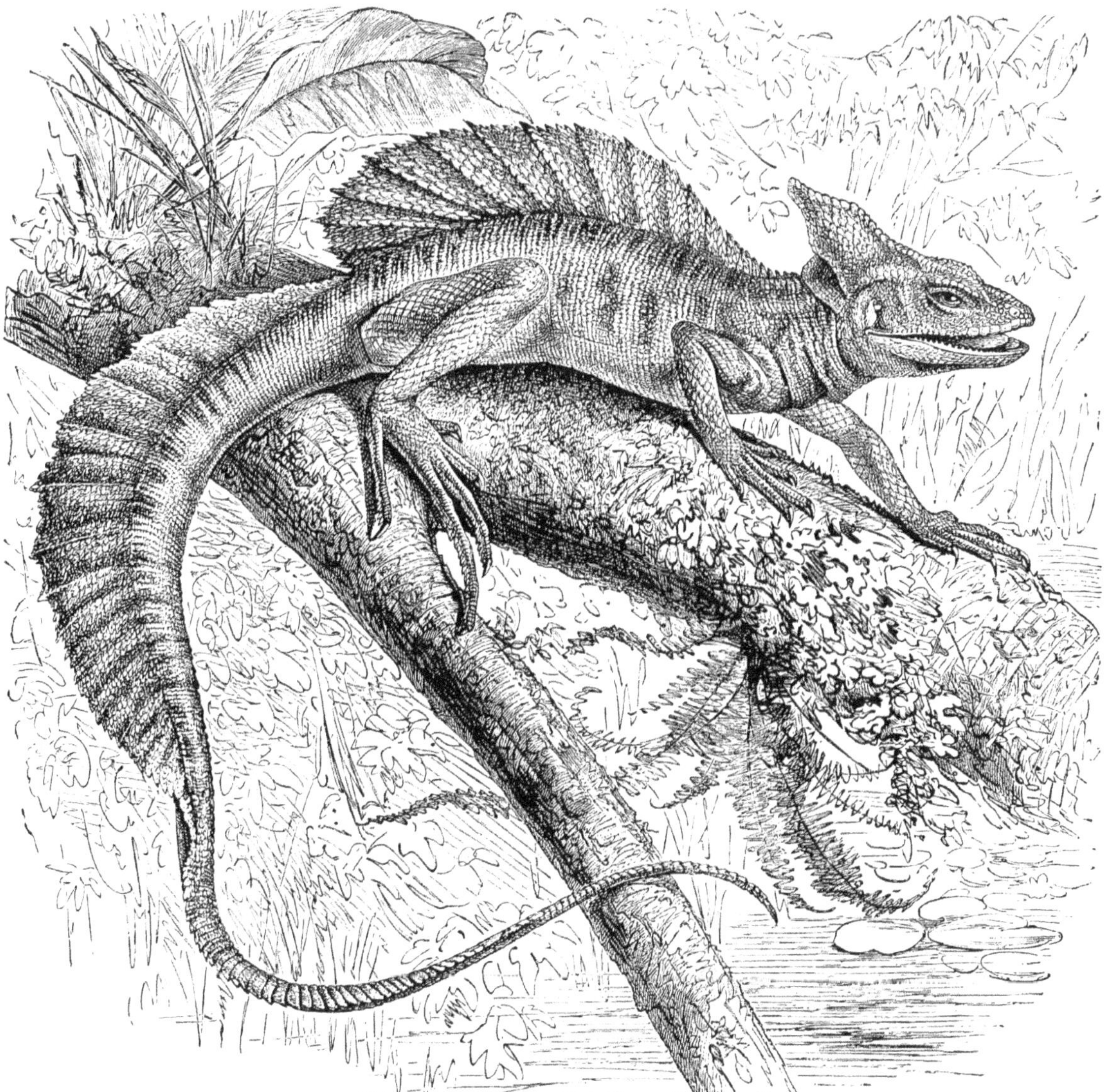

LIZARDS

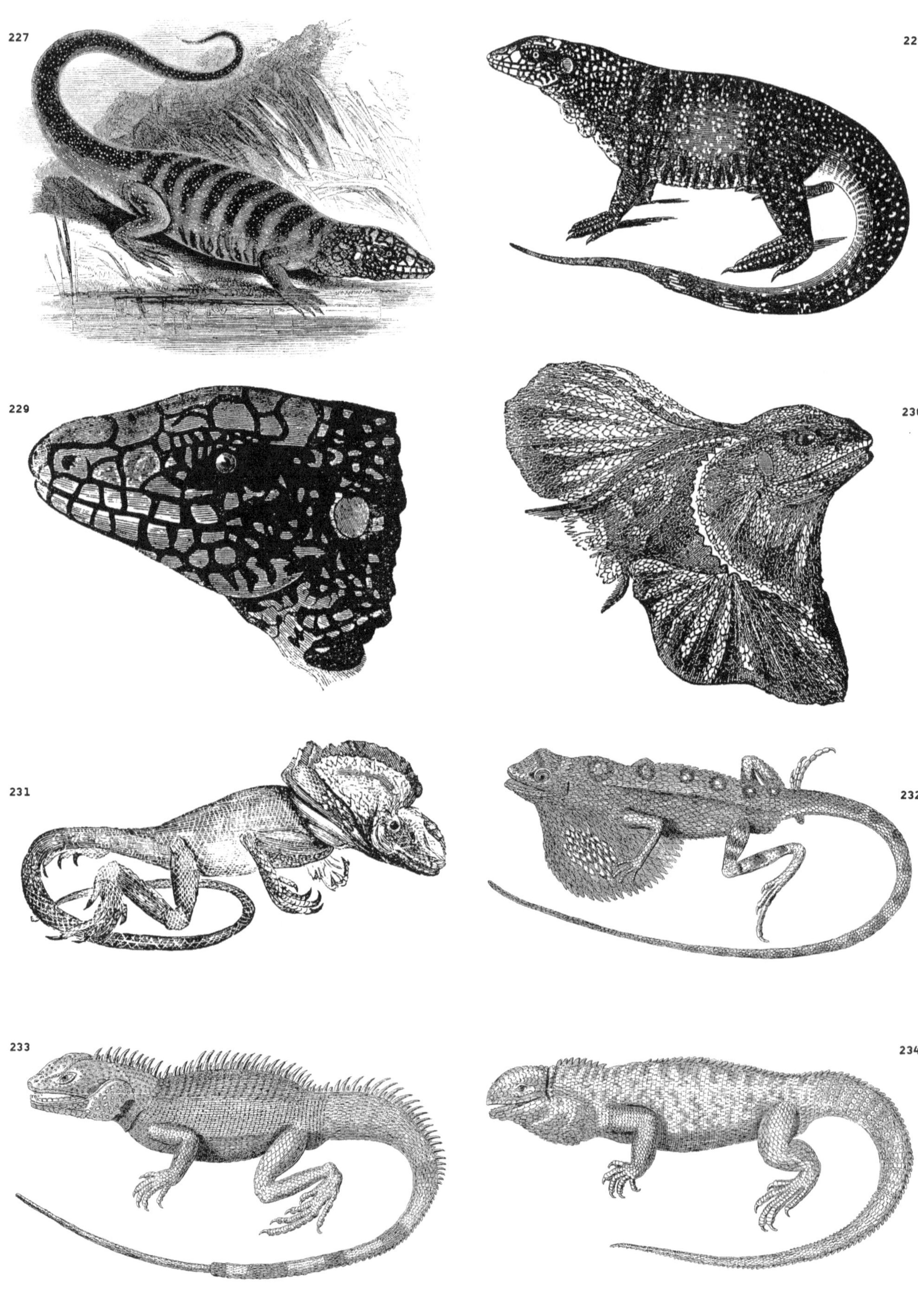

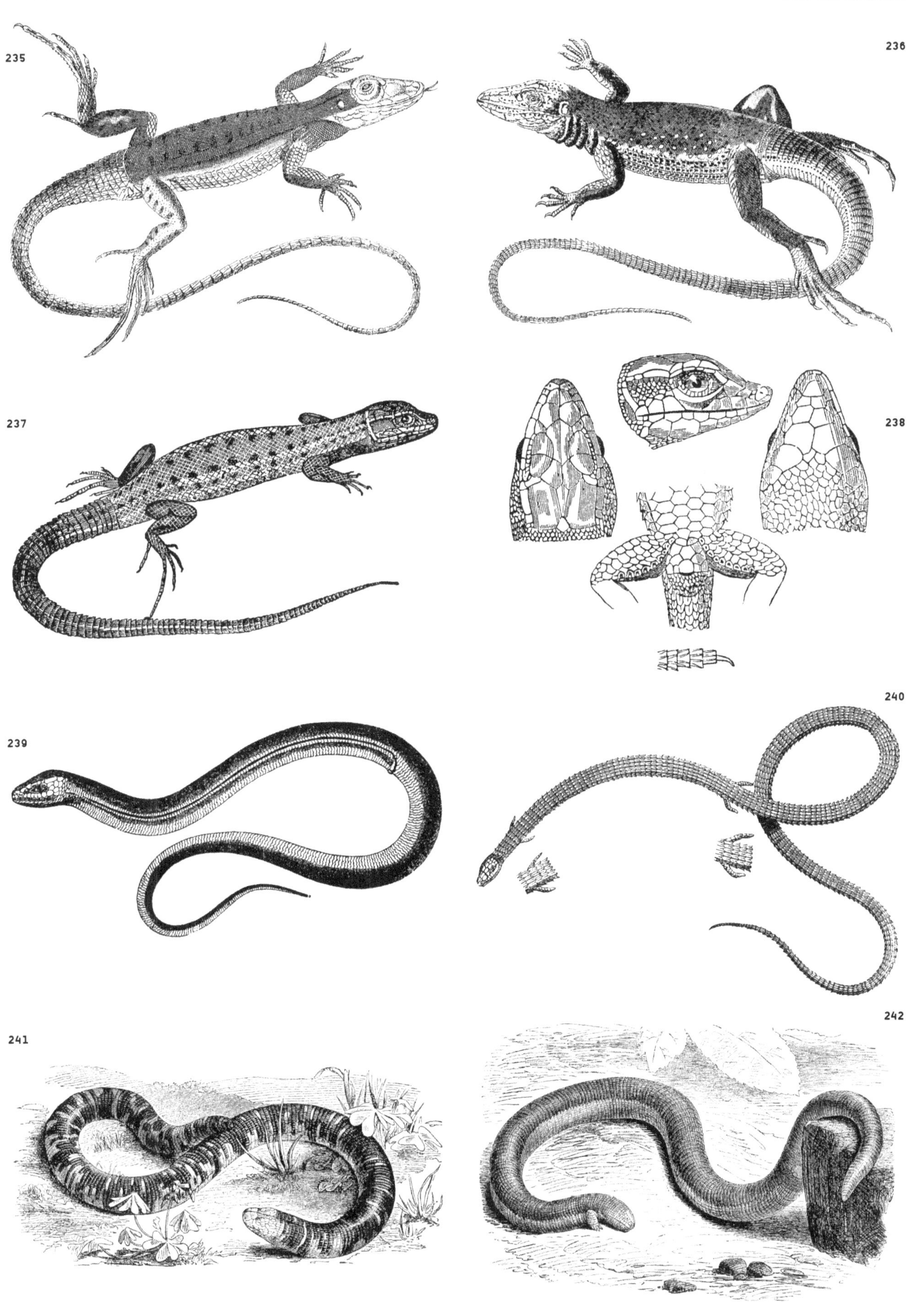

235
236
237
238
239
240
241
242

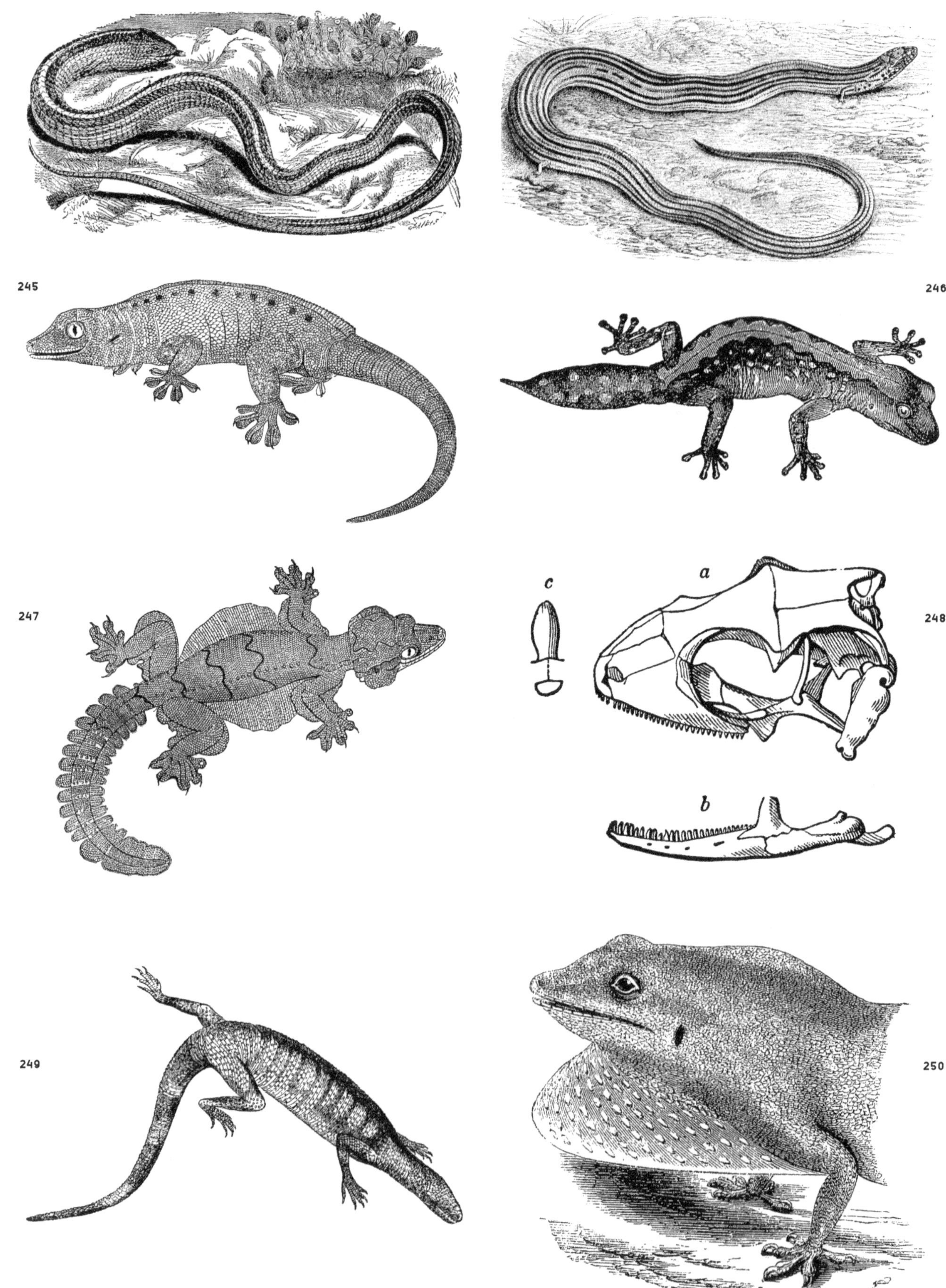

243
244
245
246
247
248
a
b
c
249
250

251

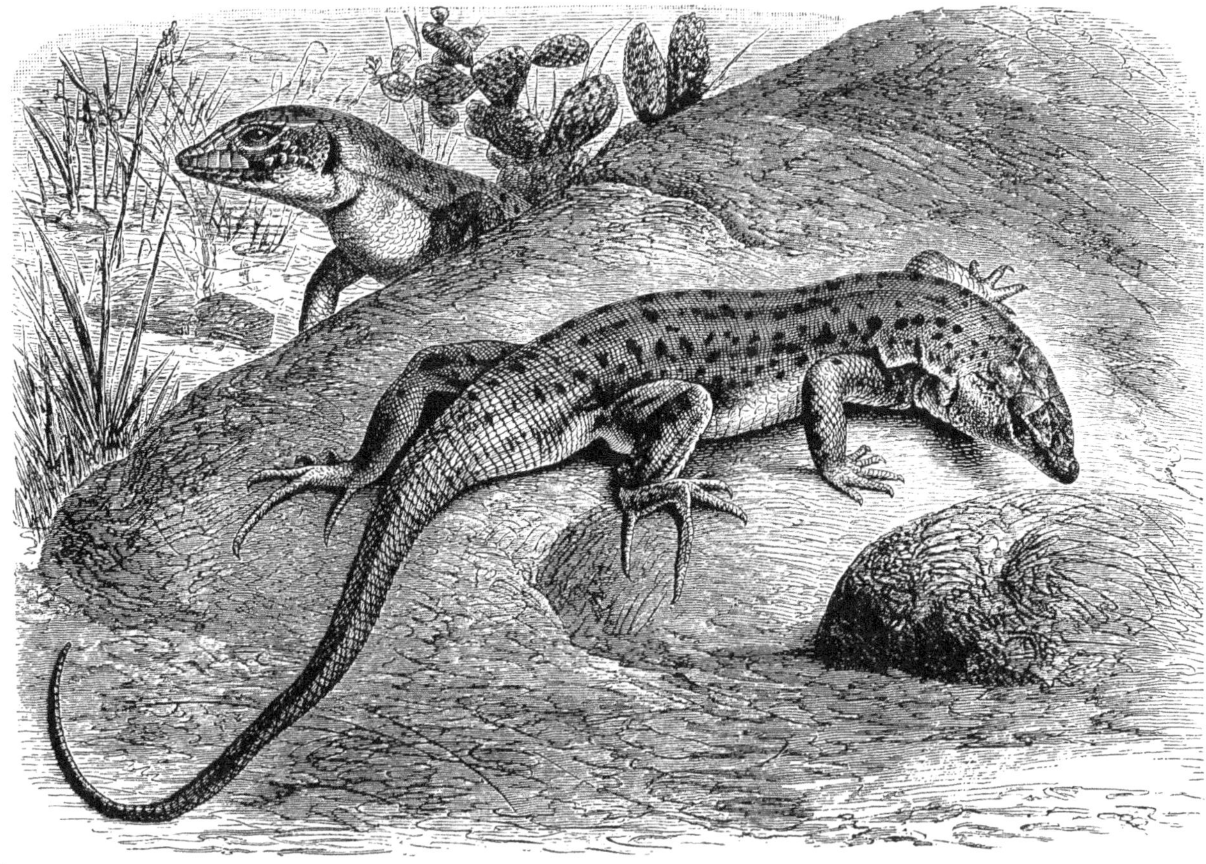

252

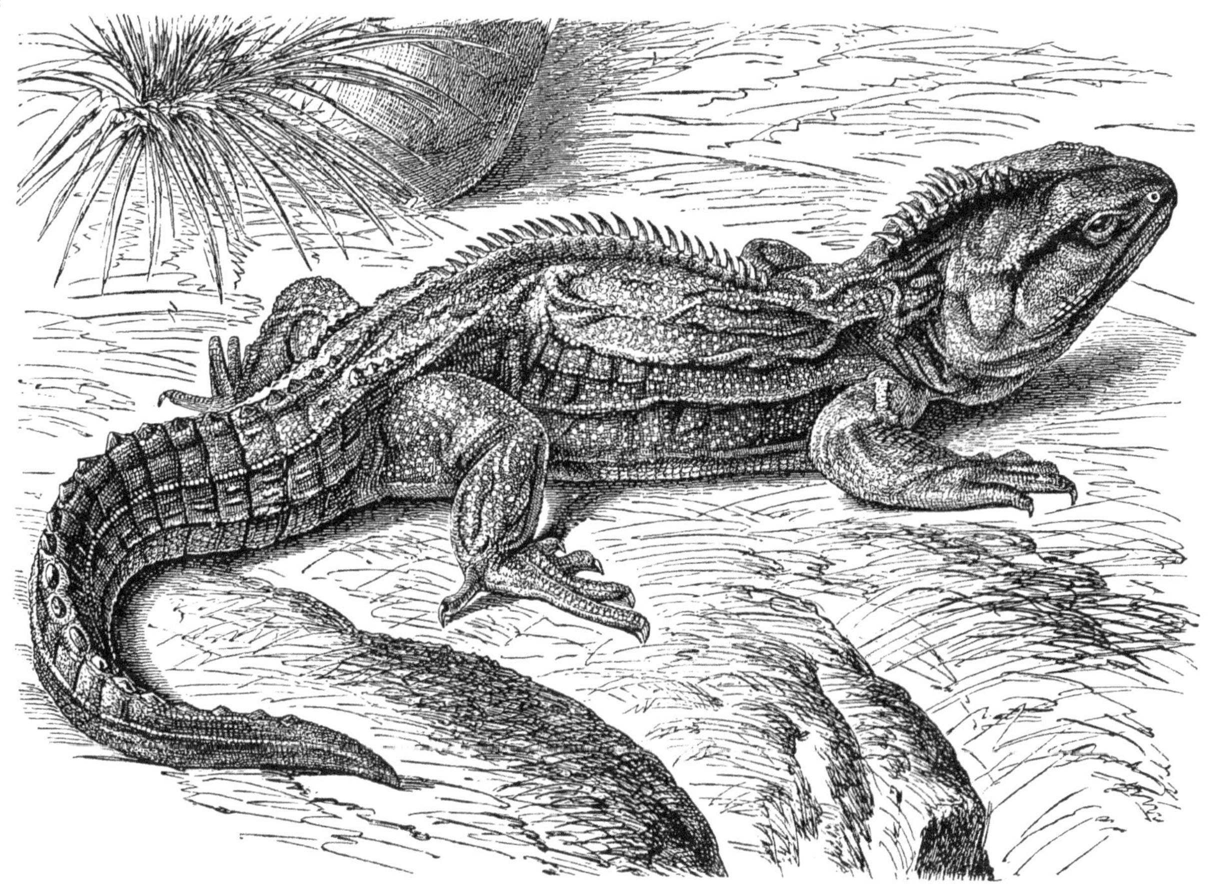

LIZARDS

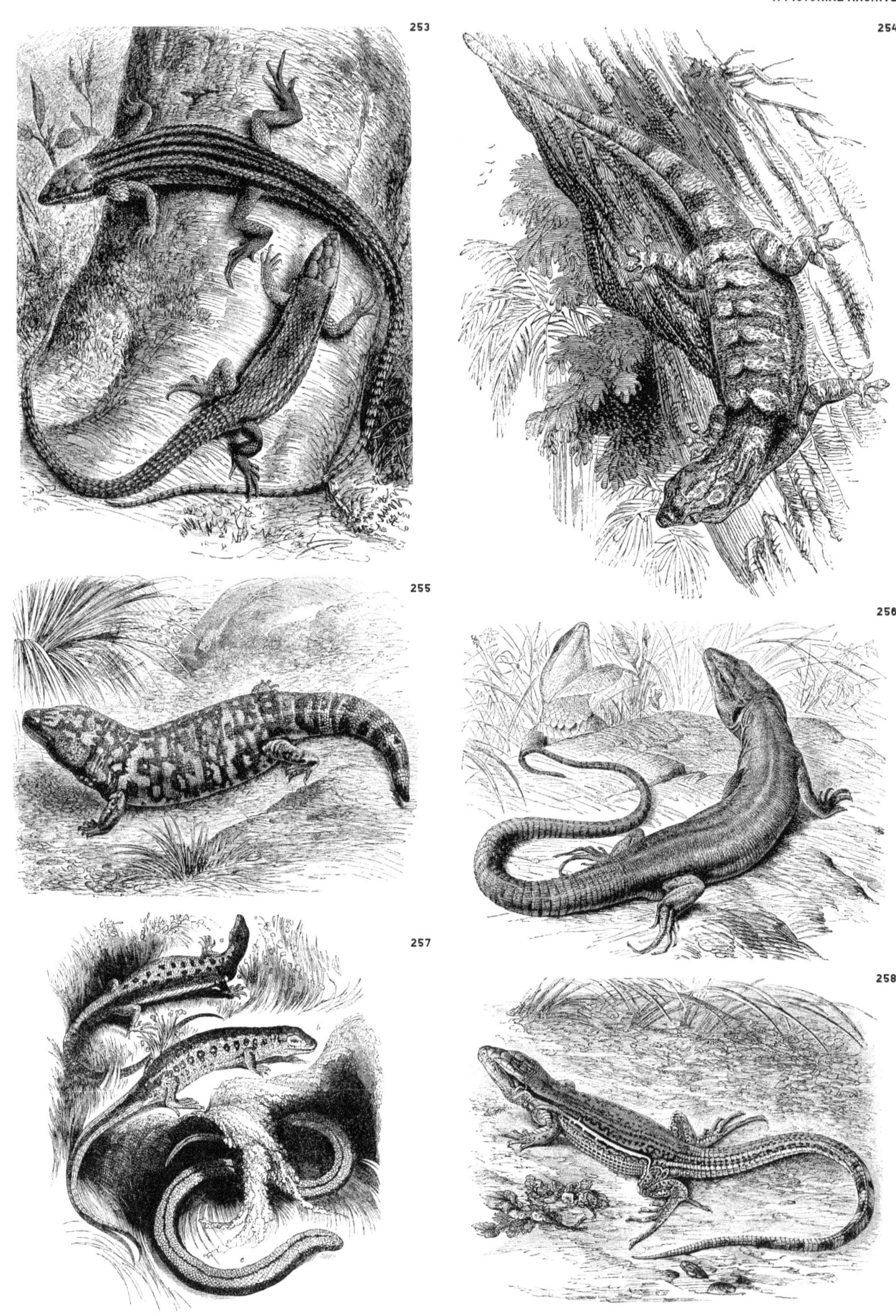

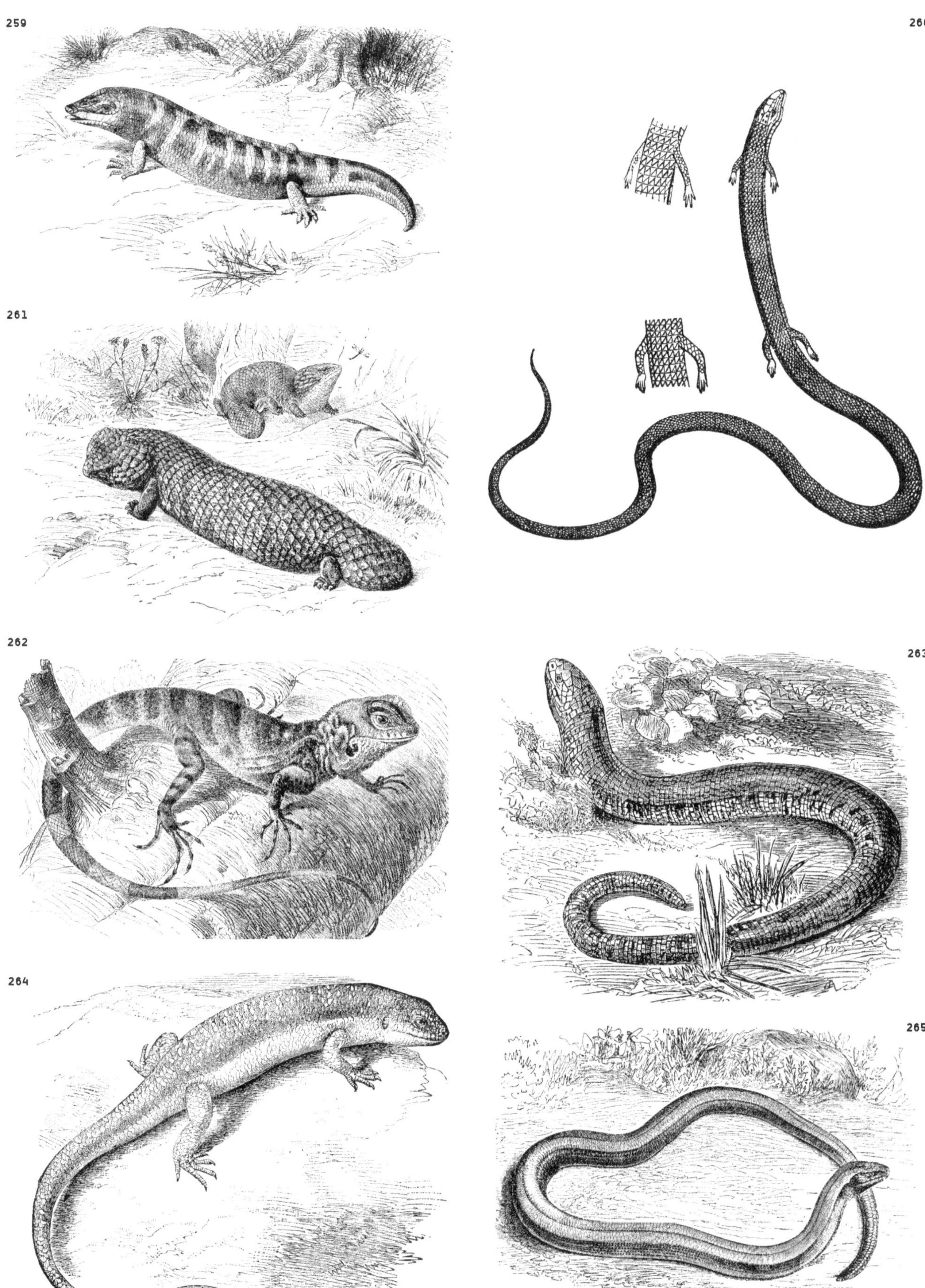

259
260
261
262
263
264
265

266

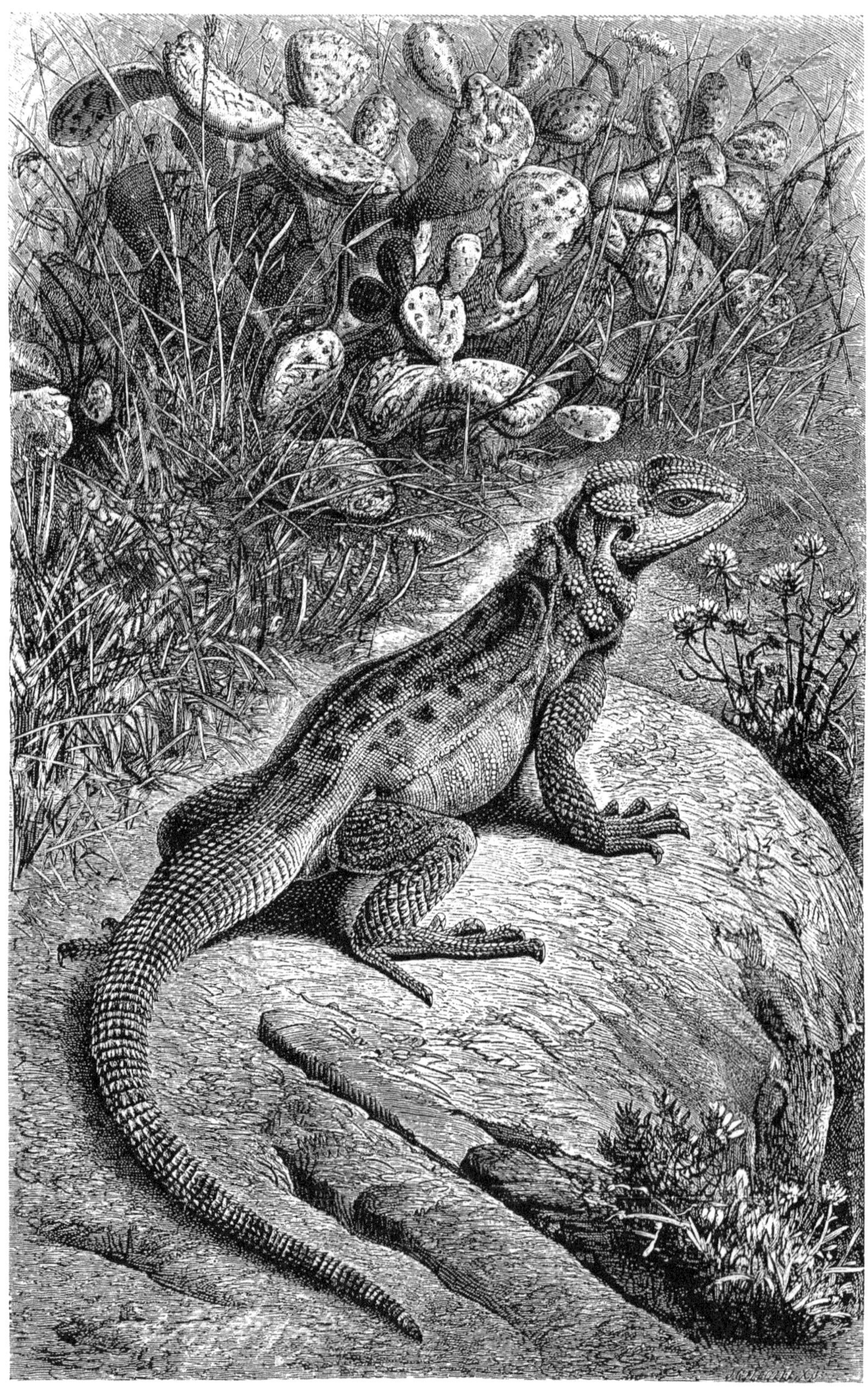

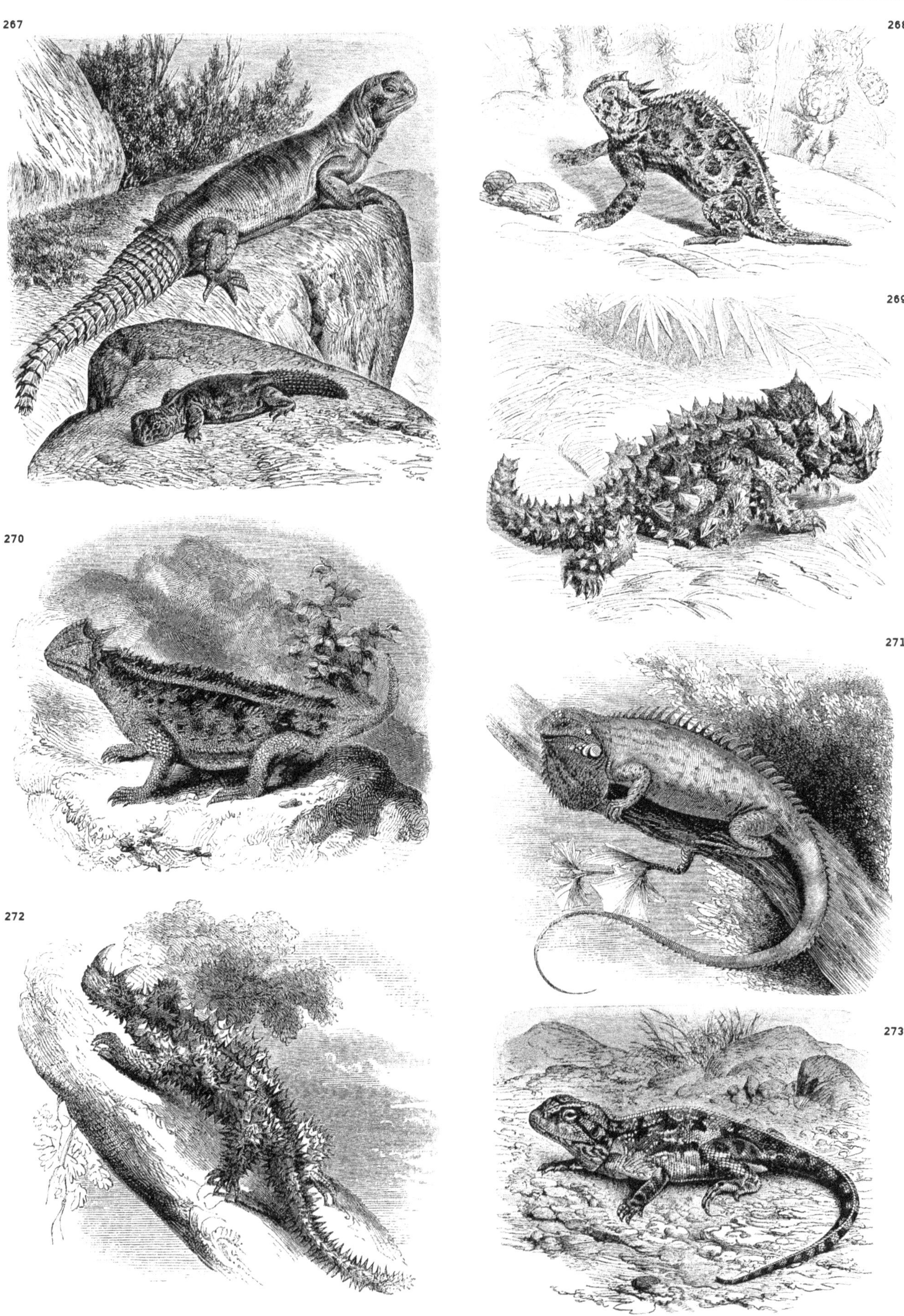

267
268
269
271
273
272
270
SNAKES & OTHER REPTILES

274

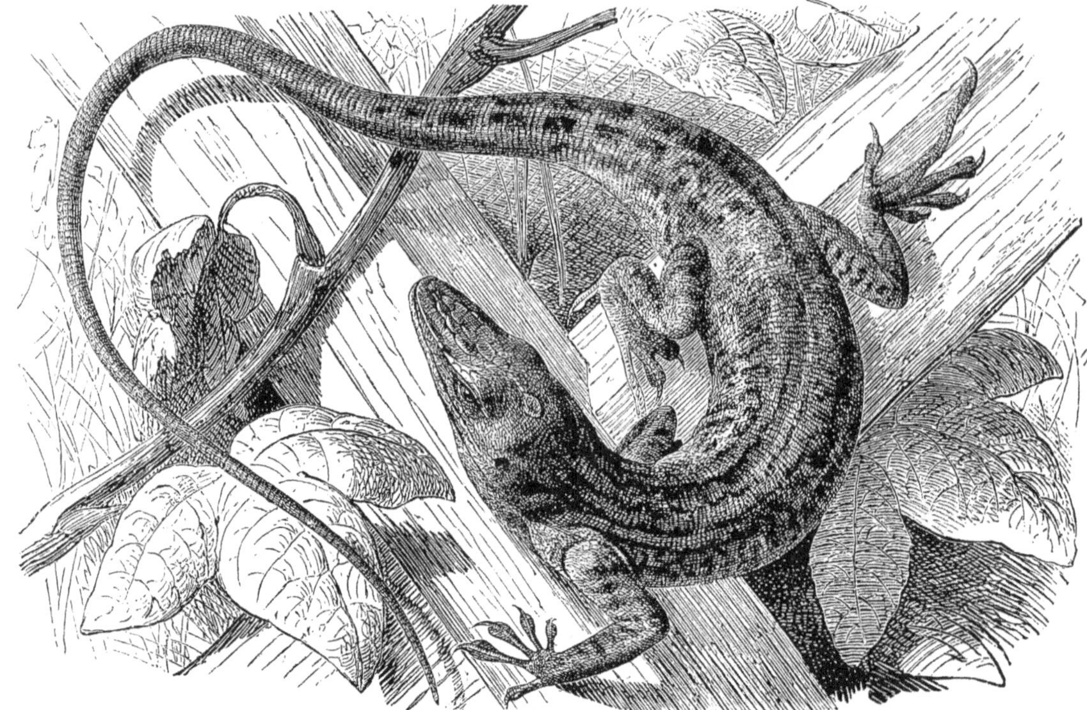

275

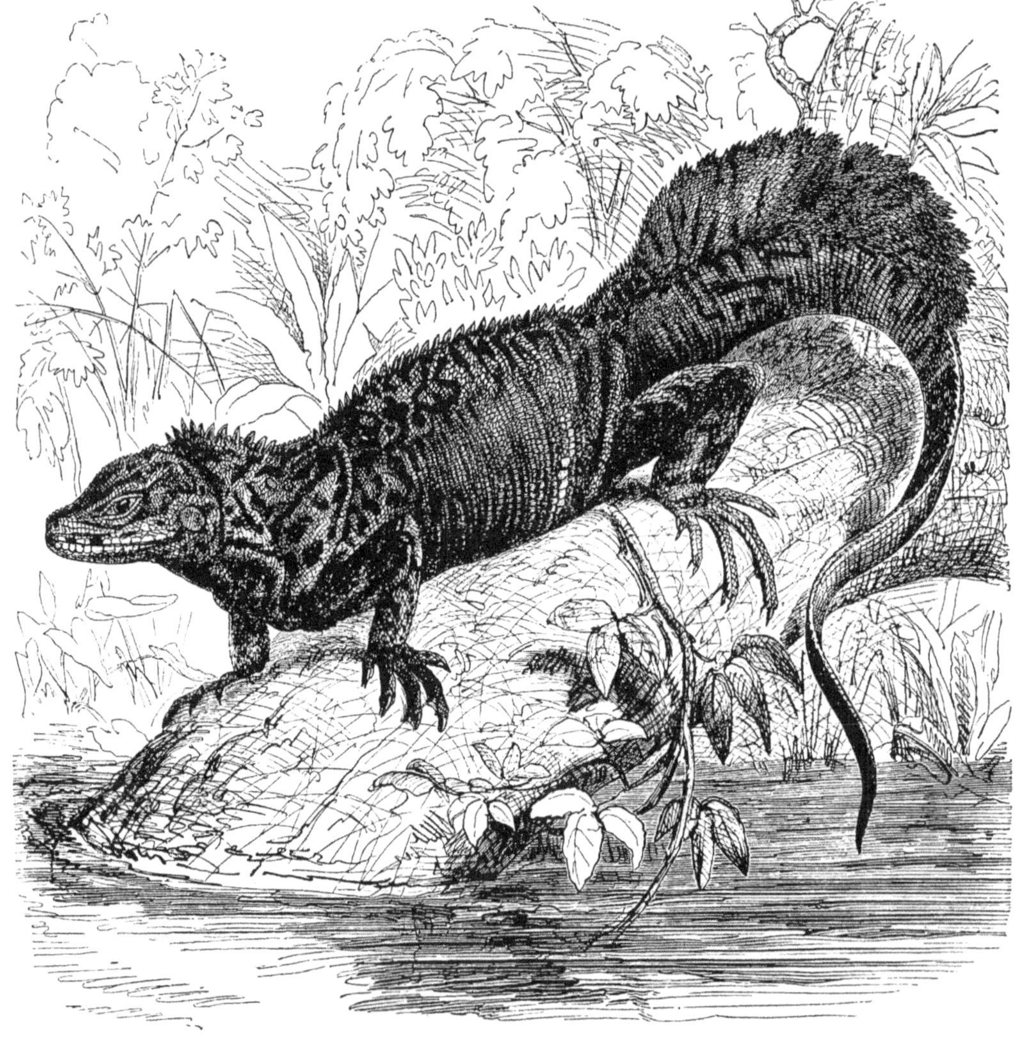

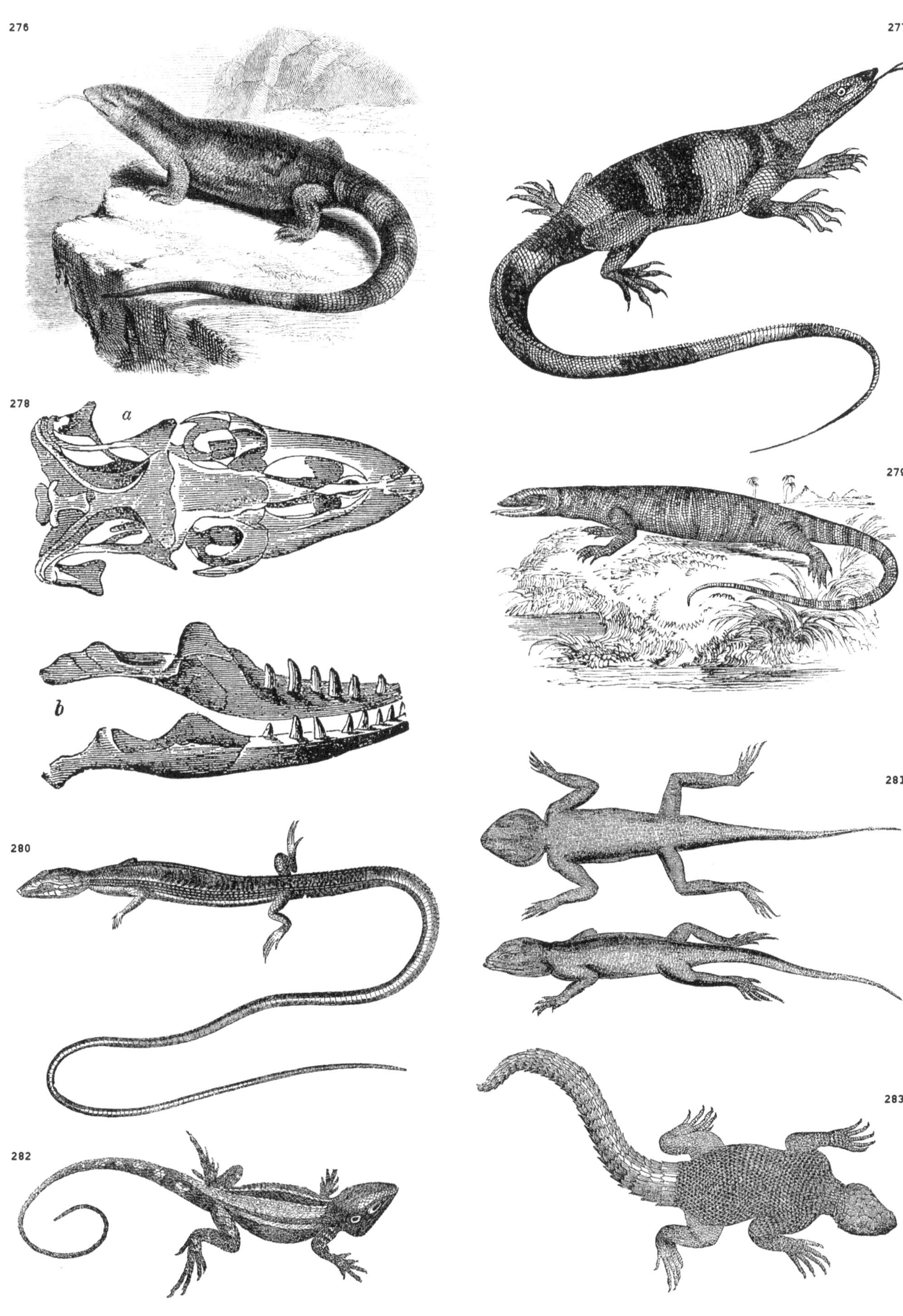

276
277
278
a
b
279
280
281
282
283
SNAKES & OTHER REPTILES

284

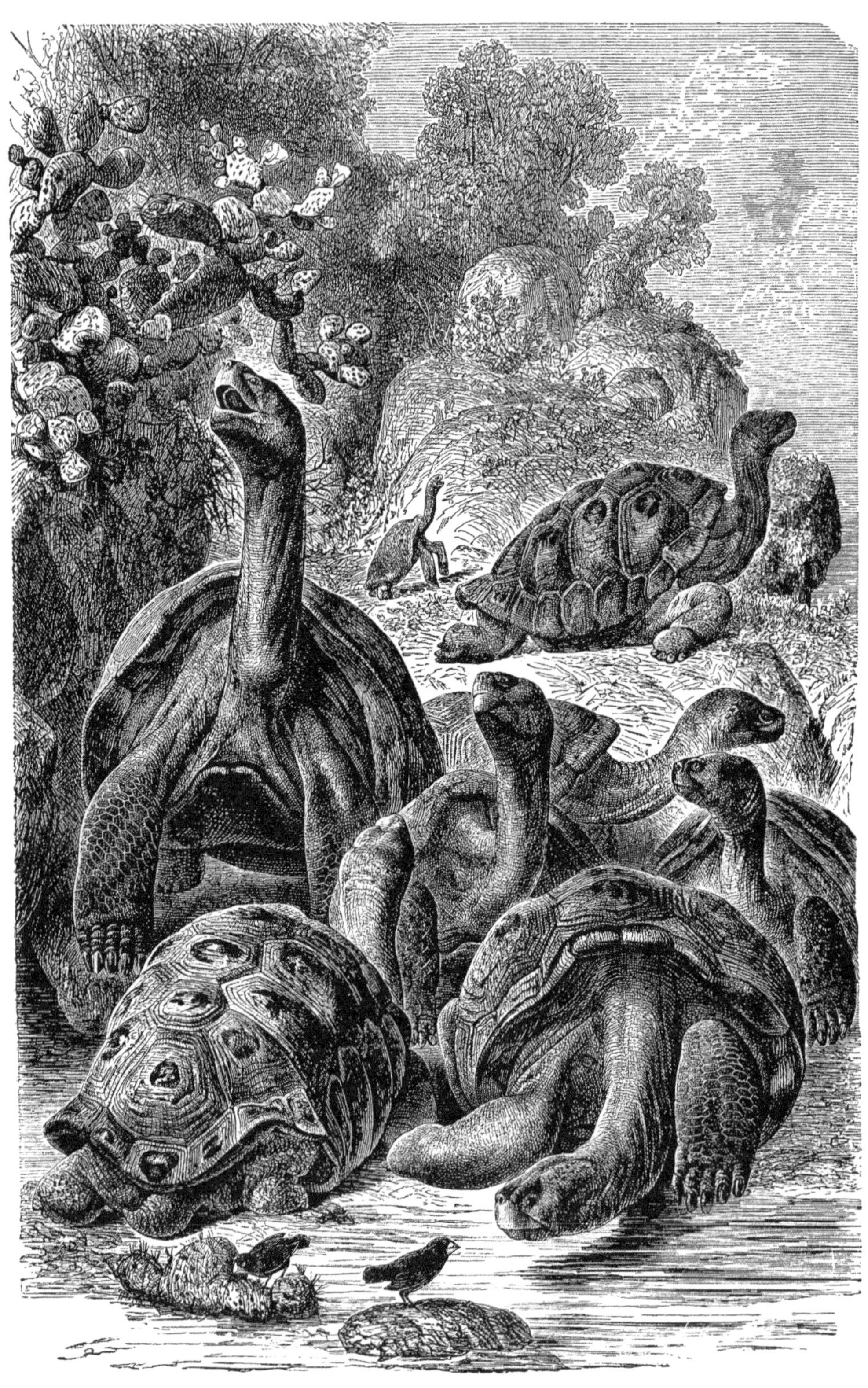

285

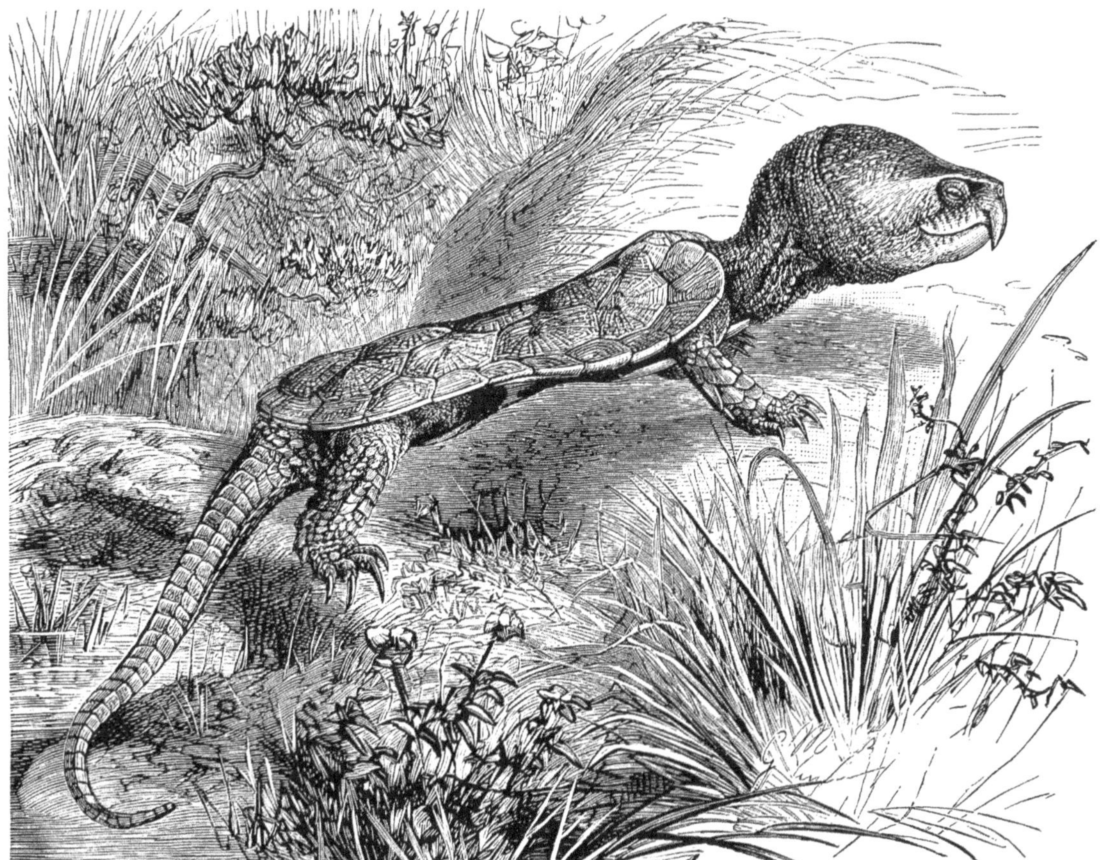

286

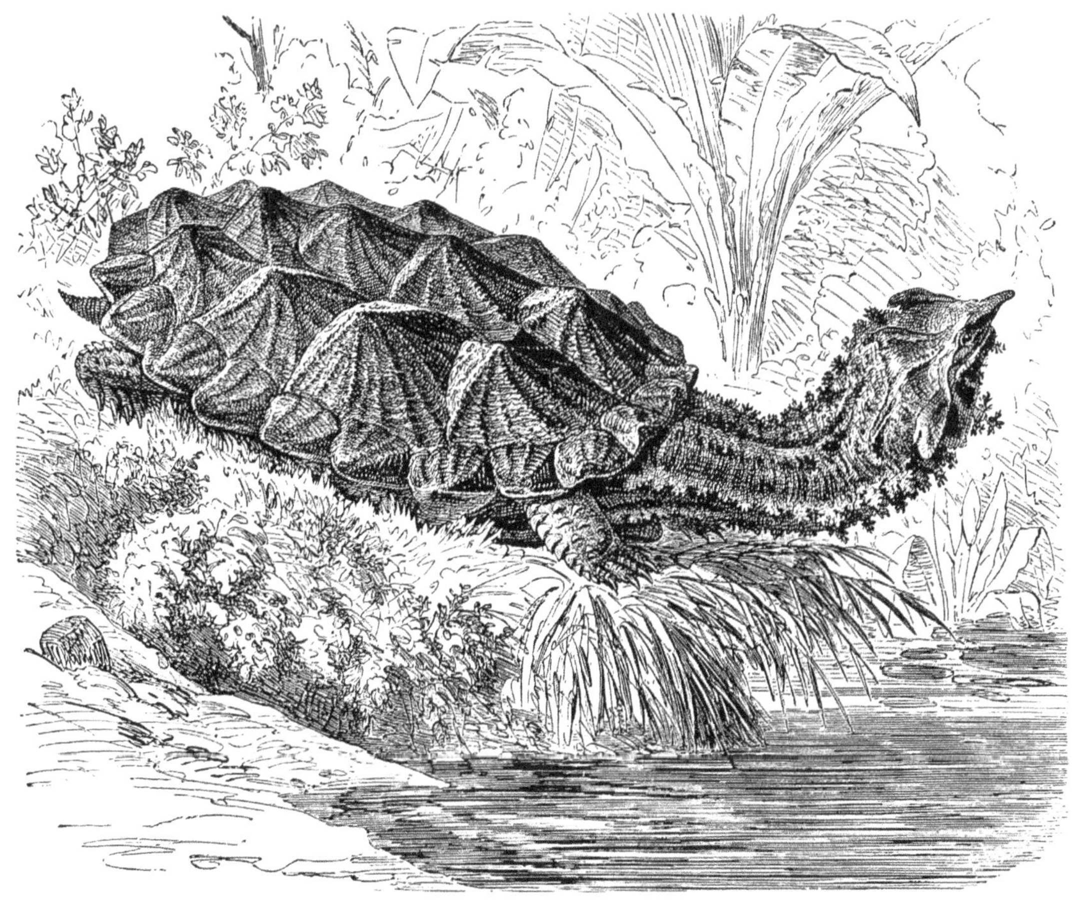

TURTLES

287
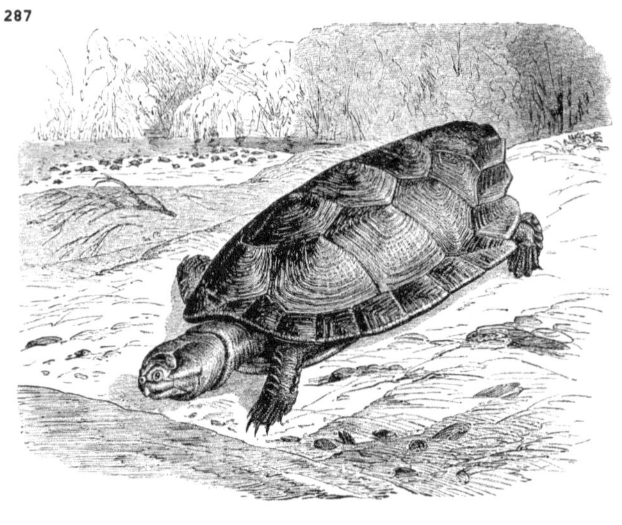

288
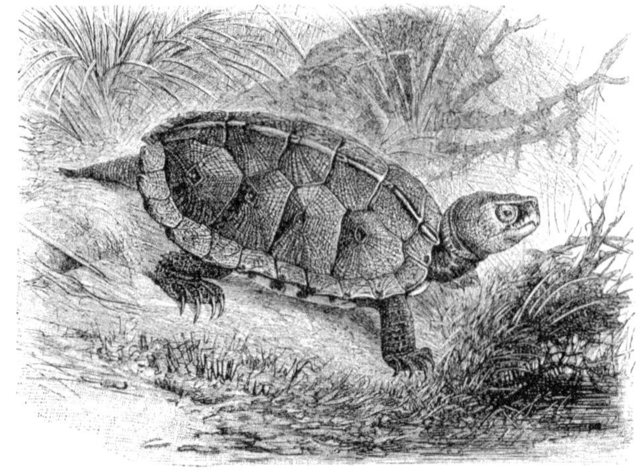

289
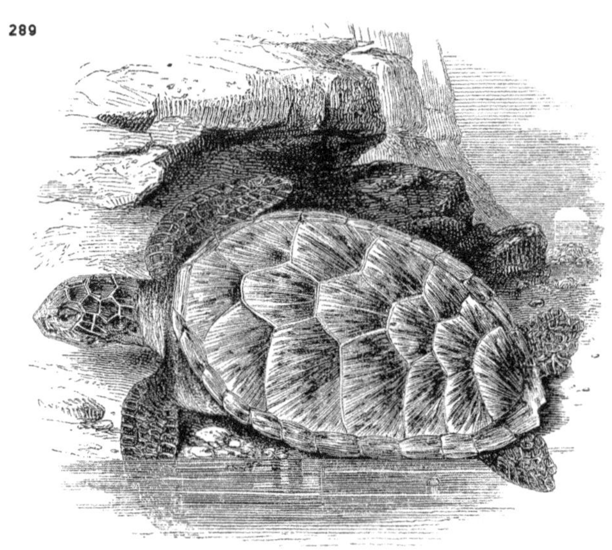

290
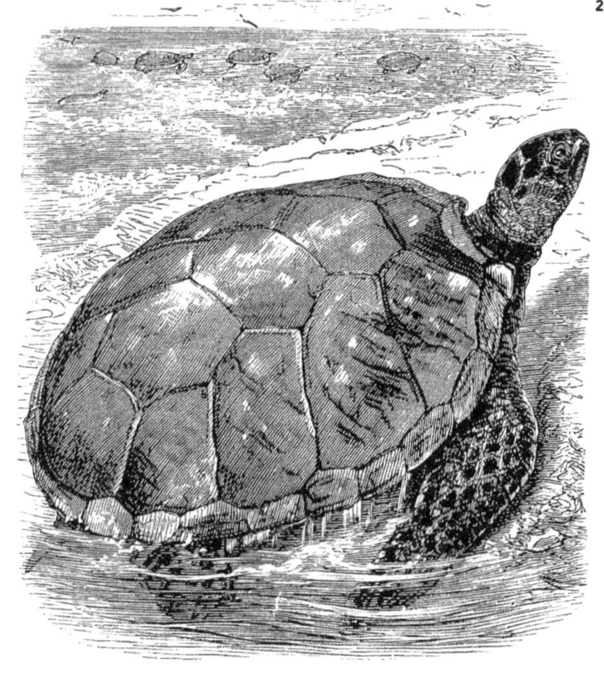

291
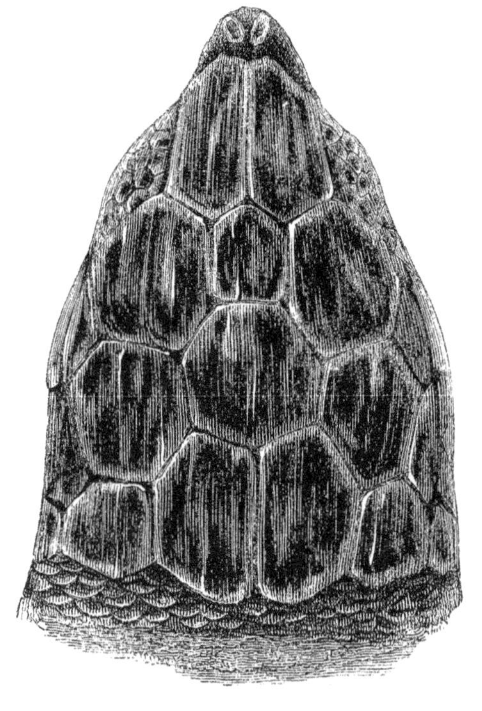

292
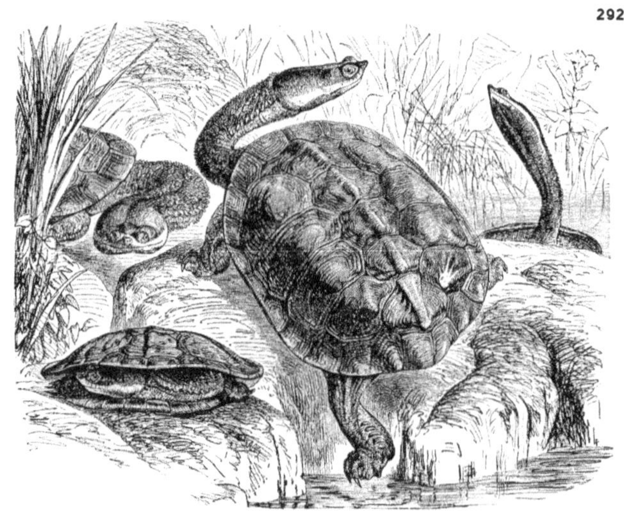

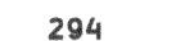

293

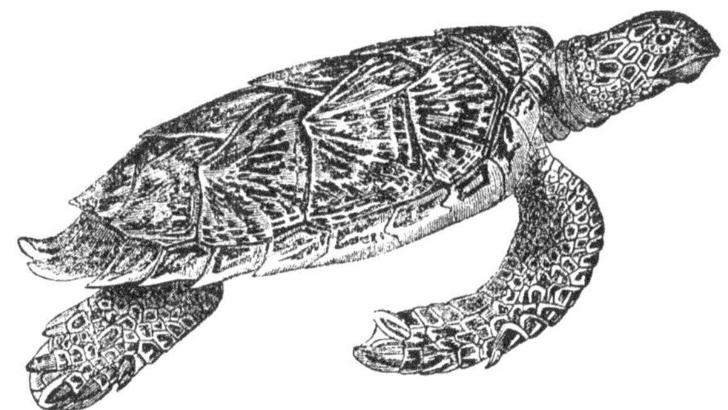

294

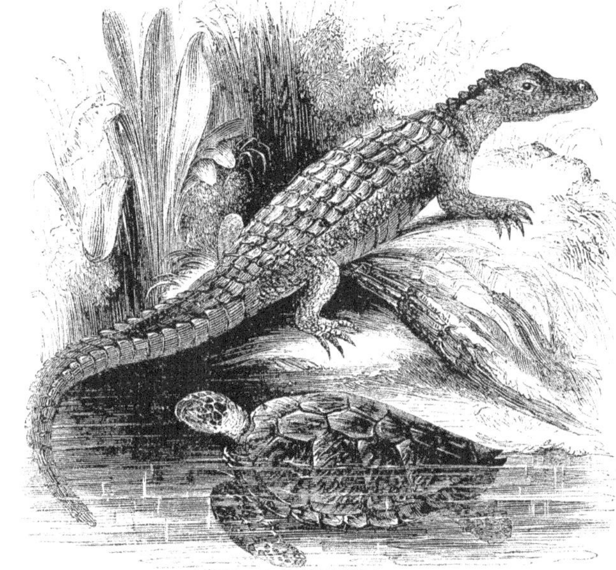

295

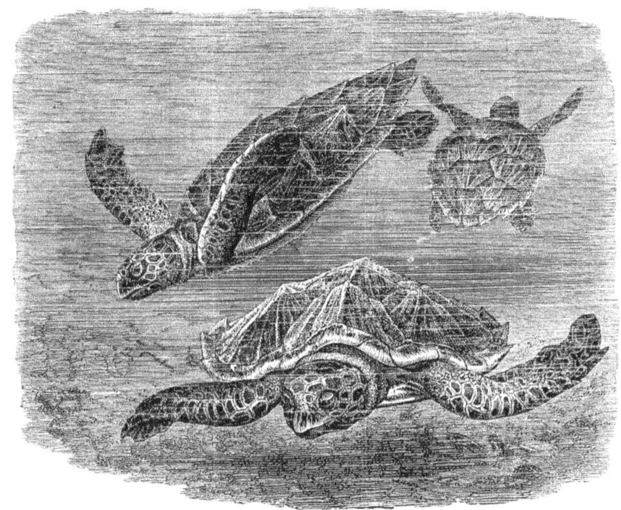

296

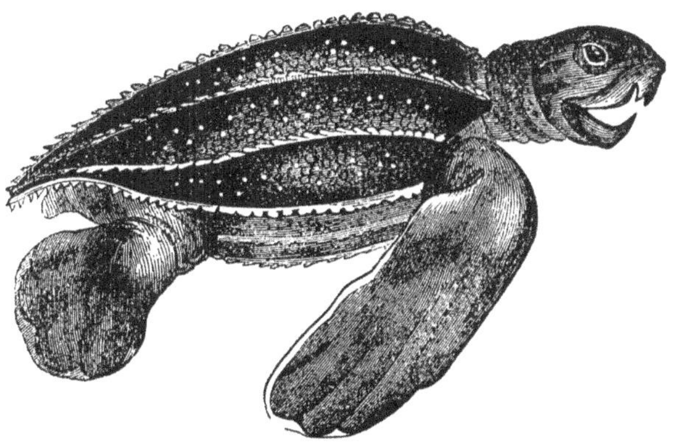

297

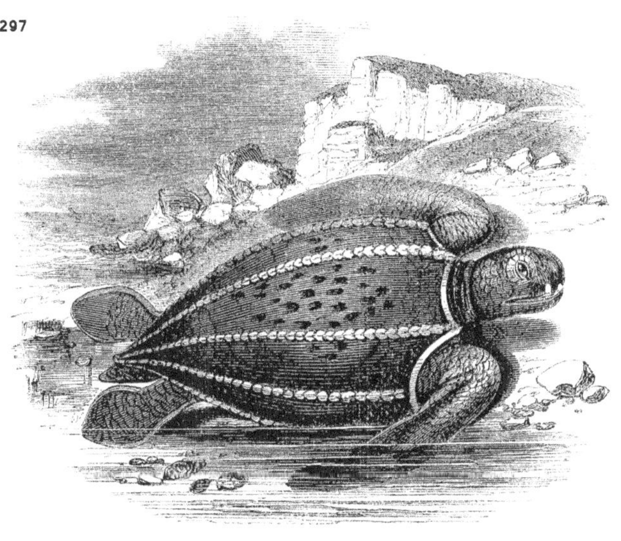

298

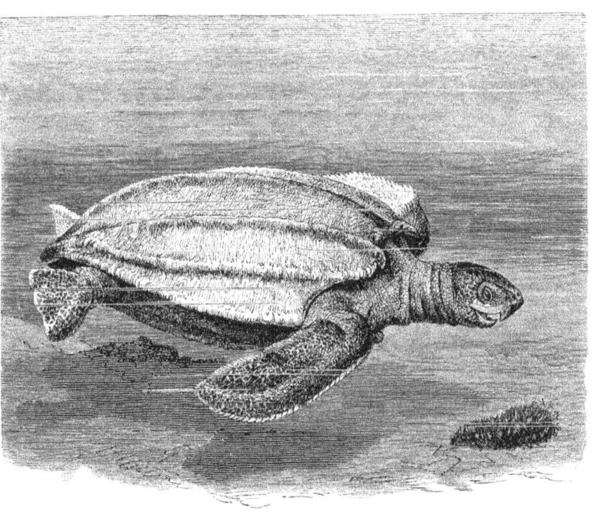

TURTLES

299

300

301

302

305

303

304

306

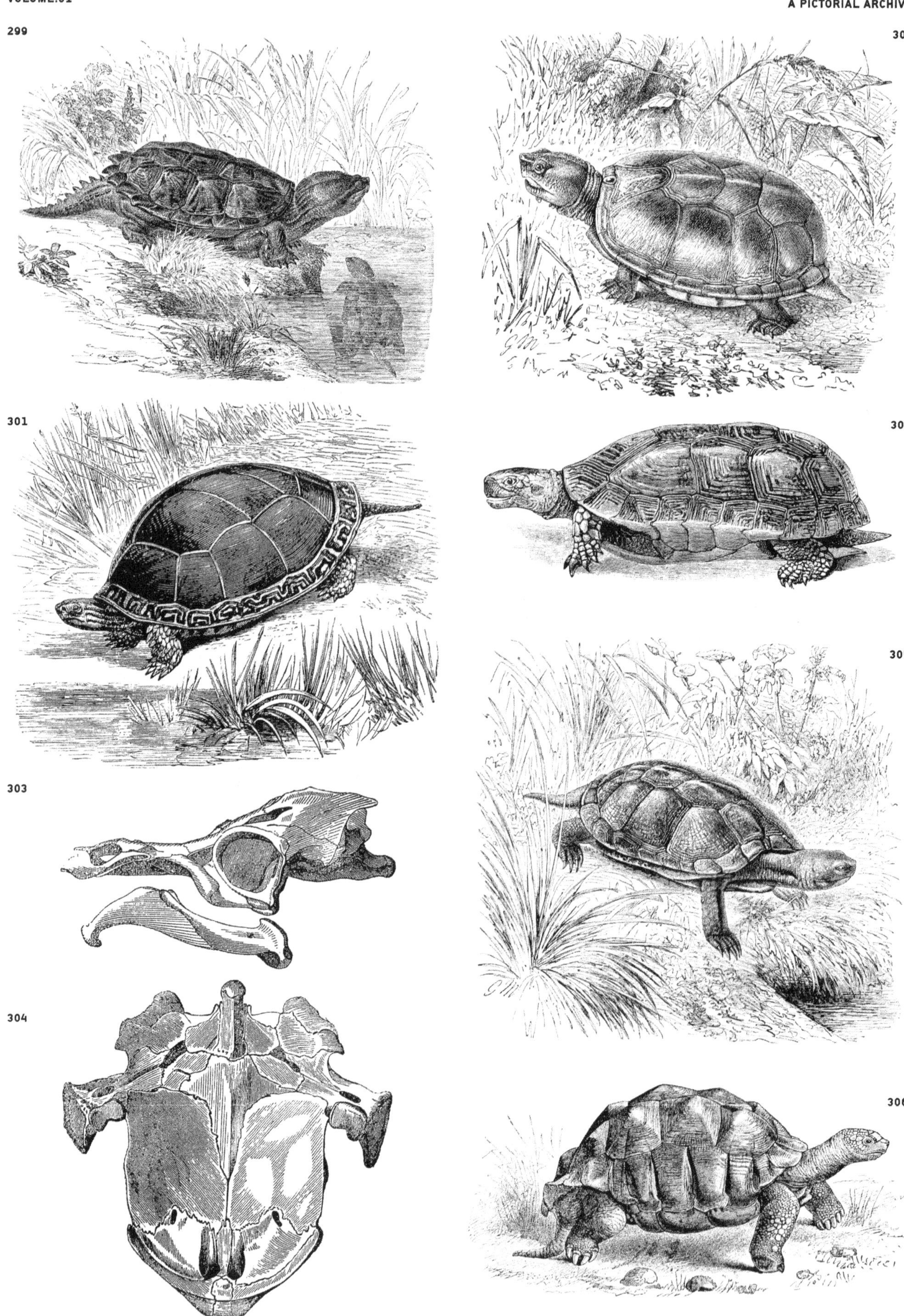

307

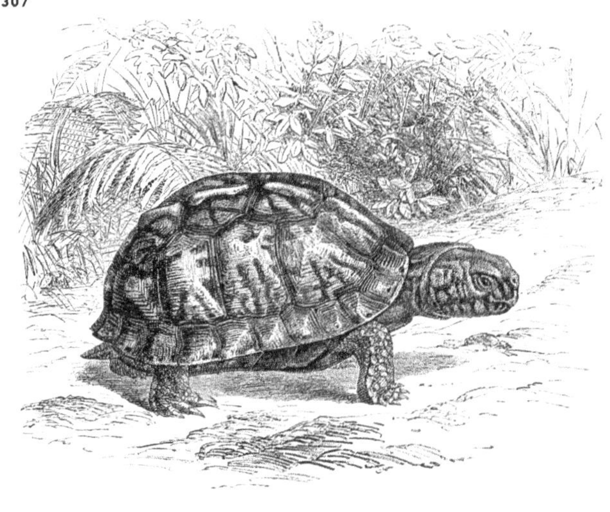

308

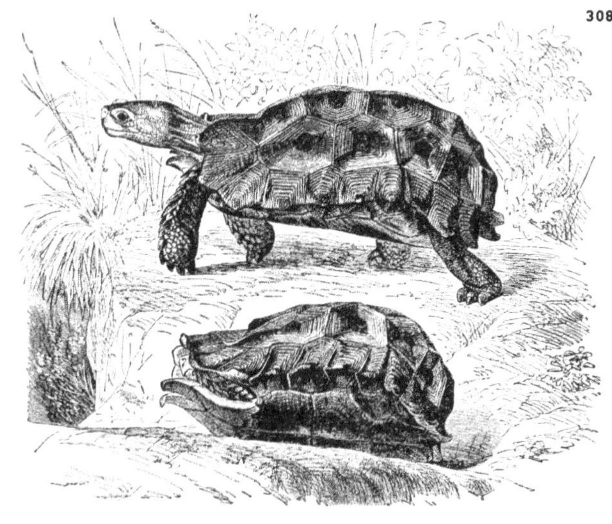

309

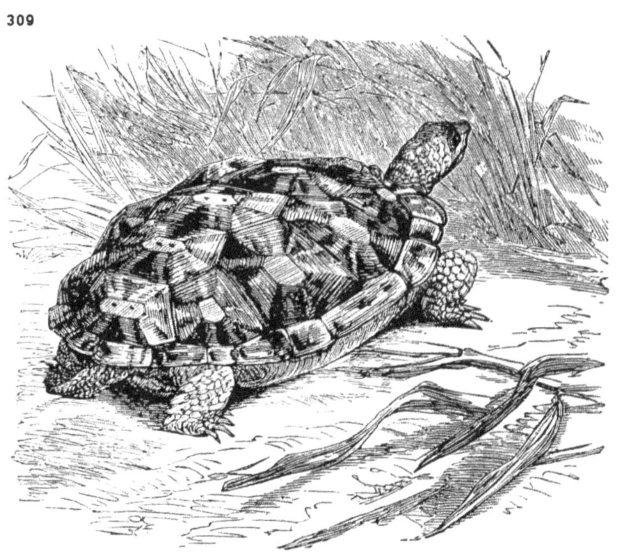

310

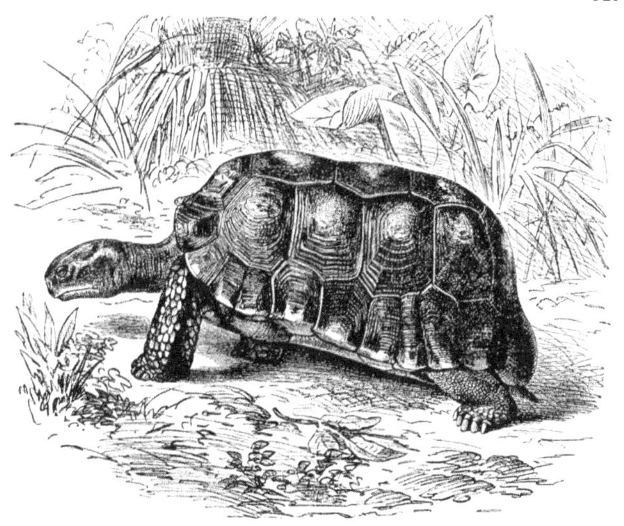

311

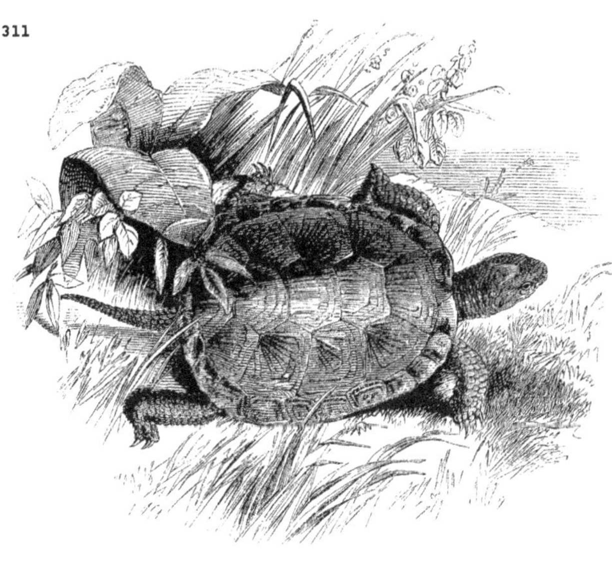

312

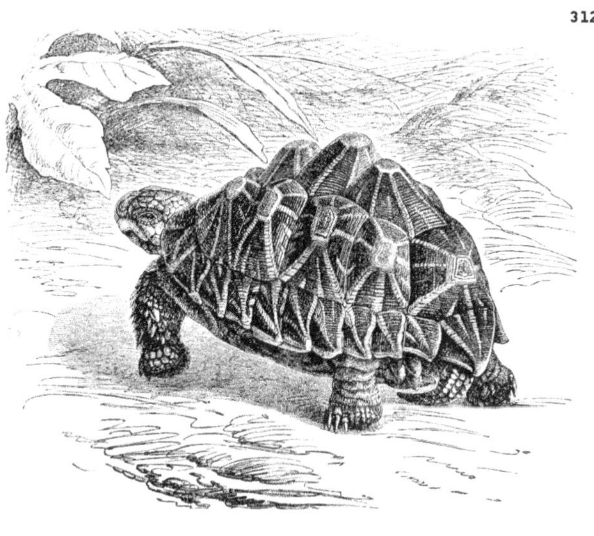

TURTLES

313

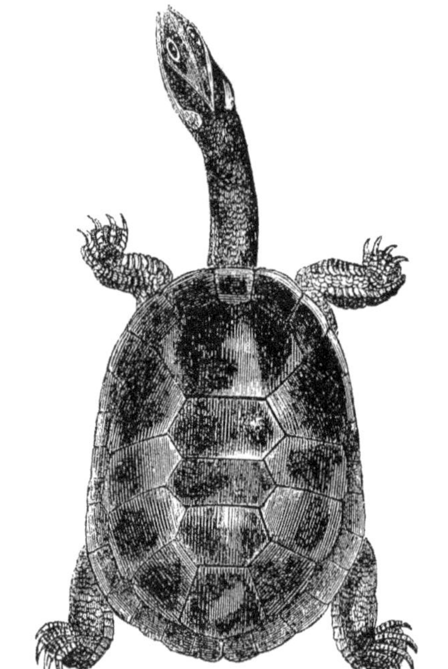

314

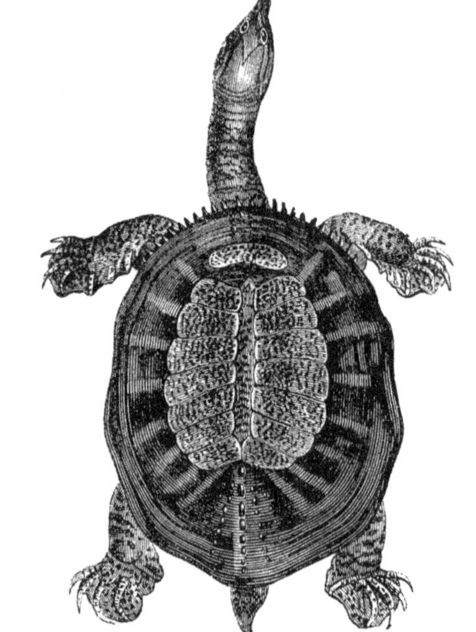

315

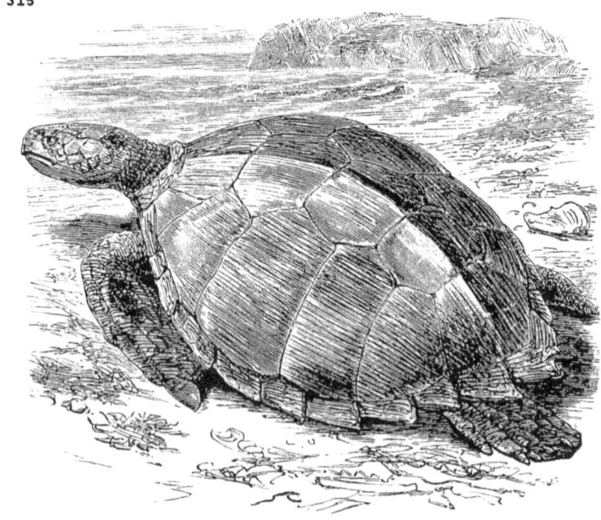

316

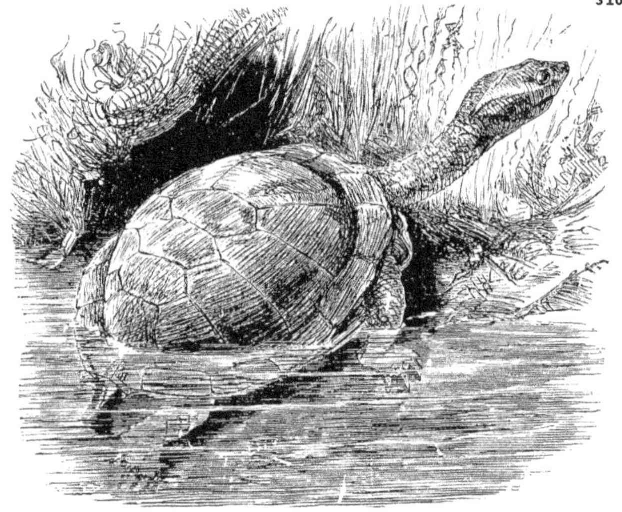

317

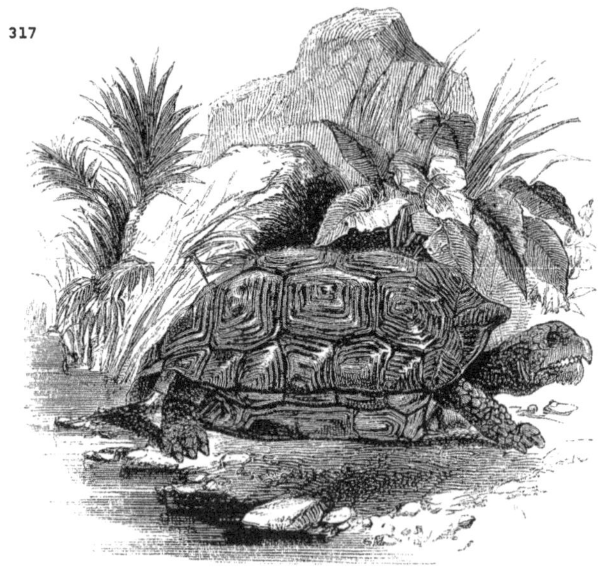

318

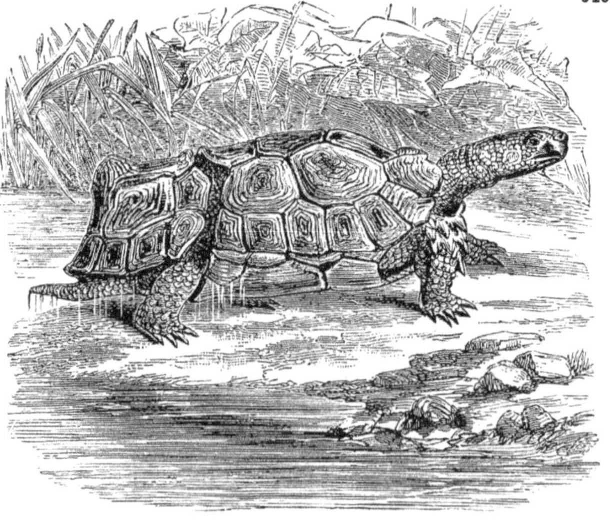

319

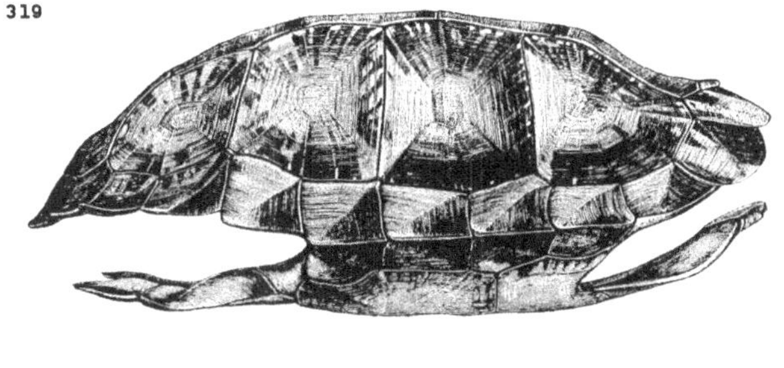

320

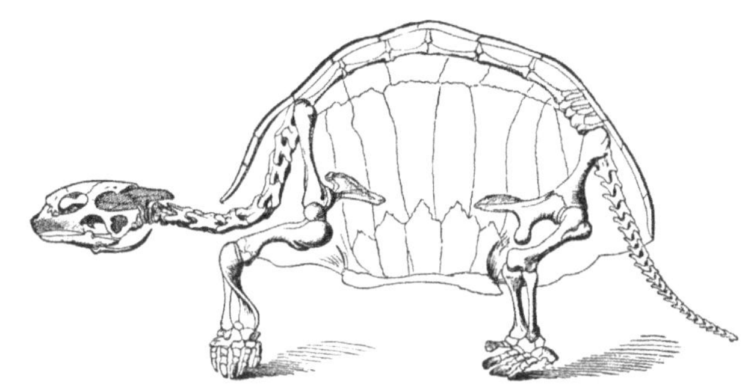

321

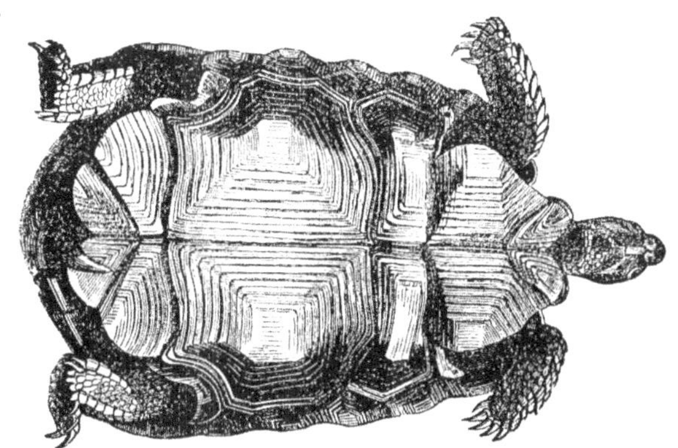

322

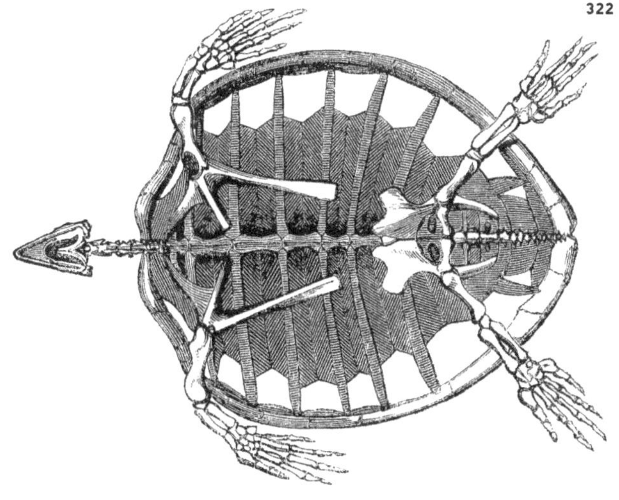

323

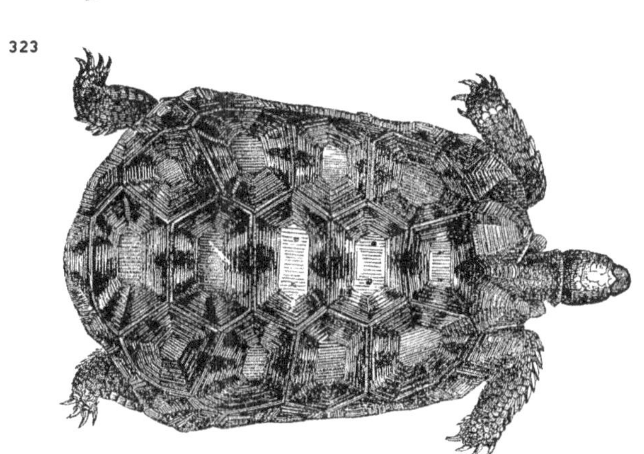

324

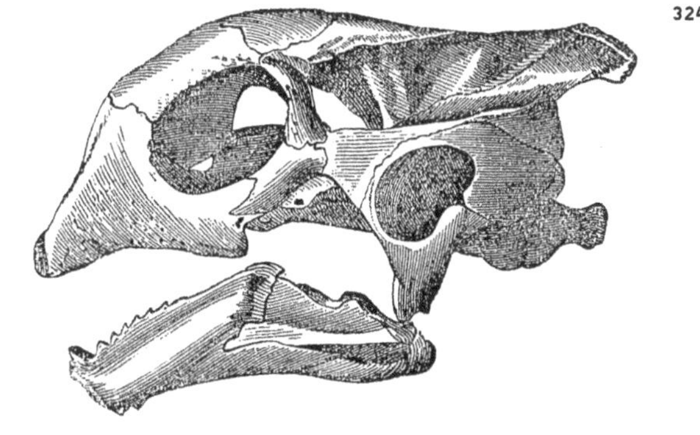

325

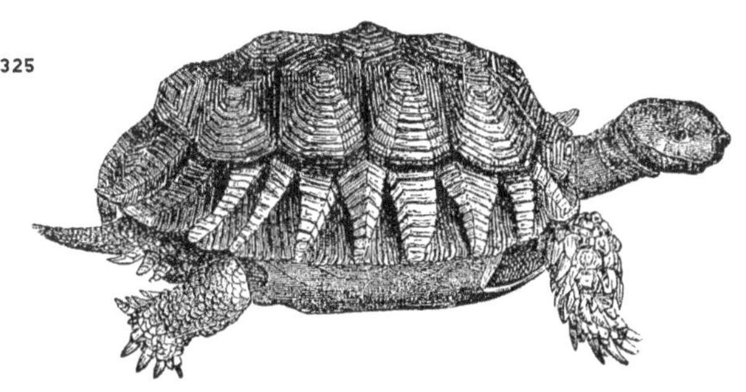

326

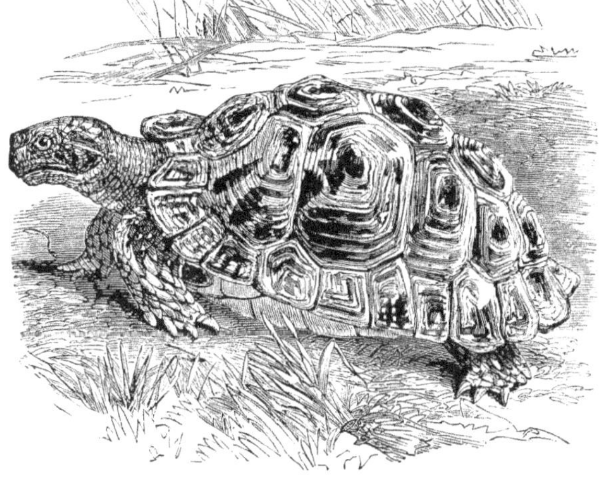

327

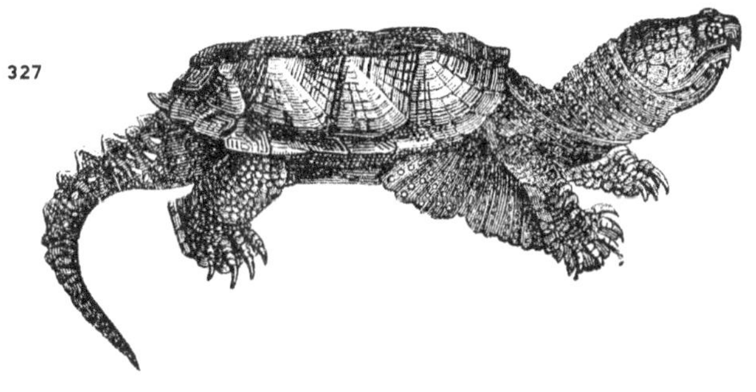

LIST OF ILLUSTRATIONS

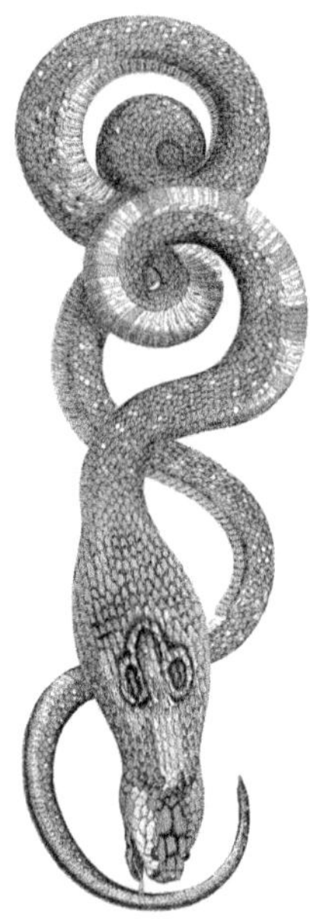

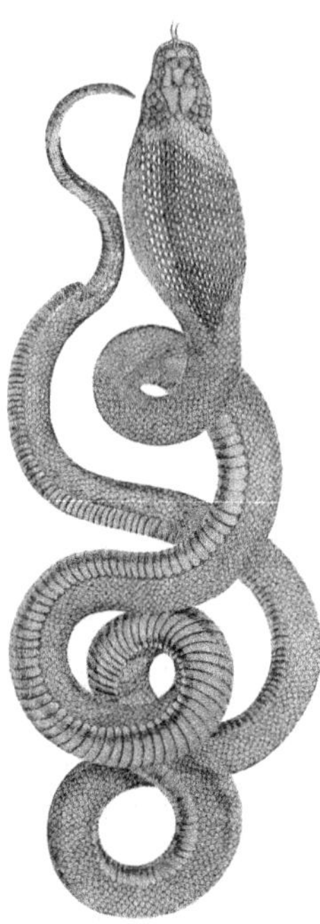

1. Skeleton of a snake
2. Skull of a Python
3. Skeleton of a Boa Constrictor
4. The Caecus, or Secret Viper
5. The Cobra de Capello, or the Spectacle-Hooded Viper
6. 1. The Egyptian Viper, 2. The Elegant Viper, 3. The Severus Viper
7. The Canina, or Green Boa
8. Rat-Tailed Pit-Viper
9. Climbing Pit-Viper
10. The Horned Viper
11. Horned Vipers in the sand
12. Russel's Viper
13. Siberian Halys Viper
14. Long-Nosed, or Sand Viper
15. The Coach Whip Viper
16. The Cenchoa Viper
17. The Panama Viper
18. The Atropos, or Life-consuming Viper
19. The Viper. Bitis, and Cobra de Monil
20. The Clotho, or Deadly Viper
21. The Lachesis, or Fatal Viper
22. The Crotaline Viper
23. The Coronated Viper
24. The Atrox, or Fierce Viper
25. The Painted Viper
26. The Pethola Viper
27. The Summer-loving Viper
28. The Viper of Rhedi
29. The Berus, or Viper of Europe
30. The Tyger-like Viper
31. The Cat-Like Viper
32. The Natrix, or Water Viper
33. A Family of Vipers
34. Viper
35. The Viper of Scripture
36. Viper
37. Head of a Viper
38. The Common Viper
39. The Black Viper
40. Viperine and Tesselated Snakes
41. Viper and its young
42. The Eja, or Desert Saw-Viper
43. Common Boa
44. Emperor Boa
45. Head of Boa Canina
46. A Boa Constrictor attacking its prey
47. Boa attacking a sleeping Lascar
48. Streaked Tree-Boa
49. Dog-Headed Tree-Boa
50. Boa Constrictor
51. The Boa Constrictor
52. Tiger Python
53. Upper Jaw and Palate of the Python
54. Skull of the Python
55. Australian Diamond Python
56. Poort-Natal Python
57. African Python swallowing a bird
58. Indian Python crushing its prey
59. A Cobra and Craster Snake
60. Young Giant Cobra or Hamadryad
61. Common Rattle Snake
62. Diamond and South American Rattle-Snakes
63. The Great Rattle Snake
64. Hood of Naja
65. Hood of Naja with 'Spectacle' pattern
66. Hood of Naja with 'Spectacle' pattern
67. Aboma
68. Aesculapian Snake
69. Black-Banded Sea-Snake
70. Banded Sea-Snake
71. Black-Marked and Horseshoe Snakes
72. Banded Sea-Snake
73. Egyptian Cerastes
74. Golden Tree-Snake
75. Glass Snake
76. Glass Snake
77. Crowned-Moon Snake
78. The Dark Green Snake
79. The Bushmaster
80. Common Adder and Ringed Snake
81. Indian Naja
82. Puff Adder
83. Blind worm, or Slow Worm
84. Short Death-Adder and Spine-Tailed Death-Adder
85. Banded Adder or Raj-Samp
86. Laocoon in the coil of snakes
87. Anaconda
88. Ringed Snake
89. Coral-Snake
90. Copper-Head, or Moccasin-Snake
91. Coral Cylinder-Snake
92. Sipo, or Brazilian Wood Snake
93. The Langaya Serpent
94. Chittul
95. Coecilia Tentaculata and Coecilia Glutinosa
96. Four-Rayed Snake
97. Purple Leptophis
98. Cat-Snake
99. Ringed Snake seizing its prey
100. Long-Glanded Snake and Masked Adder
101. Javan Wart-Snake
102. Leopard Snake
103. Javan Pigmy Snake
104. Slow-worm
105. Egyptian Sand Snake
106. The Alba Serpent
107. The Fulginosa Serpent
108. Banded Bungarus
109. Keel-Tailed Snake
110. Ringed Snake
111. A Shield-Tailed Snake
112. Boa Constrictor
113. Sheltopusic - Pseudopus Pallasil
114. Bojobi
115. Poison Glands of the Snake
116. Tentacled Herpeton
117. The Egyptian Asp
118. Bengal Ery
119. The American Asp, Male and Female
120. Head of Naja
121. Oular Carron
122. Boiga
123. Ringed Snake
124. Bicoloured Sea-Snake
125. Head and tail of Common Snake
126. Head of a viper
127. A Viper giving birth to its young
128. Skeleton and internal organs of the Viper
129. Boa Élégant
130. Boa Devin
131. Tiger Python
132. Many-banded krait
133. Timber Rattle-snake
134. Pit Viper
135. Death Adder
136. A Cobra Snake
137. Indian Cobra (Naja Naja)
138. Common Viper

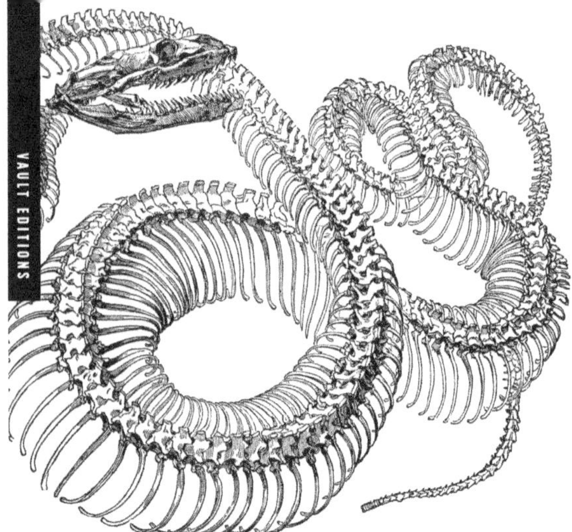

LEARN MORE

At Vault Editions, our mission is to create the world's most diverse and comprehensive collection of image archives available for artists, designers and curious minds. If you have enjoyed this book, you can find more of our titles available at vaulteditions.com.

REVIEW THIS BOOK

As a small, family-owned independent publisher, reviews help spread the word about our work. We would be incredibly grateful if you could leave an honest review of this title wherever you purchased this book.

JOIN OUR COMMUNITY

Are you a creative and curious individual? If so, you will love our community on Instagram. Every day we share bizarre and beautiful artwork ranging from 17th and 18th-century natural history and scientific illustration, to mythical beasts, ornamental designs, anatomical illustration and more. Join our community of 100K+ people today—search @vault_editions on Instagram.

DOWNLOAD YOUR FILES

STEP ONE

Enter the following web address in your web browser on a desktop computer.

www.vaulteditions.com/pages/sar

STEP TWO

Enter the following unique password to access the download page.

bwaa23847338sxda

STEP THREE

Follow the prompts to access your high-resolution files.

TECHNICAL ASSISTANCE

For all technical assistance, please email: info@vaulteditions.com

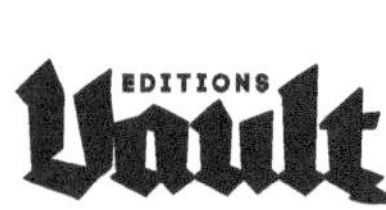

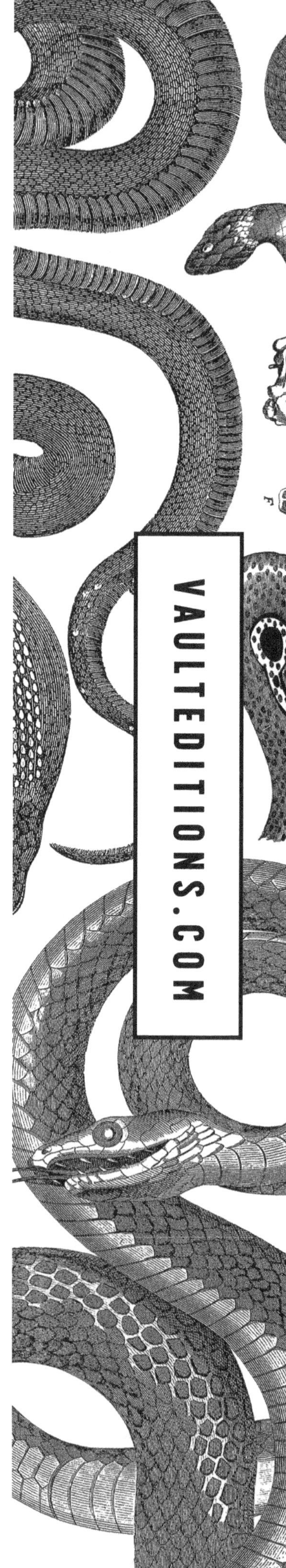